Comparative Ethics Series /
Collection d'Éthique Comparée

Comparative Ethics Series /
Collection d'Éthique Comparée

As Religious Studies in its various branches has spread out in recent years, it has met with a newly emergent discipline: Comparative Ethics as the study of moralities as cultural systems, rather than as the philosophical investigation of particular moral issues. To study a morality as a dynamic whole in its social nature and functioning requires a context in which other instances of a comparable kind are considered. Moral action-guides and religious action-guides have historically been brought together in mixed, moral-religious or religious-moral systems. The different paths followed by moralities as cultural systems in the varying contexts demand comparative study.

The series embraces three kinds of studies: (1) methodological studies, which will endeavour to elaborate and discuss principles, concepts and models for the new discipline; (2) studies which aim at deepening our knowledge of the nature and functioning, the scope and content of particular moral systems, such as the Islamic, the Hindu, the Christian and so on; (3) studies of a directly comparative kind, which bring differing moral systems or elements of systems into relationship.

GENERAL EDITOR: *Paul Bowlby*   Saint Mary's University (Halifax)

COMPARATIVE ETHICS

Towards an Ethics of Community
Negotiations of Difference in a Pluralist Society

James H. Olthuis, editor

177
T737

Published for the Canadian Corporation for Studies in Religion/
Corporation Canadienne des Sciences Religieuses
by Wilfrid Laurier University Press

2000

This book has been published with the help of a grant from the Humanities and Social Sciences Federation of Canada, using funds provided by the Social Sciences and Humanities Research Council of Canada. We acknowledge the support of the Canada Council for the Arts for our publishing program. We acknowledge the financial support of the Government of Canada through the Book Publishing Industry Development Program for our publishing activities.

Canadian Cataloguing in Publication Data

Main entry under title:
    Towards an ethics of community : negotiations of difference in
a pluralist society

(Comparative ethics series ; v. 5)
Includes bibliographical references and index.
ISBN 0-88920-339-3

1. Pluralism.   2. Difference (Philosophy).   I. Olthuis, James H.
II. Canadian Corporation for Studies in Religion.   III. Series.

BD394.T68 2000   147′.4   C99-932233-8

© 2000 Canadian Corporation for Studies in Religion /
        Corporation Canadienne des Sciences Religieuses

Cover design by Leslie Macredie using a photograph of a quilt in the Log Cabin design, barn-raising variation, Waterloo County, 1880-1900. From the collections of Joseph Schneider Haus Museum, Kitchener. Ontario.

Printed in Canada

Towards an Ethics of Community: Negotiations of Difference in a Pluralist Society has been produced from a manuscript supplied in camera-ready form by the author.

Order from:
WILFRID LAURIER UNIVERSITY PRESS
Waterloo, Ontario, Canada   N2L 3C5

The Institute for Christian Studies
designates this book as the

1999 ROBERT LEE CARVILL MEMORIAL BOOK

in grateful tribute to the service
and inspiration he has given

TABLE OF CONTENTS

Acknowledgements ix

Introduction 1
    Exclusions and Inclusions: Dilemmas of Difference
       JAMES H. OLTHUIS

Part I: Dilemmas of Difference

1   Plotting the Margins: A Historical Episode in the Management of   13
    Social Plurality
      ROBERT SWEETMAN

2   Consequences of Liberalism: Ideological Domination in Rorty's   37
    Public/Private Split
      HENDRIK HART

3   Indoctrination and Assimilation in Plural Settings   51
      KEN BADLEY

4   "Woman" in the Plural: Negotiating Sameness and Difference in   74
    Feminist Theory
      JANET CATHERINA WESSELIUS

5   Religious Conflicts, Public Policy, and Moral Authority: Reflections
    on Christian Faith and Homosexual Rights in a Plural Society   91
      HENDRIK HART

6   Rethinking the Family: Belonging, Respecting, and Connecting   127
      JAMES H. OLTHUIS

Part II: Negotiations of Difference

7   Female Genital Mutilation: An Examination of a Harmful   153
    Traditional Practice in a Canadian Context
      LISA CHISHOLM-SMITH

8 Violent Asymmetry: The Shape of Power in the Current Debate   170
   over the Morality of Homosexuality
       RONALD A. KUIPERS

9 Native Self-government: Between the Spiritual Fire and the   186
   Political Fire
       GEORGE VANDERVELDE

10 On Identity and Aesthetic Voice of the Culturally Displaced   200
       CALVIN SEERVELD

Notes on Contributors   217

Subject Index   219

Name Index   223

ACKNOWLEDGEMENTS

This collection of essays was born in the matrix of a multiyear, interdisciplinary research project on pluralism at the Institute for Christian Studies, made possible by a three-year grant from the Social Sciences and Humanities Research Council of Canada.

I wish to thank Martin Rumscheidt, Publications Officer of the Canadian Corporation for the Studies in Religion, for his help in shepherding the manuscript through the grant process of the Aid to Scholarly Publications Programme.

I also wish to thank Jamie Smith, David Smith, Michael Kelly, Jeanne Jordan-Awang, and especially Henry Friesen, for their help in the preparation of this volume.

James H. Olthuis
Institute for Christian Studies, Toronto

Introduction

Exclusions and Inclusions: Dilemmas of Differences

JAMES H. OLTHUIS

For much of human history there were neighbours and there were strangers. Neighbours were the people down the street, no matter the real differences, with whom we have lived in greater or lesser communality, familiarity, and sameness. Strangers were the aliens from far countries about whom we heard tales, sometimes exotic tales of difference, but seldom met. If, perchance, our paths crossed, these encounters tended to be erratic, momentary intersectings, whether hostile skirmishes, hospitable interludes, or romantic trysts.

With the dawn of faster advances in modes of transportation and communication an entirely new circumstance emerged. In the period which we now call modernity, "[s]trangers," as Zygmunt Bauman so poignantly puts it, "stay and refuse to go away (though one keeps hoping that they will in the end)—while, stubbornly, escaping the net of local rules and thus remaining strangers."[1] Strangers seem to be neither neighbours nor aliens. But, then, who are they? Obviously not visitors, for they do not go away. But neither are they true aliens, for their sensed presence has become strangely familiar. With them we may even regularly exchange ritual pleasantries.

In modernity, the dominant culture in the West developed liberal stratagems of toleration of the strange and different which tended to bracket, deny, ignore, dismiss, or consume the very characteristics which constitute uniqueness or difference. "Strangers" were either assimilated or expelled. As a whole, the West has practised and mastered a policy of indifference or inattention. In the public space we were all asked to keep our differences—of gender, race, or creed—at home. Differences are all right—they even add to the mix and heighten the intrigue—but they ought fundamentally to be kept personal and private. In the public space of business, whether we were neighbours or aliens was largely pushed aside or marginalized in the wake of the money economy that, it was believed, demanded emotional, ethnic, national, and religious neutrality for maximum efficiency. After all, according to the modernist credo, business is business—and it should remain that way, uncluttered and untrammelled by personal or ethnic concerns. And that basic point, despite increased corporate attention to matters of ethics and social responsibility, remains basically unchanged in the liberalism of late capitalism.

At present, this modernist synthesis—in which the marginalized suffered in silence, either insisting that they are not really that different, or resigned to keeping their differences private—is rapidly unravelling. Marginalized groups are not only taking pride in asserting their difference, but are insisting that their cherished differences be publicly recognized. This makes for a totally new situation once again—what we now refer to as pluralism.

This emerging pluralism with its embrace of difference is proving unsettling and unnerving. The boundary lines between neighbours and strangers, between centre and margins, are no longer so neat. In large metropolitan centres, at least in the West, feeling oneself to be a stranger is not only the experience of visitors or aliens. With increasing regularity, people formerly thought to be at the centre feel themselves displaced or, at the least, threatened on their own turf, within what they perceive to be their own borders. The landscape is changing so rapidly that no one can any longer count on the safety of being in the centre. There is no longer (if there ever was) immunity from exclusion. The centre, to paraphrase Yeats, no longer holds. "The" centre (if it ever was more than an mirage) has vanished over the horizon, and been replaced by a variety of centres all scurrying to be dominant. Everyone increasingly feels the need to be on the alert. Guards and guard dogs abound, walled communities proliferate. Everyone, even white, middle-class males such as myself, can feel displaced on a subway in their hometown.

On a larger and wider scale, members of culturally dominant groups tend to resent and resist programs instituted to redress injustices. Denying the obvious truth that status quo social practices are never neutral, but discriminatory to the excluded, they cry "special treatment" when their own institutionalized privilege is called into question. If, however, the previously excluded are to be granted rights without the support of programs which take into account their difference, the existing socio-economic inequities are not likely to be alleviated. While so-called neutral policies perpetuate social inequalities, affirmative action policies often spark backlash. In either case, justice is deferred.

CENTRES AND MARGINS

The modernist dilemma was centre and margin; the pluralist dilemma is centres and margins. Instead of a dilemma of difference, we have dilemmas of differences. We have a variety of groups each claiming public space and recognition. In many parts of the world the breakdown of oligarchies, of both left and right, has led to civil wars over difference. Even one-party states are under mounting pressure to give increased recognition to minority rights. As we race headlong towards the next millennium, the dominant issue on every level—personally, interpersonally, institutionally, nationally, and internationally — is the negotiation of covenants which honour difference even as they avoid a paralyzing fragmentation or anarchic splintering.

Inclusion in one group often means exclusion from other groups. However, since identity groups take shape not only on the basis of gender, ethnicity, region, cultural identity, religion, or shared commitment, but also on a variety of levels—personal, informal, institutional, societal, national, international—groups may often have overlapping memberships. How, personally, are we to accomplish the onerous task of spinning webs of identity that intersect with, but do not obliterate, other webs? How, interpersonally (a realm in which we are ever more aware of the challenge of changing roles, multiple relationships, and shifting boundaries) can we weave webs of identity open to others and yet true to ourselves? How, institutionally, nationally, and internationally, can we establish and maintain public policies and moral stances of inclusion that at the same time honour differences?

As distinctions between strangers/neighbours, centres/margins, private/public are breaking down, it is our challenge to shape a civic ethos which celebrates differences and embraces strangers, not for purposes of exclusion or domination (with the resurgence of internecine conflicts), but to affirm the special giftedness of others. The weaving of a strong, diversely coloured, multistranded, cohesive social fabric is our challenge. To negotiate the tangled and sticky dilemmas of exclusions and inclusions that neither dissolves into chaos nor, in reaction, breeds a new rigidity, will require from all of us sensitivity, flexibility, the utmost in care and vigilance—and certainly trust. In that hopeful and reconciliatory spirit, the authors of this collection present their essays.

DIFFERENCE DISARMED

Faced with the dilemmas of differences, we are convinced that the liberal, modernist response of expanding our definition of who is the "same" will not do. The subject of modern moral philosophy, the bodyless, sexless, "history-less" ego of impartial reason, is not only an illusion, but a dangerous illusion. I do not doubt that a modernist theory of impartial reason—for example, a Rawlsian theory of justice—can convincingly develop a moral case that the boundaries of the "same" need to be extended to include persons now excluded. Such Kantian strategies of inclusion do work—but only to a point, and at a cost: neglecting the very differences that such a strategy seeks to overcome. That is, such strategies work by bracketing differences such as gender, corporeality, ethnicity, faith, age, class—differences that are intrinsic to human identity. Ironically, that which is "personal" is considered morally significant only to the extent that it can be bracketed and translated into the "impersonal." Complete disembodiment and total disinterest is championed as the moral and rational position: "God's viewpoint." Divested of emotions, historicity, corporeality, and particularity, and appealing only to the unitary principle of reason, the subject is reputedly free to pronounce universally valid moral judgments.

It is questionable, however, if such Kantian "would-I-like-to-be-treated-that-way?" strategies work when we are faced with people whose constitutional make-up, needs, and desires are different from our own. While consistency works when dealing with similars, if the differences between you and me are significant (and especially if the matter on which we differ is a matter that is cherished by you as well as by me), determining my response to you on the basis of consistency with my moral principles guarantees neither justice nor morality. Just as likely, my judgment will both flow from and perpetuate my position of power, thus making for violence.

Indeed, since moral principles may themselves be rationalizations constructed to repress or mitigate unresolved issues, my response may have much more to do with my personal struggles than it does with universal morality. As Julia Kristeva emphasizes, one sets his/her face against strangers because they remind us of that which is strange in us. Anguish over "the strange within us" projects outward in attacks on others.[2] Our internal—intra-psychic—nostalgia for a unity of seamless certainty acts to mask or deny internal differences and triggers defensive reactions to difference and diversity in interpersonal—interpsychic—relations. These emotionally charged and deeply entrenched attitudes—prejudices—are used to motivate and justify moral judgments. Insofar as they are defensive reactions, even as they cloak our own arguments with the gown of universal reason and thus justify exclusionary moral judgments, they both enshroud our internal dividedness in the illusion of unity and undermine our ability truly to see and honour the other as other.

Modernity has not only been arrogant and blind to that which is different, it has often been, even if unbeknownst to itself, oppressive and violent to those who are other and different. Masquerading as the universal deliverances of reason which as such are considered self-evident, personal and particular stances can become enshrined in institutional and cultural practices as "neutral" and "normal," even if they are actually discriminatory and oppressive to those of competing or differing allegiances.

It is difficult, if not impossible, for so-called impartial reason (and thus the discourse of modernity) to address these adaptations precisely because the doctrine of impartial reason (upon which modernism is built) is itself created by repressing their importance rather than by exploring how they work. As such, these defensive strategies—and their ensuing moral judgments—are resistant to critique even as they exercise their pernicious influence. When an individual or group is entrenched in fear or denial, it is not only hard to avoid stereotyping other individuals or groups, but it is difficult to empathize authentically with them. Even worse, it is easy to advocate or participate with a clear conscience in discriminatory practices which wreak violence.

Minimizing key differences so that sameness may abound not only suppresses what deserves moral attention, but it obscures the reality that the so-called neutral policies are in fact the policies of the dominant cultural group, bear the distinctive marks of this group, and discriminate against those who differ from it. Working towards social redress of inequities and changed public policy thus requires attending to and dismantling—at the least mitigating or circumventing—these often unconscious defensive adaptations.

DIFFERENCE EMBRACED

It is this suppression of difference which is the pivotal focus of what has become known as postmodernism's critique of modernity. Modernity's very dream of developing an all-encircling theory of the whole, erecting closure, attaining unity, mastering, and controlling nature has resulted—say a host of contemporary voices inspired by thinkers such as Jean-François Lyotard,[3] Jacques Derrida,[4] and Emmanuel Levinas[5]—in the domestication if not eradication of otherness and difference. Although differing in many respects among themselves, these thinkers—who may be said to share loosely the postmodernist umbrella—make common cause in their critique of the fundamental tenets of modernism: confidence in reason, faith in science and progress, belief in rational enlightenment as the sanctioned avenues to knowledge, security, and happiness.

In contrast to the modernist either-or ethos of inclusion in sameness or exclusion in otherness, which not only sees difference in others as defect, deficit, or threat, but masks or denies differences in self, we wish to join (all the while cherishing our own distinctives![6]) this growing chorus of postmodern voices calling for a genuine embrace of difference, both in others and in ourselves. We agree that for far too long the West has been embroiled in an ethos which sees self and other, the same and the different, as two reciprocating poles, simultaneously attracting and repelling each other. In the end, it was said (and in many quarters it continues to be said) only two possibilities exist: separation, identity, independence, and self-interest, or fusion, non-identity, submission, and other-directedness. In such models, humans who wish to enter into relationships face a stark choice: either dominate or be dominated. Difference is the enemy. Either the barb of otherness is removed—and the garden of sameness triumphs—or the thorn of difference flourishes—and the wilderness of otherness runs wild.

In contrast, we suggest adopting and shaping an ethics of connection which does not play the self-same off against the different-other. In such an ethics, difference is not the enemy to withstand—rather the self's fundamental transgression is its failure to recognize the other as other and to love the other as other—but the friend to stand with. An ethics of difference begins with a recognition of difference—not as deviance or deficit that threatens—but as otherness to connect with, cherish, and celebrate. It begins—not with nuclear monads in splendid isolation—but with selves-in-connection (human intersubjectivity as part of the cosmic interconnectedness of all of life). Difference as invitation and evocation calls us to responsibility and mutuality in which authentic connection is mutual empowerment: power-with rather than power-over or power-under. In this view, community is neither the promotion of sameness nor the praising of uniformity, but is being together in difference and diversity—in, through, and despite adversity.

Admittedly, this ethic faces prodigious odds, for it is only when we are secure in our own identities-in-process/on trial (Kristeva) that we can allow ourselves to be vulnerable. Only then can we run the risk of suffering violence attending every effort to connect with the other and different. Whether by means of the ignorance that produces fear, by the guardedness that results from previous hurt, or the anger that engenders outright hostility, there lurks in each of us the temptation to strive for control over difference rather than to connect with difference. Accepting and recognizing differences is a process fraught with apprehension and anxiety, either working together towards a community-in-difference (where justice and compassion flourish) or a falling apart into islands of opposition (and the spread of rancour and hate).

In other words, although difference is the basis for connection, it can also be the basis for ignorance, fear, and conflict. But the risks in recognition of difference must be faced, because rejecting differences excludes any genuine working together, and feeds the illusion of sameness and the accompanying repression of the irreplaceable uniqueness that each of us is in our difference from each other. The more we flower and flourish in our uniqueness, the more our differences stand out, and the more special and profound can be our contribution to the communal project. And, paradoxically, the more we are able to own our own identity-in-difference, the less the difference of otherness is a threat, and the more it becomes an opportunity for growth, enrichment, and mutuality.

TOWARDS AN ETHIC OF DIFFERENCE

This collection of essays seeks to make a meaningful contribution to an ethic of difference by suggesting some ways in which we might negotiate healing ways in the wilderness of postmodern pluralism. It is the collaborative fruit of a three-year, cross-disciplinary project on pluralism at the Institute for Christian Studies, in Toronto, involving research in philosophy and the history of philosophy, educational theory and ethics, systematic theology and religious studies, social and political theory, cultural and aesthetic theory, feminist theory, and postmodernism.

The collection is divided into two sections. The first group of essays focuses on some of our pluralistic culture's struggles with recognizing and addressing general dilemmas of difference; the second group attempts to negotiate such differences in a number of particularly troubling situations.

One of the strong, common threads in the weave of each essay is the conviction that a healthy approach to differences requires, not their public bracketing, but their public celebration and exercise—that is, compassion and respect for those of differing faiths and customs. Even though the shaping of such an inclusive civic ethos is outrageously difficult—no one should believe otherwise!—it is, we believe, the only viable alternative to exclusionary policies of hegemonic domination, marginalization, and oppression. We trust that the spirit of two biblical passages imbues these essays:

> When an alien lives with you in your land, do not mistreat him/her. The alien living with you must be treated as one of your native-born. Love him/her as yourself, for you were aliens in Egypt. I am the Lord your God.
> Leviticus 19:33

> The King will say to those on his right, 'Come, you who are blessed.... I was a stranger and you invited me in, I needed clothes and you clothed me, I was sick and you looked after me, I was in prison and you came to visit me.'
> Matthew 25:34-35

Dilemmas of Difference

In the opening essay, "Plotting the Margins: A Historical Episode in the Management if Social Philosophy," Robert Sweetman reminds us that existence of cultural plurality within societies is not something new. He claims—surprisingly, I expect for many—that the West's inability to come to terms with social plurality without persecution is not fundamentally to be blamed on Western religious discourse, but on the adoption and secularizing application by Christian clerics of the Aristotelian legacy in logic. If this is indeed the case, not only are we motivated to look more critically at the hegemony of logic in the West, but a welcoming space opens up for people of a variety of faiths to work towards dwelling together in mutual respect, not through a public bracketing of their spiritual passion, but precisely in practising their passion publicly in compassion for the different and the strange.

In "Consequences of Liberalism: Ideological Domination in Rorty's Public/Private Split," Hendrik Hart explicitly takes up this theme. Arguing that when our deepest commitments are kept private they nevertheless do their public work secretly, and more often than not in discriminatory ways, Hart is troubled by Richard Rorty's liberal "we." He claims that we need to work for a compassionate, "hearted," civic ethos in which there is "space for everyone's heartbeat to be felt in public policy."

In the light of increasing cultural, religious, and linguistic plurality in Canada, Ken Badley's "Indoctrination and Assimilation in Plural Settings" reopens the indoctrination debate in education. Badley suggests that we are "ontologically challenged" if we continue to believe in the myth of ideologically neutral education. He further suggests that a small advance in the genuine recognition of differences in faith and epistemologies would be made in the publically funded system by no longer insisting on ideologically neutral teachers —no such teachers exist—but by staffing the schools with committed teachers "capable of impartiality or some kind of procedural neutrality."

In "'Woman' in the Plural: Negotiating Sameness and Difference in Feminist Theory," Janet Wesselius seeks a way through the dilemma of twentieth-century feminism: preserving the importance of gender identity while also precluding delimiting gender directives. By "keeping in mind that the goal before us is the freedom of women and not the espousal of a given theory," she argues that political attention to marginalization in its endless variety of forms helps us to avoid the totalizations of sameness with its suppression of difference even as it fully recognizes the systematic oppression of women on the basis of sex/gender.

In a threefold discussion of religion, morality, and public justice, Hendrik Hart attempts to show that Christians who theologically endorse a morality prohibiting homosexual behaviour may nevertheless be able to support public justice for homosexuals without theological or moral compromise. In "Religious Conflicts about Moral Authority: A Problem for Policy-Makers?" Hart develops a thesis concerning a certain ambiguity in the relation between religion and morality. The long middle section of his essay is a detailed illustration of this ambiguity in the work of the New Testament scholar Richard Hays.

In "Rethinking the Family: Belonging, Respecting, and Connecting," I take up the vexing question in our plural society of whether family make-up—patriarchal, permissive, single-parent, same-sex, ethnically diverse, mixed faith—is a significant indicator of potential abuse and violence. I conclude that more than anything it is the quality of the relational interactions in the family, rather than organizational structure and form, or roles and function, that fosters genuine intimacy or generates violence. Rethinking the philosophy of the family through this focus would also, I suggest, enable our society and its governments to promote and support education programs for healthy relationships in families—without becoming embroiled in the fractious issues of family form and function.

Negotiations of Difference

In North America, the limits of pluralism and tolerance with respect to the cultural traditions of immigrant groups are severely tested by the practice of female genital mutilation (FGM). Discussing the issue in a Canadian context, Lisa Chisholm-Smith argues that culturally aware education programs are to be preferred to legislation. Ways need to be found so that members of the practising groups themselves can come to realize that FGM is "not contributing positively" to their culture.

In "Violent Asymmetry: The Shape of Power in the Current Debate over the Morality of Homosexuality," Ronald Kuipers returns us to the issue of the difficulty our society has in coping with difference, in particular the difference of sexual orientation. He calls the heterosexual majority to pay attention to the asymmetry of power in the cultural debate, and pleads that those who understand homosexual difference as deviance nevertheless recognize that the difference between the heterosexual majority and the homosexual minority is unimportant compared to the "similarity both groups have with respect to their ability to suffer pain and humiliation."

In "Native Self-government: The Spiritual Fire and the Political Fire," George Vandervelde points out the pluralist conundrum raised when an all-encompassing, holistic, Native spirituality—"the spiritual fire"—is brought to bear on the issue of Native self-government—"the political fire." The Western liberal privatization of religion clearly violates, he argues, the holistic nature of Native spirituality. However, privileging Native spirituality in a political jurisdiction marginalizes all of those who within that jurisdiction wish to follow a different path. In refusing both marginalization and hegemony, Vandervelde asks for a "practical sagacity" which publicly welcomes diverse spiritualities "as legitimate, even intrinsic, sources for political deliberations and decisions."

In "On Identity and Aesthetic Voice of the Culturally Displaced," Calvin Seerveld asks if it is possible for the artistry of Fourth-World cultures such as the First Nations in Canada to avoid both the idols of tribal separation and ethnocidal assimilation. Canvassing the fierce debate among philosophically trained African cultural leaders, Seerveld suggests—with illustrations—that any kind of cohering community has a "polymorphous complexity to its particularity." If this complexity were recognized and encouraged, especially by mainline theorists and connoisseurs, it would open cultural space for "uncommercialized, non-protesting, ethnically flavoured open-to-the-neighbour art."

All these essays suggest that hope for the future lies not in shedding or suppressing the particularites of our diverse cultural heritages, but in finding non-hegemonic ways to celebrate them. Then, we will be able, in Seerveld's words, to "foreground the surprising complementary joy there can be in sharing diversity by way of artistry, or even philosophical discourse, in the press of life and death affairs." That writ large is the hope and prayer of all the authors of this book: difference, not as curse or menace, but as gift to enjoy and call to celebrate. Then, indeed, ways open for an embrace of diversity in mutuality —and looking at creation in all its dazzling difference, we may break out in praise, as God did in the beginning: "Behold, it is good! very good!"

Notes

1.   Zygmunt Bauman, *Postmodern Ethics* (Oxford: Blackwell, 1993), p. 152.
2.   Julia Kristeva, *Strangers to Ourselves*, trans. Leon S. Roudiez (New York: Columbia University Press, 1991), p. 191.
3.   "Let us wage war on totality, let us be witnesses to the unpresentable, let us activate the differences and save the honour of the name" (Jean Francois Lyotard, *The Postmodern Condition*, trans. G. Bennington and B. Massumi [Minneapolis: University of Minnesota Press, 1984], p. 81).
4.   "Reason...has always *neutralized* the other, in every sense of the word" (Jacques Derrida, *Writing and Difference*, trans. A. Bass [Chicago: University of Chicago Press, 1978], p. 96).
5.   "'I think' comes down to 'I can'—to an appropriation of what is, to an exploitation of reality.   Ontology as a first philosophy is a philosophy of power...a philosophy of injustice" (Emmanuel Levinas, *Totality and Infinity*, trans. A. Lingis [Pittsburgh: Duquesne University Press, 1969], p. 46).
6.   See James H. Olthuis, ed. *Knowing* Other-*wise: Philosophy at the Threshold of Spirituality* (New York: Fordham University Press, 1997).

Part I

Dilemmas of Difference

1

Plotting the Margins: A Historical Episode in the Management of Social Plurality

ROBERT SWEETMAN

INTRODUCTION

Contemporary Western societies have become acutely sensitive to the existence of cultural (linguistic, religious, social, etc.) pluralities in their midst. Indeed, many contemporary social and cultural theorists have come to share a way of articulating this sensitivity which assumes (if only as an unintentional rhetorical effect) that present acknowledgement of, and respect for, cultural plurality represents something "new under the sun," an invention mothered, if you will, by present necessity.[1]

It takes little thought, however, to realize that cultural plurality existing within societies and political jurisdictions is not, in and of itself, a new problem or opportunity for human beings. Such plurality seems, rather, to be part of the *longue durée* of the human condition wherever societies have grown large enough to embrace two or more distinct human groupings.

Recognition of the historical ubiquity of cultural plurality raises the possibility of examining past efforts to address and manage it. It is the intention of this essay to examine one crucial episode in the West's struggle with cultural plurality, an episode particularly influential in the formation of a pattern of social thought in which specific kinds of plurality (e.g., racial or religious) are experienced as both threatening and eradicable. This examination calls into question our habitual understanding of the intersection of reason, religion, persecution, and intolerance. Indeed, it suggests that we see the persistent recrudescence of persecution and intolerance in the political history of the modern West not as the unfortunate but predictable by-product of religious contamination, but rather as the result of a secularizing logicization of medieval Europe's guiding political theology.

R. I. Moore's slim but highly suggestive volume *The Formation of a Persecuting Society: Power and Deviance in Western Europe 950-1250* provides us an entree into the historical episode in question.[2] It does so in and through the synthetic use it makes of a growing body of historical work which attends to the experience of human subjects long neglected by—under-represented or only instrumentally present in—traditional histories of the Middle Ages.[3] The present essay begins, consequently, by presenting and evaluating Moore's attempted synthesis. It proceeds to focus more narrowly upon one important aspect of his synthesis, and concludes by suggesting the impact which Moore's synthesis has upon the still widespread narrative of Western history that identifies the banishment of religion and religious discourses from the public forum as a necessary if not sufficient condition for the construction of societies in which toleration of difference prevails.

R. I. MOORE'S THESIS: THE FORMATION OF A PERSECUTING SOCIETY

Moore argues that "the eleventh and twelfth centuries saw what has turned out to be a permanent change in Western society. Persecution became habitual. That is to say, not simply that individuals were subject to violence, but that deliberate and socially sanctioned violence began to be directed *through established governmental, judicial, and social institutions*, against groups of people defined by general characteristics such as race, religion, or way of life; and that membership in such groups itself came to be regarded as justifying these attacks."[4]

The Historical Account and Its Rivals

Heresy and its ecclesiastical response constitute the central case study underlying Moore's synthesis. Indeed, Moore says that "Lateran IV [1215] laid down a machinery of persecution for Western Christendom, and especially a range of sanctions against those convicted, which was to prove adaptable to a much wider variety of victims than the heretics for whom it was designed."[5] In other words, the Lateran Council together with the subsequent establishment of papal inquisitors in the 1230s mark out the culmination of a complex development the origin of which goes back to the late tenth and early eleventh century.

　　Moore's rehearsal of the story which emerges within this frame is on the whole rather familiar. Heresy as a widespread and organized phenomenon appeared to die in the West with the inclusion in the Catholic fold of Arian peoples in the course of the fifth and sixth centuries of the Christian era. The eleventh and twelfth centuries, however, saw a gradual reemergence and proliferation of heresy, and of progressively better organized and more widely dispersed heretical associations. Despite this story, Moore refuses to identify this very proliferation and dissemination as the context proper to the Church's persecuting response.[6] Rather, he distinguishes between heresy and heterodox belief: "heresy exists only in so far as authority chooses to declare its existence ...[it] can only arise in the context of the assertion of authority, which the heretic resists, and is therefore by definition a political matter. Heterodox belief, however, is not. Variety of religious opinion exists at many times and places, and becomes heresy when authority declares it intolerable."[7]

The business of responding to the presence of heretics and heresy belonged ex officio to bishops. It was carried out in the context of episcopal visitation and inquest (*inquisitio*). Until the mid-twelfth century, episcopal policy was straightforward enough: heretics were to be identified in the context of episcopal inquest where they were to be examined and either reconciled and assigned a condign penance, or excommunicated and exiled from the diocese after public rebuttal of their teachings.[8] After 1150, however, bishops made increasing use of the secular arm; the secular arm of torture. Exile was increasingly accompanied by confiscation of a heretic's property, by social and commercial shunning, and by the application of the status and penalties of the heretic to any who supported and voluntarily associated with them. This toughening of episcopal response forms the backdrop to the Fourth Lateran Council of 1215 and the eventual creation of the office of papal inquisitor in the 1230s.

Moore proceeds to tell the history of Jews in the West and of the treatment of lepers in such a way as to highlight parallel chronology and texture. Until 1000, Jews enjoyed relatively harmonious relations with their Gentile neighbours. Indeed, there appears to have been a gradual convergence of ethnicity, dress, and lifestyle. Then, from the end of the eleventh century, relations with non-Jews deteriorated. Jews suffered increasing physical segregation (ghetto), in range of occupations open to them (concentration on money-lending, pawnshops, etc.), dress (Stars of David), the violence of Christian mobs, and growing dependence upon, and exploitation by, their secular lords (especially the kings of England, Iberia, and France). Moreover, from the twelfth century, Christians in the West came to clarify and disseminate that stereotype of the Jew which has hovered so tragically over subsequent history.[9]

Likewise, before the twelfth century lepers were recognized and feared, but allowed to live among the non-leprous population. In the twelfth century, by contrast, Western societies began to invest heavily in institutions of segregation by means of which lepers could be isolated as completely as possible from the rest of society. Concomitantly, a leprous stereotype gained prominence by which lepers were legitimately to be thought of as the "living dead" who were to be ritually buried upon segregation.[10]

Finally, Moore notes that from the twelfth century the nexus of images and assertions used to name the heretic, the Jew, and the leper tended to interlock and, indeed, to become interchangeable. To give but one example, the use of leprosy as a metaphor for heresy becomes endemic in late twelfth- and thirteenth-century discourse. Moreover, each stereotype is imbued with the spectre of sexual promiscuity and with Satanism. Thus, Moore concludes that for "all imaginative purposes, heretics, Jews and lepers were interchangeable.

They had the same qualities, from the same source, and they presented the same threat: through them the Devil was at work to subvert the Christian order and bring the world to chaos."[11]

Moore's telling of the story in this way is designed to contest alternative versions that assume later medieval persecution to arise in response to the new-found demographic and social prominence of that persecution's victims; the synchronous and isomorphic pattern of persecution of three very distinct and different groups undermines such an assumption. Moore, by contrast wants to say that the history of persecution must be accounted for in relation to persecutors rather than their victims.

Before he can develop his own understanding of the story, however, he must dispose of a plausible, alternative explanation for the discontinuity in social ethos that he has chronicled for the periods 600-1000 and 1000-1300. In other words, he must recognize the paucity of historical sources for the earlier period and the relative abundance of sources for the later period and still argue against the claim that his story "reflects a change in the record rather than in reality, a gradual lifting of the curtain of darkness."[12] As a consequence, he examines his story of heretics, lepers, and Jews with this project in mind.

He begins this examination (as he began his initial story) with heretics and proceeds to develop the distinction between heterodox belief and heresy qua political effect which we have already noted. Within this frame he shifts his focus from the various chronicle accounts of heresy and ecclesiastical response to the massive ecclesiastical (political) changes undergone in the eleventh and twelfth centuries—the so-called Gregorian Reform. In other words, he presents the reform movement as a centralizing political dynamic by which the diffuse episcopal organization of the early Middle Ages is transformed into a centralized papal organization. The reemergence of heresy must be seen in this light—for example, Rome's initial sponsorship and eventual condemnation of Paterene criticism of the distinctive traditions of Milan's Ambrosian clergy.[13]

Moore's association of heresy and Gregorian Reform produces three observations:

1. The latitude allowed individual reformers was tied to political circumstances. Thus, Robert of Arbrissel and Henry of Lausanne could preach an identical message and, nevertheless, the former was beatified while the latter was condemned as a heretic.[14]
2. While heretics were regularly accused of innovation, Rome was the greatest innovator of all. Indeed, says Moore, "[t]o a considerable extent...charges of heresy in the twelfth century must be seen as serving to reflect back upon the recalcitrant the accusations of novelty which they had levelled at their source."[15]

3. The ecclesiastical procedure for identifying and rebutting heresy gave to it a greater coherence and therefore a more menacing aspect than it actually possessed.

All of this allows Moore to confirm his initial telling. The political ferment within the Western Church of the eleventh and twelfth centuries produced a concern to eradicate heterodox belief under the rubric of heresy; the contrast with the previous three centuries is real and not an illusion caused by our ignorance of the previous centuries.

Moore begins his examination of his story of lepers and leprosy by citing literary evidence and an epidemiology of leprosy which together suggest a significant expansion of the disease in Western Europe during the eleventh, twelfth, and thirteenth centuries.[16] This is as far as he would need to go in order to establish discontinuity between 600-1000 and 1000-1300. Nevertheless, Moore wants us to consider another possibility, namely, that the history of leprosy must be seen in terms of those who identify and deal with lepers in society. Thus, he cites three problems with seeing the eleventh through the thirteenth century as a time in which Europe knew a significant outbreak of Hansen's disease (leprosy in the strict sense):[17]

1. He points to the nearly complete lack of archeological confirmation of the literary evidence for such a major outbreak.
2. Moreover, he notes that the same combination of dense population (vulnerable to disease) and a high degree of mobility (conducive to the spread of contagious diseases) was also present in the Rhine regions of Carolingian Europe, ninth-century Wessex of the British Isles and, throughout the Middle Ages, in Italy, the densest and most mobile population of Europe. Nevertheless, there is no literary, much less archeological, evidence for an outbreak of Hansen's disease in these places and centuries.
3. Finally surviving theoretical treatises on the diagnosis of leprosy suggest that the name "leprosy" would have been applied to conditions other than Hansen's disease and, hence, would have entailed significant social content.

Consequently, Moore suggests that it may well be that leprosy existed in the eyes of the powerful beholder. If so, the coincidence of increasing concern over the presence of lepers in European society in the period 1000-1300 begins to look suspiciously like the increasing concern with heresy.

Moore faces more difficult problems when examining the history of Jews. He must admit the emergence of antisemitism in Late Antiquity, despite the legal and imperial protection accorded Jews and their leadership. Indeed, he admits that outbreaks in the fifth and sixth centuries led to forced conversions.[18] Nevertheless, he uses the demonstrable tolerance of Theodoric and the

Ostrogothic Kingdom to illustrate the generally favourable position of Jews in the barbarian kingdoms of the early Middle Ages. Moreover, he cites a variety of Carolingian developments to suggest the protraction of early medieval tolerance into the late tenth century.[19]   Given this evidence of relative integration in the centuries before 1000, the many restrictions, violence, and frequent citation of the stereotype of the "wandering Jew" during subsequent centuries stand out in contrast.

Moore then reaches for his coup de grâce; he argues that the use of interchangeable rhetoric to denote and frame policy for heretics, lepers, and Jews is also discontinuous with the practice of earlier centuries. The Jewish case is decisive, because it is well documented. "As hostility narrowed the opportunities available to them, Jews were forced ever more relentlessly into certain roles, that of the money-lender par excellence. The characteristics of the part, then, became those of the actor."[20] He is, consequently, well positioned to conclude that "[t]he medieval heretic was a reality; the medieval Manichee was a myth.... Individual Jews and Jewish communities...were welded into a single, coherent stereotype of 'the Jew.' And when our knowledge is greater, we may equally find that many who were afflicted by a shifting variety of medical and psycho-social conditions...were brought together in the single, universal image of 'the leper.'"[21]   Indeed, says Moore, one can see these interchangeable stereotypes extended more or less faithfully to cover male homosexuals, female prostitutes, usurers, and the insane.[22]

The Synthetic Meaning of Moore's Account

The last two chapters of *Persecuting Society* shift the focus from the story to its proper understanding. Moore begins by recalling the central place assumed by sexual menace, and by motifs of rootlessness, lack of boundary, and wandering in the rhetoric of persecution he has been chronicling. Such rhetoric fits well the anthropological model developed by Mary Douglas. She explains such phenomena as characteristic of fear, and fear of social change in particular.[23] Whereas fear of pollution protects boundaries generally, fear of sexual pollution protects social boundaries in particular.

If the rhetoric of persecution is evidence of fear, one asks, "Whose fear?" Moore answers unequivocally that it is "the fear that the privileged feel of those at whose expense their privilege is enjoyed."[24] It arises above all in two sets of circumstances: in the first place when the privileged come to feel that a concrete privilege is under threat; secondly, in response to times of rapid and profound social change, when all privilege seems at risk.

Moore goes on to show that the eleventh and twelfth centuries are precisely such a period of massive social change on three different levels.[25] First, it is the period in which the mature seigneurial system is established with its concomitant conceptual reassignation of all people into the simple opposition serf/noble.   Second, it is a period of rapid urbanization during which a commercial, money economy is firmly established. Third, it is a period that sees the bureaucratization of governments both secular and ecclesiastical.

The opposition noble/serf, though its social context differs from the other oppositions either newly generated or reemphasized in these centuries (Catholic/Manichee, clean/leprous, Christian/Jew), shares with them a tendency to be articulated as a species of an overarching opposition between *pauperes* (the poor) and *potentes* (the powerful). For example, all successful reform preachers appealed to the *pauperes* in the name of "poverty." Moreover, their appeal to the poor received authoritative approbation provided there was due recognition of ecclesiastical authority and its pendants, namely, secular power and social order. Moore sees as the background to reform (following Little, Murray, and Mollat) the capitalization of wealth and its identification in the minds of contemporaries with social change.[26] But, adds Moore, "[w]here money reigned supreme, the growing and increasingly menacing presence of the poor pointed to the necessity of providing for their control and, if necessary, their confinement or expulsion from the community."[27]

The portrayal of the eleventh and twelfth centuries as a time of rapid social change in which the elite worked to control others can be understood, however, in more than one way. The elite's imposition of social control can be seen within Durkheim's theory of deviance. In such a model, individuals and groups are defined as deviant so that "by excluding some, [a society is enabled] to reinforce the unity of the rest. The exercise is particularly necessary at times of rapid social change and increasing differentiation, when the redefinition of social values and the reaffirmation of social unity is called for."[28] It is precisely this Durkheimian model which has inspired English medievalists in the postwar era, an inspiration Moore has written his book to contest.

Moore asks who is calling for the reaffirmation of unity and for what reasons? He suggests that one is helped by an analogous historical development, namely, the state's interest in criminality. In general, he says, in the transition from segmentary society to state the old habit of recognizing criminality only when specific acts have been performed against specific complainants comes to be supplemented by new offenses against abstract entities (state, society, morality), offenses which the ruler or a given apparatus of order seeks out and punishes even when there is no complaint. Moore notes a similar transition in ecclesiastical response to heterodox belief in the course of the twelfth century. He asks whether the treatment of heretics and, by extension, other vilified groups belongs then, like abstract criminality, to the birth of the bureaucratic state. If so, Weberian models of centralization and universalization provide better help in understanding the development of persecution during the later Middle Ages.[29]

But, how does one decide between Durkheim and Weber? Moore suggests that one investigate whether persecution results from popular antipathy toward victims. Since the evidence regarding lepers is too fragmentary, he turns to evidence for popular hostility toward heretics and Jews. As for heretics, Moore shows that there is too little evidence of popular antipathy to warrant an appeal to Durkheim's theory of deviance. There are only six such examples preserved for the period 1100-1300 and the four examples of the twelfth century can also be seen in Weberian terms as conflicts between centralizing and popular jurisdictions. Moreover, though there is undeniable popular antipathy toward Jews, this antipathy must be placed against the background of three hundred years of substantial and increasing social integration and the association of Jews after 1000 with the seigneurial elite whether secular or ecclesiastical. Indeed, even the massacres associated with the First Crusade (1096) were not initiated by local populations but rather by foreign knights. Local Christians in fact defended Jews and their property at Mainz, Worms, and Cologne. All of this evidence suggests that one look to elite concerns rather than popular antipathy as the context proper to later medieval persecution.

Indeed, the canonization of the child-martyr William of Norwich and the role played in these events by the elite biographer Thomas of Monmouth, together with the processes which led to the burning of heretics at Soissons (1114) and Cologne (1143) prove suggestive. What begins as a dispute between persons or groups of *pauperes* attracts the interest of *potentes*. Stereotype is then used by the powerful to interpret the statements of *pauperes* in ways which augment the potential threat and which consequently justify persecution. This same pattern was observed by Kieckhefer and Cohn in connection with the witch trials of the late medieval and early modern periods.[30]

Since the evidence of popular antipathy is so weak, Moore chooses to explore a Weberian understanding of later medieval persecution. It was the princes, whether ecclesiastical or secular, then, who called for the reaffirmation of social unity and consequently the identification of deviants. They did so as part of a centralizing and universalizing attack upon all forms of communal authority. Moore uses the history of the ordeal and its suppression in the thirteenth century to illustrate the pattern of attack.[31] He concludes by drawing the analogy back to heresy and heretics. "Just as trial by ordeal expressed the authority of the community in its juridical role, popular heresy represented, not exclusively but more than any other single force, the assertion of collective values and communal independence against the subordination of religion, first to seigneurial and later to bureaucratic power."[32] The fifteenth- and sixteenth-century move to invest medical practitioners rather than local juries with the identification of lepers must be seen in the same light. So, too, the fourteenth century attempt in the Paris region to transfer practical medical care from informally educated hands (barbers, apothecaries, midwives) to those of university-trained physicians, and the gradual transfer between 1000-1300 of canonization from local communities to bishops, to the papal office.[33]

In sum, Moore is able to demonstrate that there were a wide range of attacks upon the power and authority of local communities. Moreover, these attacks were allied to campaigns of moral repression by means of which "newly instituted regimes establish their legitimacy, proclaim their adherence to traditional values, discredit their enemies and consolidate their hold on power."[34] The new regime can be identified with several different faces, so to speak, but the regime is the same: the transformation of payment of service into cash payment and of oral social processes into written instruments. In the new regime, warriors are increasingly replaced by literate clerics. Consequently, says Moore, "[i]t is among clerks that we will see most clearly how the emergence of the state represented a new stage in the division of labour, as specialization or professionalization of government—and among them...that we will find its [i.e., persecution's] origins and *raison d'être*."[35]

Moore goes on to argue that there emerged during the eleventh and twelfth centuries a cohesive class of clerical, governmental agents. He cites as evidence the claim that such solidarity of interest and action existed, made by those who felt themselves being dispossessed: traditional religious and the old nobility. He also cites the witness of this new class itself, in particular its widespread antipathy toward any who could be termed *illiterati, idiotae,* or *rustici.* He notes the ubiquity of these terms' use to denote heretics and Jews. This last conjunction allows him to conclude that the rhetoric of persecution which he had earlier identified as a language of fear is to be seen as the new clerical class's fear of those whom they name illiterate and rustic; the rhetoric is a language by which the new class bolstered their own class identity and solidarity, and by which they justified persecution both to ward off perceived threats, and to stimulate the claims and techniques of bureaucratic government.

Finally, Moore uses the intersection of heretic, Jew, and accusations of sorcery to claim that the new clerical class developed its rhetoric of persecution in a context of intense competition,[36] for there were two potential claimants to the power of the new bureaucratizing regime. Both claimants could point to their mastery of written culture, i.e., the Christian clergy and the Jewish communities of Europe. Indeed, there is scattered evidence of Jewish prominence in both secular and ecclesiastical courts of the eleventh and even as late as the twelfth century. On the basis of this admittedly fragmentary evidence Moore suggests that Jews "offered a real alternative, and therefore a real challenge to Christian *literati* as advisers of princes and agents and beneficiaries of bureaucratic power."[37] Moore claims to be able to contrast an exaggerative stereotype accorded the heretic and a diminutive one accorded the Jew. Heretical threat was purportedly exaggerated because heretics did not represent a real alternative to the Christian clergy, Jewish threat was diminished precisely because Jewish communities could present such an alternative.

Moore is aware that this synthesis represents the dark side of those social and cultural processes of differentiation which can be, and indeed often have been, presented in different and altogether more exalted ways.[38] Nevertheless, he insists that "however that tremendous extension of power and influence of the literate is described, the development of persecution in all its forms [must be] part of it and therefore inseparable from the great and positive achievements with which it is associated."[39]

Evaluating Moore's Synthesis

Moore is to be credited with recognizing the possibility of a historical synthesis implicit in a growing body of work on the social outgroups of medieval Europe. There does seem to be a synchronicity to the pattern of treatment of these groups. Moreover there does seem to be a gradual convergence of the language and images used to identify these groups as social problems. But if Moore is to be credited with an important synthetic insight, it is not an insight free from error and indeed at times what almost appears deliberate misconstrual. To give one egregious example, Moore follows Alexander Murray and Lester K. Little in seeing the importance of the capitalization of wealth and its identification in the minds of contemporaries with social change.[40] This phenomenon had in Moore's view a decided impact on the way in which the poor were conceived: "[w]here money reigned supreme, the growing and increasingly menacing presence of the poor pointed to the necessity of providing for their control and, if necessary, their confinement or expulsion from the community."[41]

Behind the work of Murray and Little, however, lie the pioneering studies of Michel Mollat and his team of researchers. Moore's reading of the implication of their work is almost perverse. Moore sees the development of hôtels de Dieu and other modes of poor relief in the twelfth and thirteenth centuries as analogues to the formation of Jewish ghettos and leprosaria (viewed as instruments of oppressive control). It is worth noting that Mollat's own reading speaks rather of the same period and strategies as a heightened concern for, and connection with, the involuntary poor which ends only with the economic contraction of the early fourteenth century, exacerbated by the scourge of plague at midcentury. The picture which Moore paints for the twelfth and thirteenth centuries is one which Mollat also describes, but then for the late fourteenth and fifteenth centuries.[42] Moore can be faulted for not acknowledging his difference with Mollat and defending his views, especially since Mollat's work is an important part of the body of historical scholarship that Moore is attempting to synthesize.

There are also a number of other places in which Moore's account and explanation of later medieval persecution must be qualified and corrected. At several points, for example, he sets up an artificially intense contrast between 600-1000 and 1000-1300, underestimating by centuries the antiquity of historical phenomena important to his story. Thus, the episcopal inquest which forms the immediate institutional backdrop to the establishment of the office of papal inquisitor is far older than Moore imagines. Its origins lie in the Roman, secular, administrative practice of Late Antiquity, practice which was adapted for ecclesiastical use in the fifth and sixth centuries along with episcopal visitation and the annual diocesan synod.[43]

Similarly, Moore identifies the origin of the ordeal with royal and centralizing social forces, not popular ones. Thus, he sees the ordeal as a regalian right exercised by Carolingian monarchs to enhance their power to intervene in the local administration of justice, at least until it was suppressed in favour of even more effective centralizing practices. While it does seem that Carolingian monarchs appropriated the ordeal as a regalian right to give themselves new powers in local affairs, it would be an overstatement to claim the ordeal itself as a regalian invention of relatively recent date. Rather, its attraction for Carolingian monarchs lay precisely in its currency as a time-honoured instrument of dispute management. There are numerous references to ordeals in sources which predate the Carolingian period. Moreover, the turf ordeals described in the most archaicizing of the Icelandic sagas suggest an origin deep in the pagan and Germanic past.[44]

More important, however, is Moore's tendency to underplay the antiquity of the stereotypes he identifies with the later medieval rhetoric of persecution. Many of the characteristic features of the medieval stereotype of the "Jew," for instance, were already operative in the fifth-century polemics of John Chrysostom. Moreover, the stereotype of the witch is a sixth-century coinage.[45] The stereotype of the Manichee finds its textual roots in the fifth century, while that of the leper is far older.[46]

These errors demand a significant modification and narrowing of Moore's fundamental thesis. One must acknowledge a far greater continuity of institutional and rhetorical configuration between Roman Antiquity and the later Middle Ages than Moore seems comfortable doing, even while acknowledging his claim that there exists a significant discontinuity in the treatment of outgroups between 600-1000 and 1000-1300.

Finally and most damagingly, Moore vastly overplays clerical solidarity. The Christian clergy were no monolith, certainly not in contemporary ecclesiastical theory.[47] While Moore's identification of class sense and solidarity can perhaps be seen within a distinct stratum of the Christian clergy, those who in the parlance of the day "raised themselves up from the dust," his use of class analysis must be far more refined (and modest) if it is to carry the day.[48] To my mind this is nowhere clearer than in his suggestion of an originary, bureaucratic struggle between Christian clergy and Jews. This argument seems to me to be plausible only if one views both the Christian clergy and Jewish communities as undifferentiated wholes. One ought, on the contrary, to see the clergy as shifting networks of interest and perspective, networks which cut across most of the other social divisions encountered in Moore's analysis. One then sees the interaction of Christian clergy and Jewish communities in far more complex and ambiguous terms.[49]

In fine, only parts of Moore's story and explanation stand up to criticism, and then only if his class analysis does not extend beyond that stratum of the Christian clergy who "raised themselves up from the dust" during the period 1000-1300. For, it does seem that this stratum of the clergy came to power in and through struggle (with regular clergy and traditional nobility rather than the Jews). In the course of this struggle they acted to mould "perennial" stereotypes of society's marginal groups into a single demonizing instrument by which to isolate and dominate an indeterminate set of other groups.

But even the partial success of Moore's thesis raises a variety of subsidiary questions. This essay proposes to deal with one in particular. Provided one gains a more precise picture of who constitutes the persecuting stratum within the clergy and of their intellectual formation, one can ask whether there is some intellectual instrument native to the formation of these clerics which might help one account for their development of an all-purpose rhetoric of persecution.

CLERICAL EDUCATION AND THE RHETORIC OF PERSECUTION

It should be admitted that Moore's identification of Christian clergy as the forgers of a rhetoric of persecution seems to fit well with our culture's habitual understanding of the intersection between reason, religion, and social conflict. A look at the education of that group within the high medieval clergy responsible for the formation of the West's rhetoric of persecution, however, will suggest we entertain revisions to our conventional identifications. For, as Moore points out, education, or at least a near monopoly upon certain kinds of education, were crucial to this group's success.

By implication, one looks toward the "rational formation" of an upwardly mobile stratum within the Christian clergy. If it were simply the monopoly of reason by a *clerical* elite which accounted for its use as an instrument of persecution, one would expect the use of a rhetoric of persecution to wane as a consequence of progressive secularization. But Moore is very clear on this score. The tool once forged remains a part of the apparatus of power in the West right into the twentieth century; the Holocaust must be seen as persecuting rhetoric's most bitter fruit.[50] As a consequence, the question will return whether there is something about the historical face of reason (its cultural reproduction) which leaves it open to persecuting applications?

The New Bureaucratic Clergy

We must once again attend to the new, bureaucratic clergy of the later Middle Ages, and to their characteristic intellectual formation. Fortunately, we are well served by the painstaking studies of the twelfth- and thirteenth-century growth of government which have appeared in the course of the last twenty years.[51] The educational and social profile of the new bureaucratic personnel has also begun to undergo scholarly analysis.[52] What emerges from these studies are a number of points which bear directly upon the clerical stratum in question. First of all, one is enabled to see the relatively narrow group of "new men" who emerge in the twelfth and thirteenth centuries in and through the expansion and bureaucratization of government, both civil and ecclesiastical. Secondly, one is reminded of the antipathy which these men aroused among other demographically important clerical groups, most notably monastic and liberally educated writers. They were vilified for their merely pragmatic formation and for their secular outlook. Thirdly, recent historical work places new clerical players in the context of a parallel rise among non-clerics of mediocre knightly status. Finally, one glimpses diverse educational contexts in which the new bureaucracy was formed.

Indeed, intellectual formation took place within several possible institutional settings or in a combination of institutional settings. Some went to the proliferating cathedral schools of northwest Europe, submitting themselves to the discipline of the liberal arts, in particular, the *trivium*.[53] From the thirteenth century, an important minority received their arts training in the context of nascent universities.[54] Many others went to notarial schools in towns where they received a training in Latin, the *ars dictaminis* and arithmetic. Still others received the bulk of their administrative education as part and parcel of their capacity as clerical *familiares* of one or another official (in the court of archdeacon, bishop, justiciar, etc.).[55]

While it is plausible or even probable that "humbler" forms of schooling produced a significant percentage of the clergy who came to staff the nascent bureaucracies of the twelfth and subsequent centuries, it was undoubtedly also true that training at cathedral schools and later at the universities represented the ambitious cleric's high road to advancement. Already in the beginning of our period, i.e., the late tenth century, the connection between study at cathedral schools and recruitment to high ecclesiastical office was marked.[56] Successful study at a cathedral school led to appointment as an imperial or royal chaplain which led, in turn, to a bishopric or abbacy.[57]

Cathedral schooling of the late tenth and eleventh centuries was organized around two central foci: letters and what was termed "character" (*mores*). In other words, the end proper to a cathedral school education was proficiency in letters which was part and parcel of an overarching pedagogical ethos directed toward the formation of good character. Virtue and virtuous bearing were thought both to witness to, and habituate the subject to, proper character. Their formation within the person of the student, then, constituted a *cultus virtutum* which was to transform him into a civic-minded, ecclesiastical magnate—a man of dignity, elegance, nobility or excellence (*honestas*), affability, and *humanitas* (i.e., charm, grace, and wit), qualities which bore corporeal fruit in decorum or artful speech, gesture, and carriage.[58]

Character formation occurred both within and alongside traditional liberal studies—the *trivium* of grammar, dialectic, and rhetoric and the *quadrivium* of arithmetic, geometry, astronomy, and music. Magisterial pedagogy centred upon personal "modelling" of character (*moralitas*). This modelling came to literary-exegetical expression in *moralitates*: the master's characterological or spiritual understanding of liberal letters. *Moralitas*, inclusive of an eye for the moralizing "core" of letters, was conceived as the productive end of this schooling, whereas the primary, pedagogical means of production was *imitatio*: an imitation of the master's *moralitas* and of his nose for *moralitates*, those hidden treasures of meaning unveiled via grammatical/rhetorical analysis, particularly the *enarratio poetarum*.[59] It was above all in faithful *imitatio* of poetic utterance that the student at the cathedral school put on that civilizing speech by which he fostered "mildness" and "friendship" at court and, by extension, throughout society.[60]

From the late eleventh century, the nature of cathedral-school education shifted. Masters of the "old learning" found themselves bereft of students who flocked instead to other teachers offering a similar career success in less time and with less effort; in other words, without the long years of harsh, corporeal character formation, and a different and swifter interaction with letters. The career of Peter Abelard and his struggles with Anselm of Loan and William of Champeaux are paradigmatic of the shift under consideration.[61]

One sees in this shift an "entire system of education...caught in a conflict between a traditional kind of teaching that tended toward the acquisition of human qualities and a new kind that tended toward knowledge and rational inquiry."[62] The "old learning," though displaced from the cathedral school and nascent universities, maintained itself elsewhere well into the thirteenth century: within the schools of monastic communities and orders of regular canons, among a dwindling humanist elite who adopted a canon of texts as their charismatic source for *imitatio*, and at princely courts, as the *Vitae* of Thomas Beckett make clear.[63]

In these "refugee" settings the old learning came to be divided up and parcelled out. While princely courts picked up on the master's corporeal *moralitas* and its *imitatio* by subordinate courtiers,[64] humanists appropriated the *moralitates* within literary studies and established them in opposition to, and competition with, the products of the "new learning" at twelfth-century cathedral schools and, subsequently, in the arts faculties of the universities.[65] The original balance of personal *moralitas* and literary *moralitates* seems to have been preserved within monastic communities, but was cut off from the production of civic-minded, ecclesiastical magnates.[66]

In the schools of the "new learning" the central orientation of the curriculum was displaced, a process whereby *moralitates* as central focus were replaced by dialectic, i.e., logical analysis of texts. The transformation was facilitated by the contemporaneous recovery of much of the Aristotelian corpus via translation from Arabic and Greek.[67] It sparked, in turn, a fundamentally new textual production and a new technology of research.[68] As dialectic and its characteristic habits of thought and mind began to dominate the arts curriculum, learning came more and more to centre upon the verbal cut and thrust of thesis and counter-example, i.e., upon the analysis of our experience of the world into opposable units, the interrelationship of which would then be conceptually accounted for (the discursive acts of division and composition).[69]

From the thirteenth century, this dialectically charged pedagogy emanated from the universities and cathedral schools to affect court and traditional religious education. We see its effect in the late thirteenth-century development of contestatory genres within courtly love literature and in the contemporaneous establishment of a Cistercian college at the University of Paris.[70]

Clerical higher education remained tied to the arts curriculum, as is clear from the two papal incentives established in the thirteenth century to facilitate clerical study.[71] Consequently, if one is to maintain the emergence of a habit of persecution among the socially ambitious stratum within the high medieval clerisy, one does well to examine the new dialectical focus of higher education of the late twelfth and subsequent centuries, and to ask whether such a focus sheds light on the rhetorical shape and development of that habit.

Aristotelian Opposition and the Rhetoric of Persecution

The rhetoric of persecution which Moore presents makes abundant use of the topos of antithesis, i.e., the juxtaposition of two terms in such a way that the one term expresses the negation of the other. Since this form of antithesis gives rhetorical expression to a dialectical or logical opposition we turn to consider the tenth and eleventh chapters of Aristotle's *Categories* (11b-14a), in which he treats the ways in which things are said to be in opposition.[72]

Aristotle begins the treatise as a whole by introducing the coordinates of "name" and "definition." These coordinates can be used to connect things in reality. Things can share "name" and "definition," or share a "name" only, or at least the root of the "name" (1a). This leads him to consider the relationship of what we say about a subject and the subject itself. He distinguishes four different combinations of things "said of" and "being in" a subject (1b). Thus, he is led in turn to consider the subjects about which things can be said. In this context he identifies the ten categories of "substance" and the "accidents": "quantity," "quality," "relation," "place," "time," "posture," "state," "act," "passion"(2a-11b). Since these categories mark out the primary and distinct modalities of intelligible being, Aristotle moves to consider the different ways in which distinguishable entities can be opposed.

He identifies four senses in which things are said to be opposed: (1) as correlatives, (2) as contraries, (3) as privation and possession, and (4) as affirmation and negation. Correlatives are opposites which belong together in the sense that they are meaningful only in relation to each other. Aristotle illustrates this type of opposition with the terms "double" and "half." Something is the double of something which is its half. In other words something can only exist as "double" in relation to something which is its "half" and vice versa.

Contraries, on the other hand, are opposites which admit of no such interdependence, i.e., the one's determinate being is not dependent upon the other's. Thus, to use Aristotle's own example, good is not the good of some bad, nor is white the white of some black. The relationship between contraries can be distinguished into two types. There are contraries which have and which do not have intermediaries. "Black" and "white" illustrate the first type as all the other colours (but especially grey) mediate between the two contraries; "odd" and "even" illustrate the second of the two types, for an integer must be either one or the other.

Positives and privatives have reference to the same subject. Aristotle illustrates this type of opposition with the example of "sight" and "blindness"; they both refer to the eye. In oppositions of this type that which is referred to by means of a positive is "natural," i.e., is rooted in the very nature of the thing. A privative is, by implication, "unnatural." Thus, says Aristotle, "[w]e say that anything capable of receiving a possession is deprived of it when it is entirely absent from that which naturally has it, at the time when it is natural for it to have them" (12a 29-35). Blindness, for example, is not denoted by the term "unseeing" unless the subject in question should be able to see.

The fourth and final type of opposition which Aristotle identifies is that of affirmation and negation. Concerning this type, he says, "It is plain that things opposed as affirmation and negation are not opposed in any of the above ways; for only with them is it necessary always for one to be true and the other one false" (13b 1-4). He illustrates the point with reference to the propositions "Socrates is sick" and "Socrates is not sick." One of these propositions must be true regardless of whether Socrates exists or does not exist. In the case of a set of contraries such as "Socrates is sick" and "Socrates is healthy," one of the propositions must be true and the other false, if and only if Socrates exists. If his does not, they are both false. In the case of positives and privatives such as "Socrates sees" and "Socrates is blind," both propositions will be false if Socrates does not exist. Furthermore, both will also be false if Socrates exists but is not yet able to acquire the power of vision (as were Socrates to be a fetus). As for correlative oppositions such as "double" and "half," neither of them is true nor false in and of itself.

This summary of the types of logical opposition proves illuminating when applied to the rhetoric of persecution "invented" during the later Middle Ages. One can make sense of this rhetoric if one sees it as a conflation of the third and fourth types of opposition. What I am claiming here is that the rhetorical "letter" of the rhetoric of persecution identified by R. I. Moore expresses an opposition of the fourth type, i.e., an opposition of affirmation and negation, such that one must be true and the other false. Nevertheless, there is present in "spirit" or as subtext the opposition of possession and privation in that one of the terms of the opposition names a capacity or possession which ought by rights, i.e., naturally, to be. If we take the opposition faithful and infidel for example (pagans, Jews, Muslims and/or heretics being denoted by the latter term), the former term has the force, in Moore's rhetoric of persecution, as both an affirmation and a possession whereas the latter of the terms has the force of a negation and a privation. Inasmuch as they are opposed as affirmation to negation, the one must be "true" and the other "false." But inasmuch as they are opposed as possession to privation, hence as something naturally present to its unnatural absence, only the affirmation can be "true"; the negation is as privation necessarily "false." Clearly, in such a pregnant conjunction, anything which is a privative negation ought doubly not to be.

Thus, the opposition of Christian/non-Christian or, as it was more often expressed, of *fideles/infideles*, while literally expressed as an opposition of affirmation and negation, was imbued with the "spirit" of an opposition of possession and privation. What is important to note is that the resultant union of letter and spirit led to the inescapable conclusion that the very existence of the groups referred to by such privative negations represented a threat to the existence of the referent of possessive affirmations. Strictly speaking, if a negation is true, i.e., if its referent is present, its opposite, an affirmation, must be false, i.e., absent. Nevertheless, because the negation is privative (and the affirmation possessive), the occurrence of a privative negation is irreversible; i.e., no natural process exists whereby a privation is transformed into a possession. Indeed as Aristotle says: "With privation and possession...change occurs from possession to privation but from privation to possession it is impossible; one who has gone blind does not recover sight nor does a bald man regain his hair nor does a toothless man grow teeth" (13a 31-36). Thus, while *fideles* are, as it were, by their nature potentially *infideles*, the converse is not the case. Clearly, in such a train of thought the presence of even one *infidelis* is a serious matter for those charged with responsibility for the faithful.[73] What would seem to be called for is an annihilation of the presence of the infidel so as to insulate the faithful from those presences who might occasion the irreversible transformation from possession to privation.

In a formal sense, of course, such reasoning is "sophistic." What is set aside in this train of thought is the effect of original sin by which all are born, as it were, *infideles*. It overlooks the concomitant theological assertion of the supernatural, i.e., that some are supernaturally gifted with *fides* by which they become *fideles*. Thus, it ignores the fact that what is not naturally possible is made possible supernaturally. In other words, the late medieval rhetoric of persecution seems to insist that the contrast *fideles/infideles* be conceived as a natural one prescinding altogether from those possibilities supernaturally present if invisible to the light of natural reason. It is this "naturalization" of the opposition *fideles/infideles* which identifies the application of the Aristotelian doctrine of logical opposition in the late medieval rhetoric of persecution as a secularizing phenomenon.

Furthermore, at an even more elementary level the conflation of affirmation and negation with possession and privation is not fully consistent with Aristotle's treatment of logical opposition in the *Categories*. He is there at pains to show how each of the four types of opposition is irreducibly distinct (12b-13b). Nevertheless, types of opposition can be brought into close conjunctions. Indeed, Aristotle's sense of how human beings come to know can be understood as a deft conjunction of the oppositions of affirmation to negation and of correlatives.

Aristotle opens his *Metaphysics* with the affirmation that "all humans desire by nature to know" (980a20). This central impulse to know is expressed in wonder, a wonder which crystallizes in a single question: "What is this that I behold?" The question, in turn, launches a new series of intellectual movements which have as their end the formulation of a definition which serves to answer, definitively, the question which lies at their origin.

The formulation of a definitive answer, however, is the conclusion of a process in which a number of tentative answers have already been tried. Indeed, the initial wonder which gives rise to the question "What is this?" carries implicit within it a first provisional identification: "This is something not known." In other words, the mystery one beholds is placed in opposition to the things which one knows, as negation to their affirmation. This opposition of the fourth type, then, registers mystery, i.e., names, and so delimits the space in which the mystery is to be located so that a second question can be asked: "What is this something unknown like among the things which are known?" Consequently, in the order of knowing, opposition of affirmation to negation can be seen as a necessary preamble to an opposition of correlation, and by extension to a process of analogy by which one comes to know what it is that one beholds. Thus, it is true that here as in the medieval rhetoric of persecution inquisition flows from the opposition of affirmation and negation, but not so as to exclude or exterminate. Rather, inquisition is intended precisely to include what the negation signifies, i.e., to give it determinate (definitive) being in the world of things known.

Given the appropriateness of treating different forms of opposition in intimate conjunction, it does not seem surprising that clerics schooled to the Aristotelian doctrine of logical opposition would so connect distinguishable forms of opposition in their thinking about marginal outgroups as to conflate them in practice. There was, of course, no strictly logical necessity to such usage; the conflation cannot be termed an "effect" of the discourse. Indeed, my claim is precisely the opposite: the discourse of persecution is itself, in part, the "effect" of the logical conflation I have been describing. With Moore, I see the propriety of suggesting that non-discursive factors played a determinative role motivating a persecuting application of Aristotelian logic. Moreover, group solidarity and interest within a centralizing and universalizing process of social transformation seems to me a likely identification of the most intelligible of these non-discursive factors; class interest by contrast seems to me to be too broad a denotation. Group interest, however, is not sufficient to account for discursive practice; one must also identify a group's characteristic mental habits and training, its characteristic lingual patterns. When we do this with that group of later medieval clerics who seem to have been responsible for the formulation of a rhetoric of persecution, one finds that it is not their formation as representatives of a religious institution nor their formation to the religious discourse of the Latin Church which allows us to account for the logical mechanisms at play in the rhetoric they "invented." Rather, it is the Aristotelian formation of their "natural intellect," i.e., their secular, intellectual formation which provides the most suggestive interpretive keys.

CONCLUSIONS

Examination of R. I. Moore's thesis about the West's characteristic "rhetoric of persecution" allows us to modify our traditional linking of religion, social plurality, and persecution. It does not appear to be the case that Western religious discourse is to be blamed for the modern West's difficulty in managing social pluralities without persecuting. At the very least, such an accounting is too simplistic. While Christian clerics do appear to have been responsible for the "invention" of a rhetoric of persecution, they did so not so much as heirs to a Christian discursive practice but rather as inheritors of the Aristotelian modes of logical opposition which they applied in service of a secularizing process of modernization. In this light it is no surprise that the passing of social leadership from Christian clergy to lay political administrators did not lead to the fading away of the discourse of persecution which Christian clergy had developed, but rather to its intensification. Indeed, it might be said that late medieval use of the rhetoric of persecution in the management of social pluralities worked to cultivate a taste for persecution in subsequent ages. Fortunately, it is a taste we secularized Westerners are learning to find bitter, but it is one which we can hardly claim to have lost.

Notes

1. For present ferment surrounding the increasingly plural cultural practice of professional historians see my "Of Tall Tales and Small Stories: Postmodern 'Fragmatics' and the Christian Historian." Keynote address given at the Lilly Foundation Regional Conference, "The Future of Christian Scholarship in a Postmodern World" held at Calvin College (Grand Rapids, MI) June 11-15 1994, now published in *Fides et Historia* 28, 2 (1996): 50-68.

2. (Oxford: Basil Blackwell, 1987). (Cited as *Persecuting Society*.)

3. Moore is above all concerned with historical writing which takes as its subject heretics,

32 Towards an Ethics of Community

the poor, Jews, lepers, homosexuals, prostitutes, and witches. See in this regard Moore's own *The Origins of European Dissent* (New York: Basil Blackwell, 1985); Michel Mollat, *Les pauvres au moyen âge* (Paris: Hachette, 1978); *Gle ebrei nel alto medio evo, Settimani di studio del centro Italiano de studi sull'alto medioevo*, xxvi (1978) (Spoleto: Presso la sede del Centro, 1980); S. N. Brody, *Disease of the Soul: Leprosy in Medieval Literature* (Ithaca, NY: Cornell University Press, 1974); J. Boswell, *Christianity, Social Tolerance and Homosexuality: Gay People in Western Europe from the Beginning of the Christian Era to the Fourteenth Century* (Chicago: University of Chicago Press, 1980); L. L. Otis, *Prostitution in Medieval Society: The History of an Urban Institution in the Languedoc* (Chicago: University of Chicago Press, 1985); and Christina Larner, *Witchcraft and Religion: The Politics of Popular Belief* (Oxford: Basil Blackwell, 1984).

4. *Persecuting Society*, p. 5.
5. Ibid., p. 10.
6. Ibid., pp. 1-2.
7. Ibid., pp. 68-69.
8. Ibid., p. 24.
9. Ibid., pp. 34-45.
10. Ibid., pp. 45-60.
11. Ibid., p. 65.
12. Ibid., p. 68.
13. Ibid., pp. 69-70. See also Brian Stock's much more detailed but compatible analysis in *The Implications of Literacy: Written Language and Models of Interpretation in the Eleventh and Twelfth Centuries* (Princeton, NJ: Princeton University Press, 1983), pp. 151-240.
14. *Persecuting Society*, p. 70-71.
15. Ibid., p. 77.
16. Ibid., p. 73-74.
17. Ibid., pp. 75-80.
18. Ibid., pp. 80-81.
19. Ibid., pp. 81-88.
20. Ibid., p. 89.
21. Ibid., pp. 90-91.
22. Ibid., p. 91-99.
23. Moore uses three of her many studies: *Lele of the Kasai* (Oxford: Oxford University Press, 1963); *Purity and Danger: An Analysis of Concepts of Pollution and Taboo* (New York: Praeger, 1966); and *Natural Symbols: Explorations in Cosmology* (London: Vintage Books, 1973).
24. *Persecuting Society*, p. 101.
25. Ibid., p. 102.
26. For the case to be made for such a view see L.K. Little, *Religious Poverty and the Profit Economy in Medieval Europe* (London: P. Elek, 1978); A. Murray, *Reason and Society in the Middle Ages* (Oxford: Clarendon Press, 1978), and M. Mollat, *Les pauvres*.
27. *Persecuting Society*, p. 106.
28. Ibid., p. 107.
29. Ibid., pp. 109-12.
30. See in this regard, Richard Kieckhefer, *European Witch Trials: Their Foundations in Popular and Learned Culture,1300-1500* (Berkeley: University of California Press, 1976); and Norman Cohn, *Europe's Inner Demons* (London: Chatto, 1975).
31. *Persecuting Society*, pp. 124-35.
32. Ibid., p. 133.
33. Ibid., pp. 134-35. For the identification of lepers see Christina Larner, *Witchcraft and Religion*; for Parisian moves see Renate Blumenfeld-Kosinski, "The Marginalization of

Women in Obstetrics," *Not of Woman Born: Representations of Caesarean Birth in Medieval and Renaissance Culture* (Ithaca, NY: Cornell University Press, 1990), pp. 91-119; for the process of canonization see André Vauchez, *La sainteté en occident aux derniers siècles du moyen âge d'après les procès de canonisation et les documents hagiographiques,* Bibiothèque des Ecoles françaises d'Athènes et de Rome, fasc. 241 (Rome: École française de Rome, 1981).

34. *Persecuting Society,* p. 135.
35. Ibid., p. 136.
36. Ibid., pp. 140-53.
37. Ibid., p. 150.
38. There is, for example, a whole historiography centred around the concept of renaissance and renewal. One of the more recent efforts in this regard is R. L. Benson, G. Constable, and C. D. Lanham, eds., *Renaissance and Renewal in the Twelfth Century* (Oxford: Clarendon Press, 1982), especially the introduction and Gerhardt Ladner's opening essay (pp. 1-33).
39. *Persecuting Society,* p. 153.
40. Ibid., pp. 109-12.
41. Ibid., p. 106.
42. See Michel Mollat, *Les pauvres,* pp. 110-352.
43. See in this context the overview provided by Gabriel Le Bras in *Institutions ecclésiastiques de la Chrétienté médiévale,* 2 vol., "Histoire de l'église depuis les origines jusqu'a nos jour," A. Fliche and V. Martin, eds., (Paris: Bloud et Gay, 1964): 2.434-41, esp. 435. For the earliest of the diocesan synods see O. Pontal, *Histoire des conciles mérovingiens* (Paris: Editions du CERF, 1989), p. 192. Le Bras brings out the connection between episcopal visitation and inquisition citing canons 2, 6, and 7 of the Second Council of Braga (572) in which bishops are exhorted to instruct parish clergy to inform them when they visit as to the presence of heretics among other "circumstances" within their jurisdiction.
44. Moore bases his analysis on R. Bartlett, *Trial by Fire and Water: The Medieval Judicial Ordeal* (Oxford: Clarendon Press, 1986). But see A. Erler, "Der Ursprung der Gottesurteile," *Paideuma, Mitteilungen zur Kulturkunde* 2 (1941): 44-65. For the presence of ordeals in Icelandic sagas see Jesse Byock, *Feud in the Icelandic Saga* (Berkeley: University of California Press, 1982).
45. See Peter Brown, "Sorcery, Demons, and the Rise of Christianity from Late Antiquity into the Middle Ages," in *Witchcraft, Confessions and Accusations,* ed. Mary Douglas (London: Tavistock Publications, 1970), pp. 17-46.
46. While St. Augustine of Hippo's many fifth-century polemics against the Manichees of his experience provided later generations with sufficient material for a colourful and disturbing stereotype, the Old and New Testaments of the Christian Scriptures bear witness to the fear and loathing which the spectre of leprosy and the leper inspired in the ancient Near East.
47. See, for example, the discussion of the orders of cleric in Roger E. Reynolds, "'At Sixes and Sevens'—and Eights and Nines: The Sacred Mathematics of Sacred Orders in the Early Middle Ages," *Speculum* 54 (1979): pp. 669-84. For the theoretical distinctions between secular and religious clergy in the twelfth and thirteenth centuries see M. Peuchmard O. P., "Le prêtre ministre de la parole dans la théologie du XIIe siècle (Canonistes, moines et chanoines)," *Recherches de la théologie ancienne et médiévale* 29 (1962): 52-76 and idem, "Mission canonique et prédication: Le prêtre ministre de la parole dans la querelle entre Mendiants et Séculiers au XIIIe siècle," *Recherches de la théologie ancienne et médiévale* 30 (1963): 122-44.
48. Moore's thesis must be accommodated to the social heterogeneity of heretical groups discovered by Herbert Grundmann in *Religiöse Bewegungen im Mittelalter:*

Untersuchungen über die geschichtlichen Zusammenhänge zwischen der Ketzerei, den Bettelorden und der religiösen Frauenbewegun in 12. und 13. Jahrhundert und über die geschichlichen Grundlagen der Deutschen Mystik, Historische Studien, 267, 2nd ed. (Darmstadt: Wissenschaftliche Buchgesellschaft, 1970), especially to the spin given his findings (i.e., that the struggle between orthodox and heretic in the eleventh and twelfth centuries is perhaps best seen as an intra-clerical struggle for control of the new technology of literacy) by Brian Stock in *The Implications of Literacy: Written Language and Models of Interpretation in the Eleventh and Twelfth Centuries* (Princeton, NJ: Princeton University Press, 1983), pp. 88-240. It must also take into account the antagonism of clerical university students toward the rest of the clergy as described in Jacques Le Goff, *Intellectuals in the Middle Ages*, trans. Theresa Lavender Fagan (Oxford: Basil Blackwell, 1993), pp. 20-50. Finally, it must be accommodated to the evidence of a criminal underclass among the clergy of the fourteenth and fifteenth centuries uncovered by Richard Kieckhefer in *Magic in the Middle Ages*, Cambridge Medieval Textbooks (Cambridge: Cambridge University Press, 1989), pp. 151-75.

49. This reconfiguration of our understanding of the medieval clergy owes much to Gabriel Le Bras. See Le Bras, *Institutions ecclésiastiques*. For a more complex understanding of the relationship between Jewish communities and Christian clergy see Adriaan Bredero, "Het anti-joodse gevoelen van de middeleeuwse samenleving," in *Christenheid en christendom in de Middeleeuwen: Over de verhouding van godsdienst, kerk en samenleving* (Kampen: Kok Agora, 1987), pp. 229-73.

50. Indeed, Erasmus and Machiavelli stand as fitting symbols of the point being made here. While the clerical Erasmus is conscious of establishing an understanding of the Christian religion and its history which will foster tolerance of doctrinal plurality, Machievelli, the secular counsellor of Italian princes, makes explicit room for the employment of a rhetoric of persecution within his famous transposition and transformation of the medieval "*speculum principis*" into the context of early modern Italy.

51. I will refer only to two of the finest examples of this scholarship in English: M. T. Clanchey, *From Memory to Written Record. England, 1066-1307* (Cambridge, MA: Harvard University Press, 1979); J. W. Baldwin, *The Government of Philip Augustus: Foundations of French Royal Power in the Middle Ages* (Berkeley: University of California Press, 1986).

52. See, in this regard, C. Warren Hollister and John W. Baldwin, "The Rise of Administrative Kingship: Henry I and Philip Augustus," *American Historical Review* 83 (1978): 867-91; R. C. van Caenegem, "L'histoire du droit et la chronologie. Réflections sur la formation du 'common law' et la procédure Romano-canonique," *Etudes d'histoire de droit canonique dédiés à Gabriel Le Bras* (Paris: Sirey, 1965), pp. 2.1459-65; but especially, J. W. Baldwin, "*Studium et Regnum*: The Penetration of University Personnel into French and English Administration at the Turn of the Twelfth and Thirteenth Centuries," *Revue des études islamiques* 44 (1976): 199-211; Ralph V. Turner, "The *Miles literatus* in twelfth- and thirteenth-century England: How Rare a Phenomenon?" *American Historical Review* 83 (1978): 928-45; idem, "Clerical Judges in English Secular Courts: The Ideal versus the Reality," *Medievalia et Humanistica*, n.s. 3 (1972): 75-98; idem, *Men Raised Up from the Dust: Administrative Service and Upward Mobility in Angevin England* (Philadelphia: University of Pennsylvania Press, 1988); and Rolf Köhn, "Schulbildung und Trivium im lateinischen Hochmittelalter und ihr möglicher praktischer Nutzen," *Schulen und Studium im Sozialen Wandel des Hohen und Späten Mittelalters*, ed. Johannes Fried, Vorträge und Forschungen, 30 (Sigmaringen: Jan Thorbecke Verlag, 1986), pp. 203-84.

53. For eleventh-century cathedral schools see C. Stephen Jaeger, *The Envy of Angels: Cathedral Schools and Social Ideals in Medieval Europe, 950-1200* (Philadelphia: University of Pennsylvania Press, 1994), pp. 53-194. (Cited as *Envy of Angels*.) For the twelfth century see Joseph Goering, *William de Montibus (c. 1140-1213): The Schools and*

the Literature of Pastoral Care, Studies and Texts 108 (Toronto: Pontifical Institute for Mediaeval Studies Publications, 1992), pp. 3-57; R. W. Hunt, *The Schools and the Cloister: The Life and Writings of Alexander Nequem (1157-1217)*, ed. Margaret Gibson (Oxford: Clarendon Press, 1984); and Stephan C. Ferruolo, *The Origins of the University: The Schools of Paris and Their Critics, 1100-1215* (Stanford, CA: Stanford University Press, 1985). For thirteenth-century universities see Jürgen Miethke, "Die Kirche und die Universitäten im 13. Jahrhundert," *Schulen und Studien*, pp. 285-320.

54. J. Le Goff, *Intellectuals in the Middle Ages.*

55. See the work of Ralph V. Turner cited above and especially his discussion of Geoffrey fitz Peter in *Men Raised Up from the Dust*, pp. 40-41.

56. What follows is heavily dependent upon *Envy of Angels*, 1-195.

57. Ibid., pp. 36-52.

58. Ibid., pp. 76-117.

59. Ibid., pp. 118-79. For reading as disclosure of the hidden sense, see Edouard Jeauneau, "L'usage de la notion d'integumentum à travers les glosses de Guillaume de Conches," *Archive d'histoire doctrinale et littéraire du moyen âge* 24 (1973): 35-100. For the Roman and medieval development of *enarratio poetarum* see Rita Copeland, *Rhetoric, Hermeneutics, and Translation in the Middle Ages: Academic Traditions and Vernacular Texts* (Cambridge: Cambridge University Press, 1991), pp. 1-62.

60. *Envy of Angels*, pp. 140-64.

61. Ibid., pp. 217-36.

62. Ibid., p. 236.

63. Ibid., pp. 239-327.

64. C. Stephen Jaeger, *Origins of Courtliness: Civilizing Trends and the Formation of Courtly Ideals, 939-1210* (Philadelphia: University of Pennsylvania Press, 1985).

65. *Envy of Angels*, pp. 244-68.

66. Ibid., pp. 269-77. See in this regard the pioneering study of Caroline Walker Bynum, "*Docere Verbo et Exemplo:* An Aspect of Twelfth-Century Spirituality," *Harvard Theological Studies* 31 (Missoula, MT: Scholar's Press, 1982).

67. Marie-Thérèse d'Alverny, "Translations and Translators," *Renaissance and Renewal*, 421-62.

68. See, in this regard, Richard H. Rouse and Mary A. Rouse, "*Statim invenire*: Schools, Preachers, and New Attitudes to the Page," *Renaissance and Renewal*, 201-25.

69. See the classic and still current narrative of Martin Grabmann in *Die Geschichte des Scholastischen Methode*, 2 vol. (Freiburg-im-Bresgau: Herdersche Verlag, 1909 and 1911). See also Paléamon Glorieux, *La littérature quodlibétique de 1260-1320*, 2 vol. (Paris: Vrin, 1935).

70. See in this regard Helen Solterer, *The Master and Minerva: Disputing Women in French Medieval Culture* (Berkeley: University of California Press, 1995), and Reinard Schneider, "Studium und Zisterziensorden," *Schulen und Studium*, pp. 321-50.

71. Leonard E. Boyle O.P., "The Constitution Cum ex eo of Pope Boniface VIII," *Mediaeval Studies* 24 (1962): 283-302.

72. The text of the Latin Aristotle is to be found in *Aristoteles Latinus* V,1, ed. Laurentius Minio-Paluello (Bruges-Paris: Desclée de Brouwer, 1961). All translations in this text will be cited from *The Complete Works of Aristotle*, Bollingen Series, 71.2, ed., Johathan Barnes (Princeton: Princeton University Press, 1984), pp. 13-24.

73. For an analysis of anti-witch polemics of the fifteenth century which is compatible in many respects with the analysis argued for here, see Stuart Clark, "Inversion, Misrule and the Meaning of Witchcraft," *Past and Present* 87 (1979): 99-127. In this article, Clark offers a highly differentiated reading of Jacob Sprenger and Heinrich Kramer's *Malleus maleficarum* [for an English translation of the treatise see *The Malleus Maleficarum of Heinrich Kramer and James Sprenger*, trans. M. Sumner (New York: Dover, 1971)]. It

should be said that Kramer and Sprenger's treatise imbues the rhetoric of persecution with a virulent misogyny for they identify witchcraft as a phenomenon to be gendered female; their move represents the first such identification within witchcraft polemics. Their treatise, of course, becomes the jumping-off point for subsequent raising of the identification of witchcraft with women to a commonplace within witchcraft polemics. Thus, one sees in their treatise a particularly clear instance of how the rhetoric of persecution can be used to vilify groups other than the central groups for which it was intended.

2

Consequences of Liberalism: Ideological Domination in Rorty's Public/Private Split

HENDRIK HART

Thihis metaphilosophical paper discusses an aspect of the long history of reason as a barrier to religion, by focussing on Richard Rorty's efforts at rescuing liberal tolerance. Liberal Rorty tries to avoid liberalism's interference with tolerance resulting from its imposition of an alleged common and neutral reason on the public. Via his own attachment to a public/private split, however, he also interferes with tolerance, and imposes his own rational barrier to religion. I argue (1) that his attempted liberation of Enlightenment liberalism from its universally imposed, rational neutrality is incomplete, (2) that his public/private split is an obstacle, because it does not separate liberalism as public strategy from his liberalism as private ideology, and (3) that democratic pluralism will improve without imposed forms of argument in conversation to which not all members of the public have full and equal access.

INTRODUCTION: RORTY AS LIBERAL

One can profitably read all of Richard Rorty's *Contingency, Irony, and Solidarity* as a commentary on his struggle with whether or not there is a relation between the public and the private.[1] Part III of *Objectivity, Relativism, and Truth* can be read in the same way.[2] Both collections show that the struggle is complex and subtle material for careful digestion and frequent rereading. What emerges is an Enlightenment liberalism shorn of reliance on realism, reason, objectivism, and divinities or pseudo divinities. But is it still liberalism?

Key to answering this question is Rorty's subscription to a split between public and private. Richard Bernstein speaks of a "rigid separation."[3] The private is a personal realm of solitude. Here others have no right to interfere. In our solitude we create ourselves as we want, provided we do not hurt others in the process. The public is a space where we relate to others on a common basis of shared beliefs. The private has no place here. Beliefs are shared as a result of free and open conversation, unrestrained argument, non-violent

37

persuasion. So Rorty continues the liberal tradition of tolerance, first proposed by Locke as a way of coping with a violently intolerant plural society, divided by metaphysical and religious matters, and determined to end the division by one party's domination through victory in war. Locke's proposal has become the strategy of Enlightenment liberalism: toleration for all metaphysical and religious beliefs, provided they are treated as private. Public matters are settled rationally, without linkage to private metaphysical or religious beliefs. Reason is common to all. This liberal strategy is entitled to domination of the public, because it wages no war other than one of arguments based on universal reasons.

Rorty's major contribution to the "postmodern" development of this liberalism is a thorough demystification and naturalization of "rational." It is not privileged, it is not grounded, it is not grounding, it is not transcendental, it is not universal, it is not a priori, it is not access to reality as it is, it is not immutable, it is not a matter of logic, it is not philosophical, it is not theoretical. In a sense, rational is no longer even strictly rational in some technical way, that is, logical-conceptual. Any civil process leading to agreement can be called rational in a broad sense.[4] This is thrashed out so thoroughly and from so many angles that it may appear Rorty has ironed out most of the traditional difficulties noted by objectors to Enlightenment liberalism, among whom we find theologians, metaphysicians, communitarians, feminists, postmoderns, and others. Most notably, he makes clear that liberalism is much more than just a neutral strategy to deal with metaphysical-religious diversity and its plurality of prejudices. Liberalism itself is one of the ideologies, worldviews, final vocabularies, "religions," metaphysics, or however else we may name it.[5] "Religion" here has the sense in which Heidegger characterizes the Western intellectual tradition as theo-ontological and Popper characterizes his talk of his own commitment to science as "confession of faith."[6] Ideology is, so to speak, religion without ritualized worship. Liberalism is the ideology which in Rorty's view has the best credentials in our present, contingent, historical situation to deal with the potential violence of competing pluralities. What this comes to in the practice of finding common solutions to common problems is that Enlightenment liberals do not have an a priori privilege. They, like anybody else, need to persuade others of the acceptability of their contributions, including the acceptability of the liberal strategy. Thus Rorty's liberalism looks less intolerant than the "tolerance" of a dogmatic imposition of neutral reason. Two problems remain, however.

One problem is the question whether in Rorty's view the (Western) public truly plays on a level playing field, where initially all citizens are equal participants in the conversation. Traditional Enlightenment liberals have in fact never fully granted all people equal entitlement to their metaphysical or religious beliefs in private, coupled with a public strategy limited by what all have in common as a result of rational persuasion. The liberal strategy has in effect dominated the public arena with liberalism's private ideological belief about how reason should deal with plurality. Liberals have not kept their own ideology private, nor have they provided space in the public mind for convictions which did not fit the liberal strategy. In this sense liberalism is not, as I said, just a strategy for dealing with a plurality of conflicting convictions through the toleration of these convictions, provided they are kept private. Liberalism has rather been a strategy for domination—see Rorty's own language below—of the public with a private ideology of liberal reason common to all. It is, you might say, an attempt at eradicating the public and political significance of metaphysical or religious difference, and settling other differences by reason instead of war. Being aware of this, Rorty develops the idea of the liberal community as a contingency.[7] Its basis is hope only.[8] Bernstein sees this as fideism.[9]

Rorty's own most recent vocabulary, however, suggests that, despite his critique of neutral reason, liberal intolerance may not have disappeared from his own views altogether. Liberals who consider Rorty as having sold out liberalism might take note of this. In an interview he says "the dominant language game of liberal democracy swallows up others because it does and it should—just as it has to clear away tribalism, religious fundamentalism and so forth if it is to get anywhere. It has to preserve and prove its superiority over other language games."[10] And a little further this sentiment is underscored: "It's not just my vocabulary, it is one we all have to use when we get together." This language, I suggest, is not just a hard to kill semantic habit of liberals, but more likely a revelation of where the liberal heart beats. Yet according to liberal vocabulary, "where the heart beats" has to stay out of the conversation, simply because it is not shared, public, common. Where Rorty's heart beats, his final vocabulary, is participation "in discussions as fellow citizens without dragging religion into it."[11] But this final liberal vocabulary is not now—and probably never will be—the shared possession of the entire public, not even where the public is Western or even just Anglo-American. It is where the liberal heart beats or, to put it differently, the way the liberal "drags liberal religion into it" by masking liberal "religion" in other language—say, Will Herbert's civil religion—while denying that move to others. So, at least in public, it is not a matter of toleration but, in Rorty's own words, of hoped for domination.[12] Not the crude domination achieved with guns, but the "civil" one achieved in conversation.

In a review the same sentiment is present.[13] It is "bad taste to bring religion into discussions of public policy."[14] Rorty wants us to see two things. One is that "the role of Enlightenment ideology in giving meaning to the lives of atheists is just as great as Christianity's role in giving meaning to...[the life of Christians]."[15] In my language: liberals, too, have a heart that beats somewhere. The other is that "mature, public-spirited adults are quite right in not attempting to use...[the private ideologies that give our lives meaning] as a basis for politics."[16] Quite plainly spoken: "Don't bother us with matters that are not our concern."[17]

Rorty admits that our hearts "will influence political convictions."[18] I agree. I also agree that in political discussion the mere assertion by a religious person to an atheist: "But God requires this!" is neither here nor there. But Rorty does not seem to be open to the point, as few liberals ever have been,[19] that many people—"mature, public spirited adults" even—who are willing to argue less crudely, nevertheless do want to fundamentally connect their politics with their religion, rather than just have it be influential. They want to have their politics be one vehicle for their hopes. And they wish to be open and candid about this in their conversations with political opponents. It also is clear that Rorty's liberal democratic vocabulary is based on his liberal Enlightenment ideology, and that he is not only open about that, but wants others to be dominated by it.[20]

The other problem is the difference between conversation and argument. The common foundation of traditional liberalism is Enlightenment reason, argument. For Rorty it is conversation rather than argument. This matter is explicitly discussed.[21] Rorty appears to suggest that in the public sphere we promote sharing by means of conversation, where conversation is almost as wide as civilized interaction. It is not only talk, but also film, music, plastic arts, novels, and television. At other times, however, conversation seems to depend crucially on argument, that is, on getting to share beliefs within the space of reasons. In fact, when in the interview he is specifically asked to comment on the difference between argument and conversation, his answer at first suggests that in argument we try to show how the other person is irrational, while in conversation we just try to change attitudes without saying they are irrational.[22] Later in the interview, however, argument becomes crucial. Certain approaches to the conversation are declared invalid because they are not arguments. I suspect that this may not just be a hard to kill habit of a philosopher trained in the analytic tradition, but at least in part a remainder of the crucial role of neutral reason in the liberal tradition; that is, another classic feature of the liberalism where Rorty's private heart beats. And his repeated return to a public whose beliefs are shared, that is, who have reasons to conceive of things in similar ways, may be an indication that mere redescription and changing the subject is too easy a self-description of Rorty's new liberalism.[23] For it seems that in order to get people to adopt his new vocabulary, he primarily wants to resort to argument himself, to giving reasons in the logical space of reasons.

So there are two problems here, both identified by Rorty, but neither solved by him. One is that a possibly hidden, pseudo-neutrality comes to the surface and is imposed: the vocabulary we all have to use. The other is that a possibly hidden, pseudo-rationalism comes to the surface: shared beliefs. Both are significant ingredients in the old Lockean ideology and they seem to survive in Rorty, in spite of his real efforts to get rid of both. Why would they persist?

The neutrality—purity untainted by religion?—may persist because a supposedly shared fund of beliefs, severed from metaphysical or religious roots in Rawls's style,[24] is easily perceived as neutral, even where it becomes the tool of domination for a group in power, striving to force other people to keep their hopes private. In that case the private is not, however, a haven where our deepest hopes are safe from persecution or where no one can force us to hope what others want. Rather, the private is now a realm to which hopes are banned in order not to have public significance.[25] False privatization of commitments leads to false neutralization of public opinion. The private realm becomes a detention camp for religious dissenters from liberalism. In public they have to fit the order of Enlightened liberalism, which presents this order as common (neutral?). Rorty calls this a compromise,[26] which he tries to make palatable by "the gradual expansion of the imagination of those in power."[27]

The rationalism may also persist because politics and religion are both too often discussed in terms of beliefs—language, vocabulary, concepts, propositions, whatever. That skews the discussion. Politics is not without beliefs, of course, but its main agenda is making decisions to act in certain ways that become law for all. Religion, too, is not without beliefs, of course, but its main agenda is fostering a hope that is big enough to orient the meaning of our lives.[28] In our Western history all of this has been swallowed up by the language of belief. In part this has led to the common assumption in our culture that if you hold no recognizable cultic beliefs about an afterlife, about a divinity, and similar things, you have no religion. The idea that any community fostering life-giving hopes in people is a religious community would not be easily accepted in our culture. Rorty talks about this in terms of final vocabularies, but does not actually acknowledge their functional equivalence with religious language. So if he really does want to change the subject and introduce new metaphors, I suggest that the vocabulary of shared beliefs may not be his most helpful metaphor. This too easily hides the possibility that religion is a human function present in all communities.[29] Further, shared beliefs could easily be the imposed beliefs of one group. Do Natives, for example, really have an argument in the West? At least one discussion of Rorty's contribution to the Eleventh Inter-American Congress of Philosophy in Mexico in 1985 suggests this is questionable.[30]

So the neutrality and the rationalism combine to cover over the fact that in the liberal public/private split there is nevertheless an area where the split has disappeared, where private liberal ideology becomes the common purpose of the public. To that I now turn.

THE SPLIT AND ITS PROBLEMS

It is hard to argue against the legitimacy of a distinction between public and private. My mail is private. Others have no right to read my mail. I can, of course, read my mail to others. But others have no right to it. And the law protects me. However, there are limits to this. If in my mail I have been plotting to kill my employer and this somehow leaks out, a judge could force me to read my mail aloud on the witness stand, that is, in public. Privacy is important, but it cannot be absolutely severed from the public. That goes the other way around too. The public space is a space to which I must have access. The law creates that space for me as well. Shops that are open to the public must be open to me. But the goods in the shop are the property of the proprietor until I have paid for them. They are not public in the sense that I can just walk in and take them. Nor can I do whatever I want in that public space. The public and the private are interrelated realms that cannot be artificially unhitched. They are, in fact, real only in terms of one another. They are not split.

In the mid-twenties, John Dewey lucidly explained, in the opening chapter of *The Public and Its Problems*, that all human beings unavoidably engage in certain actions which have equally unavoidable consequences, which as unavoidably affect other people.[31] This mutuality in being unavoidably affected by one another lies beyond the personal, private responsibility of either party. This creates a special public. The notion of this public is the notion of a realm of mutual interaction with consequences for which, if we do not have another way to see to it, we cannot hold anyone personally responsible. Wherever I go, I need to breathe. This is unavoidable. Modern industry is impossible without affecting the air. Neither it nor I can help this. The "neither it nor I" creates a need for someone to take responsibility when it becomes clear that industry may hurt whoever inhales. In the second chapter Dewey develops the idea that this "someone" is the state, the public authority. And since the state has a particular concern to create a network of interrelationships to assist us in situations where conflicts of the unavoidable kind are, as much as possible, avoided or given a "just" solution, all of us need opportunity to give shape to the public in the political process.

Since politics, the public, and the state all have to do with putting limits on undesirable consequences of unavoidable actions, a pluralist public whose pluralism is metaphysical and religious, that is, a public deeply divided about deep commitments having to do with human happiness and the meaning of life, is an especially difficult public to deal with. These commitments have finality and exclusivity. Rorty acknowledges this.[32] They are also unavoidable. Rorty acknowledges this as well.[33] So, understandably, he favours a tradition whose sense of "public" avoids dealing with divided commitments in ways that can only be hurtful, such as was the case for example in the Bosnian strategy for settling conflict. In the liberal tradition the solution is: the public will tolerate ultimate commitments, but their place in human affairs is limited to private domains. The tolerance may even include protecting our right to have these commitments, provided we do not let them play a role in public.

Now here comes the crucial point: Rorty does not deal with religious commitment as something we may, in case of conflict, freely decide to keep private, for a while, till the dust has settled. Rather, he insists we must keep it private. The public will protect freedom of religion. But the price is that "the religious" must not bother the public.[34] Consequently religion is banned from significant public institutions, say, schools. Public schools, however, are schools with some character, they have a face. But what face does the public have in the school? The face that hides a liberal heartbeat? There are European democracies which favour a democratic education system in which the state pays for all educational systems of the public's choice. Government policy with respect to funding public education in most North American jurisdictions financially "forces" most parents to send their children to one school system, even though that system's face is not the face of choice of many parents. Freedom and democracy seem at risk here, in spite of their unprecedented expansion in liberal societies.

For Rorty common sense is a public good.[35] A final vocabulary is private.[36] Liberalism is, for an ironist like Rorty, a private final vocabulary.[37] Yet he also speaks of a final vocabulary that is "the common sense of the West," which happens to be that of liberalism.[38] I cannot construe this in any other way than as the classic liberal move of declaring its particular views to be common. In liberalism construed in this way, the public/private split goes all the way down except for liberals. The real distinction becomes an unreal split, but its unreality escapes detection because to its creators it appears as no real split at all. Their heart beats on both sides. Rorty claims that the split only means that no single theory can hold public and private life together, though a real life could. I remain suspicious. In that same context he refers to achieving this unity in life through the public part of the private final vocabulary of the liberal.[39] Does this not mean there also has to be a private part to the liberal public vocabulary? Does liberalism not want to be exactly the theory that Rorty says is impossible? For others, however, liberal privacy is too individualistic and the liberal public too common. It does not seem that Rorty has been able or really even willing to rescue liberalism from social hegemony. What is "common to us all" in this liberalism remains a strictly liberal hope.

PLURALISM WITH INTEGRITY FOR ALL

I want to make a case for a public consisting of people whose lives are whole rather than split, for whom the public/private distinction is a correlation on a continuum. I also want to argue for a public whose sharing is around respecting difference in public and whose active membership is open to all who can demonstrate with their lives that in their differences they do not hurt others. Public justice will then on the one hand be an open notion, to be filled in by citizens as they participate responsibly. But it will also be a closed notion, because it will exclude whatever is—though initially minimally defined—hurtful to others.

People whose lives are whole are people with deep commitments that are relevant to all of their lives. Rorty will likely agree. What we call those commitments is unimportant: religion, ideology, final vocabulary, metaphysics, philosophy, worldview. Rorty will likely agree again. What is important is their characterization in Rorty's own words: they serve to justify our actions, beliefs, and lives; in terms of them we tell our life's stories.[40] The Rorty who writes these things is the contingent liberal ironist. The story of his liberal life is, for him, not rationally justified and the liberal community has no rational foundations. A liberal has hope, liberal hope.[41] Community is a matter of "shared hope and the trust created by such sharing."[42] I quote Rorty here, because I agree with him. And I think Bernstein is right to call this fideism, though in my view mistaken to think there is something wrong with this. But I am also persuaded that only a residue of old liberal dogma can tell the Rorty who says these things that as a citizen he leaves those hopes behind, that in public he has no life story to tell, that in fact he forbids himself to have such hopes and tell such stories. It seems fair to wonder, in fact, just how consistently Rorty himself believes this. When he says that "the moral tasks of a liberal democracy are divided between the agents of love and the agents of justice,"[43] he is saying this in the context of preserving "self-identity" and "sense of selfhood."[44] This context is not just private, but the public one of being "admitted as citizens."[45] I do not see why it makes a practically important difference that he is talking about an ideal, though not a philosophy.[46] Does that sort of language not becloud the realities of liberalism? It seems fair for Rorty to speak of his country as a democracy. But is not a liberal democracy a less democratic one? One with space only for liberals? Surely Rorty does not think most American citizens are liberals.[47] If so, does the expression liberal democracy not do violence to the non-liberal citizen? Can "liberal society" mean more than a society where liberals dominate? Is the private liberal vocabulary gone public not a form of the violence a liberal wishes to avoid? Are not too many citizens excluded from the liberal category of mature, public-spirited adults? Are these adults not simply a smug group whose opinions have liberal approval?[48]

I suspect that in part Rorty is bewitched here by a notion of private in relation to public that is too much isolated solitude. Richard Bernstein speaks of Rorty's logic of apartheid in this context.[49] As I said earlier, in reality, nothing concrete is so private that it is not also in some way public. That extends to what we are apt to call our private parts. Even "in private" you cannot do with these "privates" whatever you please. Even in the privacy of the spousal bed, sexual abuse is a public offense. Privacy that leads to suffering shows the potential public side of the private coin. So how could it be then that our deepest hopes, hopes which Rorty says give us a sense of community, should not be (at least in part) public? In my view, Rorty is right about what our deepest commitments are. But he appears mistaken to say that they are strictly, just, only, absolutely private. Rorty's own limit on privacy, namely noticed cruelty and suffering, shows the presence of the public in his privacy.[50] Not only can our commitments, on his own description, not be that private, he himself does not keep them private. And a careful reading of his texts suggests that he does not want to keep them private. When he urges those of us who are not liberals to keep our life stories out of public discussion, that is not just intended to give us protection to preserve our hopes, but also to keep those hopes outside the walls of a liberal democracy's self-image of the public. Privacy now feels like a detention camp, domination. When he says that "the dominant language game of liberal democracy swallows up others" it is clear to me that "dominant" means more than "powerful majority." It means an active barring from "the conversation," a subjugation, which seems neither liberal nor democratic.[51]

Perhaps I can now immediately jump into the argument that deepest commitments kept private are like the prejudices rationalism once claimed it did not have: they do their public work in secret. Women, gays, blacks, the poor, and Jews were not in truth oppressed by reason during two or three centuries of Enlightenment, that is, by public arguments that could stand up to scrutiny in the logical space of reasons, but by hidden prejudices reason said it did not have. In the mean time they invisibly drove the logic machine of the Enlightenment's public civility. The members of the gentlemen's club do not just politely shop in the bazaar and reveal their identity only inside the club. In the club they think up schemes for keeping shopkeepers in their place.[52] And the effects are noticeable in the bazaar. The sensitive perceiver will notice them as pain. Rorty's liberalism, because of his recommended liberal irony and the policy of opening as many doors and windows as possible, may be a more liberal, more open, more flexible liberalism than that of unprejudiced reason. But the domination remains. Bernstein observes that Rorty is not inclined to contemplate an alternative.[53] This, I suggest, is the (hidden?) side of Rorty of which some feminists, perhaps without exactly articulating or fully documenting it, are suspicious: a subtle form of domination. Sandra Harding, in a note, is suspicious of Rorty's "we."[54] Lorraine Code, citing Nancy Fraser as her ally, in a more extended discussion voices the same concern.[55]

The liberalism that is Rorty's public policy, liberal democracy, has the face of the private liberal heartbeat. Rorty is aware of the exclusivity of his liberal community's identity.[56] But he does not resolve the tension which results when, as in this case, public policy and private identity are one on some deep level, though they are intended to be kept separate. That is understandable, however, when the genuine desire for toleration is translated into an impossibility, namely that of politics without a heartbeat. Because such a politics is both impossible and undesirable, Rorty is apparently content to give his own public policy a private heartbeat, even though he has then transgressed his own public/private split. They have become welded. But where they are so welded, how will the public institutions shaped by that public policy remain tolerant? They are places where other heartbeats, that is, other than liberal, are indeed branded as private and are thus not welcomed as shapers of public policy. Instead, the liberal heartbeat, in the context of public institutions, suddenly announces itself as common sense, is imposed as the public position we should all take.

Why is this undesirable? Primarily because it discourages certain forms of openness and freedom. In spite of the fact that societies influenced by liberalism enjoy unprecedented openness and freedom, they are nevertheless unnecessarily curtailed by the closed sense of "public." To make the point with an example which is by now perhaps more familiar, though by no means generally palatable, it might help here to see a parallel with what feminists have pointed out about knowledge, namely that much and important knowledge, public knowledge too, is gendered. The parallel is that much and important knowledge, public knowledge too, is ideologically coloured. And what can in this way be understood about knowledge is applicable to political action as well. Hence the artificial blocking out of a factor which is nevertheless at work results in subterranean currents of control over the public. Examples are easy to give. Public political examination of the (mostly hidden) religious factor in public discussions of homophobia, for example, will be neglected in the name of freedom of religion. Or ideological commitments in the pursuit of "free enterprise" will remain hidden. In this way, by barring them from public view, the liberal approach underplays the unavoidable ideologically coloured components of all public life. On the one hand liberalism and its toleration have been largely responsible for the establishment of freedom and democracy in the West. On the other, liberalism's failure to fully acknowledge the masking of its own private ideological character with the domination of its public practices impedes some needed further extension of toleration to create more radical freedom and democracy.[57] If that is so, acting in public discussion as though it is not so can only darken our counsel. Susan Babbit observes that "a person's rational interests...depend precisely upon the kinds of personal and political transformation experiences the liberal accounts want to rule out."[58] Liberalism then practises ideological intolerance in public, masking significant forces shaping public policy and preventing us from knowing what these forces are.

Rorty's conflict does not seem to be an unavoidable one. It is possible to encourage all participants in the public conversation to bare their hearts, not just the liberals. We could be working toward a kind of full participation, full democracy. This is more than American democracy, which John Dewey once analyzed as a one-party system organized in a slower-moving, conservative and a faster-moving, progressive wing.[59] Full democracy would give voice to the actual diversity (pluralism) present in that society.[60] This would be a democracy not of argument or of common denominator, but of maximized participation. The maximization will occur as the result of recognizing that people's participation (as individuals, in communities, through institutions) is invited not because they have become "one of us," but because they are different, and in their difference they are willing to welcome the difference of others.[61]

Each community will still maintain that its hopes have more reality and credibility than any other. But in this new public, domination will not make any commitment attractive. The only hope of making our hope the hope of others will lie in the possibility that our hope becomes visible as hope, that is, as a way to liberation from suffering. Not only will there be space for everyone's heartbeat to be felt in public policy, but in the carried out policy the heartbeat must come through as the policy's having heart. People will more likely develop pride in, and be prepared to take responsibility for, a public policy which, though they do not fully dominate it, does not altogether exclude them either. Instead, they will have political ownership.

The freedom to declare ownership is one important advantage over a public debate in which such declarations arouse suspicion. But there is another advantage. Public discussion, as we become more and more aware these days, benefits from full disclosure. The public is entitled to know what deeply moves people in arriving at the positions they hold. My proposal here is not a request for dogmatic pronouncements, but for deliverance from the dogma that people have arrived at the positions they hold in public by public-rational methods alone. The time has come, perhaps, that those who dogmatically declare this about their positions arouse justified suspicion.

Notes

1. Richard Rorty, *Contingency, Irony, and Solidarity* (Cambridge: Cambridge University Press, 1989). (Cited as *CIS.*)
2. Richard Rorty, *Objectivity, Relativism, and Truth* (Cambridge: Cambridge University Press, 1991). (Cited as *ORT*.)
3. Richard J. Bernstein, *The New Constellation: The Ethical/Political Horizons of Modernity/Postmodernity* (Cambridge: MIT Press, 1992), p. 286.
4. *ORT*, pp. 36-37.
5. *CIS*, pp. 73-95; *ORT*, pp. 203-10.
6. As late as the opening sentence of his plenary address to the 1988 World Congress of philosophy in Brighton, England.
7. *CIS*, pp. 44ff. In a fascinating discussion of these matters Stanley Fish seems less contingent than Rorty. He argues that Christians who are willing to participate in open discussion have caved in to liberalism, and he has little eye for the dogmatism of his liberalism's "procedural rules of pluralistic academia." See "Why We Can't All Just Get Along," (especially p. 26) in *First Things* 60 (February 1996): 18-26.
8. *ORT*, p. 33.
9. Ibid., p. 279.

10. Richard Rorty, "Towards a Liberal Utopia" in *Times Literary Supplement*, 24 June 1994, p. 14. (Cited as *TLU*.) My italics. In a review of Alan Ryan's *John Dewey and the High Tide of American Liberalism* Rorty curiously combines appreciation for Dewey's views in the latter's essay "Christianity and Democracy" with his own sentiment that "religious, aesthetic or philosophical views...are for weekends." But Dewey's essay opens with a page of strong views on the social and intellectual significance of religious views. See "Something to Steer by" in *London Review of Books*, 20 June 1996, p. 8. Dewey's essay can be found in volume 4 of *John Dewey: The Early Works 1882-1898*, p. 3.

11. *TLU*.

12. *ORT*, pp. 203-10.

13. Richard Rorty, "Religion as Conversation-Stopper" in *Common Knowledge* 3, 1 (Spring 1994): 1-6. (Cited as *RCS*.)

14. *RCS*, p. 2.

15. Ibid., p. 5.

16. Ibid., p. 2.

17. Ibid., p. 3.

18. Ibid., p. 4.

19. A recent and current discussion—involving Stephen Carter, Philip Quinn, Kent Greenwalt, Stanley Fish and George Marsden, Robert Audi and others—shows important and, in my view, promising cracks in the wall.

20. *CIS*, pp. 73-95. How would Rorty deal with Cornell West's analysis of black politics in North America as fundamentally directed by their religion? See part I of his *Prophetic Fragments: Illuminations of the Crisis in American Religion and Culture* (Grand Rapids, MI: Wm B. Eerdmans and Trenton: Africa World Press, 1993).

21. *CIS*, pp. 44-60.

22. *TLU*.

23. *CIS*, p. 44.

24. *ORT*, p. 183.

25. *RCS*, p. 2.

26. Ibid.

27. *ORT*, p. 207.

28. On this understanding of religion, there could be atheists, but not a-religious people. Religion simply is a term for a cluster of realities named differently by different people, such as final vocabulary (Rorty), ultimate commitment (Tillich), ideology, core life-orientation, deepest or most pervasive human hope, etc. One could have any of these without "believing in" a God. But it is hard to see how one could be human without this function in life playing some role. See, for example, atheist Kai Nielsen's unpublished manuscript "Is Religion The Opium Of The People? Marxianism and Religion." In this paper Nielsen does not abdicate his atheism, but argues that human beings process the ultimate existential questions of life in a way that has to be called religious. An important treatment of what I here call religion can be found in Charles Taylor's *Sources of the Self: The Making of the Modern Identity* (Cambridge: Harvard University Press, 1989). Taylor frequently refers to the underlying spirituality, the moral sources, the epiphanic in human experience in a way closely related to what I have in mind. And he emphatically denies that this dimension can simply be equated with our having certain beliefs (403, 413, 491). The use of the term "religion" in connection with what is usually taken to be a "secular" interest such as economics recently surfaced in the title of an article in *Studies in Religion* by Michel Beaudin, "Cette idole qui nous gouverne. Le néo-libéralisme comme 'religion' et 'théologie' sacrificielles" 24 April 1995, pp. 395-413.

29. Charles Taylor makes much of the fact that movements denying what I here call the religious function can do so only in the name of some (repressed) form of that function.

30. See Thomas Auxter's "The Debate over Cultural Imperialism" in *Addresses and*

Proceedings of the American Philosophical Association 59 (1985): 753-57.

31. John Dewey, *The Public and Its Problems* (Denver: Alan Swallow, 1954. Originally, New York: Henry Holt, 1927).

32. *CIS*, p. 73; *ORT*, p. 210.

33. *ORT*, p. 182.

34. If I am right (as I briefly stated earlier) that, functionally speaking, "religion" is a matter of the human "heartbeat" or of what Rorty himself refers to as the function of our final vocabularies, then all members of the public are religious, that is, have deep commitments (Charles Taylor's spirituality of moral sources) that in some way or other affect them deeply.

35. *CIS*, p. 74.

36. Ibid., p. 73.

37. Ibid.

38. Ibid., p. 77. My italics.

39. Ibid., pp. 120-21.

40. Ibid., p. 73.

41. Ibid.

42. *ORT*, p. 33.

43. Ibid., p. 206.

44. Ibid., p. 203. Illuminating remarks about this are made by Drucilla Cornell in a section of a chapter called "The Geertz/Rorty Debate." See her *Transformations* (New York and London: Routledge, 1993), pp. 172-77.

45. *ORT*, p. 206

46. Ibid., p. 209.

47. I am taking "liberal" here in a narrow ideological sense (and not as a name for democratically inclined people) in which the traditional appeal to common rational underpinnings to the exclusion of what cannot thus be supported plays a major ideological role.

48. *RCS*, p. 2.

49. *ORT*, p. 286.

50. *CIS*, p. 164.

51. *ORT*, p. 279.

52. Ibid., p. 209-10.

53. Ibid., p. 280.

54. Sandra Harding, *The Science Question in Feminism* (Ithaca: Cornell University Press, 1986), p. 194.

55. Lorraine Code, "Taking Subjectivity into Account" in Linda Alcoff and Elizabeth Potter, *Feminist Epistemologies* (New York: Routledge, 1993), pp. 23-24. For Fraser, see Nancy Fraser, "Solidarity or Singularity? Richard Rorty between Romanticism and Technocracy" in Jonathan Arac and Barbara, Johnson, eds., *Consequences of Theory* (Baltimore: Johns Hopkins, 1991). Also see Drucilla Cornell's *Transformations*.

56. *ORT*, p. 210.

57. This point is also made by Stephen Carter.

58. Susan E. Babbit, "Feminism and Objective Interests: The Role of Transformation Experiences in Rational Deliberation" in Alcoff and Potter, *Feminist Epistemologies*, pp. 245-64. The quote is from p. 251, the italics are mine. See also *ORT*, pp. 279, 263-64.

59. See his *Liberalism and Social Action* (New York: Capricorn Books, 1963. Originally, New York: Putnam, 1935).

60. This is difficult but not impossible. Dutch political democracy is, for example, much more pluralist than North American. Space does not permit an extensive description of a fuller democracy, but I could summarize certain conditions that would lead to more inclusion. This could be possible, for example, if (1) none be cruelly told that they must

leave their commitments at home; (2) all will be expected to respect the commitments of others; (3) none can expect their commitments to be allowed free play if consequences of these commitments require people to engage in kinds of cruelty abhorrent to most civil democracies, such as the sexual abuse of children; (4) all will be urged to make their commitments palatable by demonstrating (not just arguing) that their commitments lead to the alleviation of suffering in the eyes of those who now suffer; (5) none can expect their commitments to be fully implemented; (6) all make proposals for non-cruel ways of shaping public policy that are consistent with their commitments in some fundamental way. In these conditions not every element is without controversy, but they do, I believe, lead to easier resolution of controversy. The elimination of suffering, for example, in the eyes of those who suffer, takes the sting out of "who defines suffering?" We all know what suffering is. The causes and their effects as suffering are controversial. But if those who suffer are allowed to make their case and deserve alleviation, important steps forward will have been made.

61. I am not pleading for a utopian full inclusion of all. In our complex world no strategy can guarantee that sort of inclusion. I am suggesting, however, that ideological liberalism is unnecessarily intolerant (by its own standards) due to its commitment to reason as the principle of inclusion/exclusion.

3

Indoctrination and Assimilation in Plural Settings

KEN BADLEY

A twofold problem faces Canadian education. The first fold involves the indoctrination debate, still unsettled after several decades, yet still bearing decisively on educational policy. The second fold involves the changing Canadian educational landscape, now obviously characterized by increasing cultural, religious, and linguistic plurality. This plurality manifests itself in tribalism and in regular conflicts about normativity in the public square. In the midst of this plurality, many Canadian parents of school-aged children believe that courts, provincial governments, and educational authorities deny them educational justice by determining that their own religion cannot inform what their children learn in schools. Yet, from their vantage point, their own educational tax dollars are used to indoctrinate their children into another worldview—some combination of materialism, secular humanism, and liberalism—every day of the school year. When these parents cry foul, defenders of common schools reply that the only way to make schools accessible to everyone is to make them neutral, which implies leaving religion out of education.

Examining the various charges and replies in this discussion reveals a philosophical-ideological thicket, through which the various parties apparently can no longer hear each other. I suggest that educators and educational theorists could go a long way toward solving these policy difficulties if we can find the will to move forward on the matters of indoctrination, pluralism, and related concepts, such as neutrality.[1]

INDOCTRINATION: AN UNSETTLED DEBATE

Conceptual problems and disagreements still dog the debate about indoctrination in education, even after decades of struggle. Educators, philosophers of education, the courts, and the public, dispute what differentiates indoctrination from education, and what criterion or combination of criteria actually singles out what counts as indoctrination. What does count as indoctrination? The criteria usually listed include:

- the intention of the teaching activity is to bring about in the student unshakable or unquestioning belief in an idea, regardless of the veracity of that idea.[2]
- the means of teaching violate in one or more ways the rights, agency, or person of the student. In the language of the philosophy of education, the means violate a differentiated or positive concept of education, in which worthwhile learning is implied versus education in the descriptive or undifferentiated (education system) sense of the word.[3] On this account, education implies approval of the means of teaching by whomever is speaking at the moment.
- the contents are doctrinaire or contain doctrinaire elements. Some claim simply that if the contents are about doctrines then we have a case of indoctrination.[4] In Holocaust revisionism, we uncover a paradigm case of doctrinaire contents. Some observers, of course, suggest that instruction in Christian faith serves equally well as a paradigm.
- the upshot or outcomes of teaching involves the student's emerging with either false, unquestioning, or unshakeable beliefs, despite a teacher's good intentions, laudable methods, and worthwhile content.[5]

Each of the above has found defenders who have argued that one of these criteria is sufficient by itself to identify indoctrination; others have argued for various combinations of the four. Debates continue regarding each of the separate criteria as well, resulting in questions like: what is a worthwhile intention, what are acceptable means, what are doctrinaire contents, and what is false belief, unshakable belief, and non-evidential belief? Some, in their innocence perhaps, have even asked what is wrong with unshakeable beliefs, especially and obviously, for example, with regard to analytic truths such as $2 + 2 = 4$.

Aside from the disagreement about means, intentions, content, and outcomes, other matters remain:

1. Distinguishing and delimiting such key concepts germane to the indoctrination discussion as neutral, fairminded, impartial, empathetic, committed, dispassionate, and just;
2. Establishing the semantic range and possibly the logical status of doctrines; and
3. Establishing whether religion has been defined too narrowly, and whether worldviews might not lead to clearer reflection on indoctrination.[6]

By no means, do these questions exhaust the avenues of approach we might take to such a complex area of enquiry. To the point of this chapter, the debate on indoctrination has thus far largely failed to identify the following:

1. Cases where a community or society widely accepts a dominant worldview and then hegemonically enforces that view through the school system. This situation is illustrated for us if we believe, for example, the allegations typically made on the one side by critical theorists (who believe schools have been hijacked by free-market conservatives), and, on the other side, by conservative observers (who believe schools have been hijacked by leftists and liberals); and

2. Cases where the curriculum contents fail to treat a matter sufficiently and thus portray, by silence, an inaccurate picture, regardless of the intentions (or means) of this lopsided portrayal. For example, Aboriginal Canadians are usually invisible in histories of Canadian engagement in World War II. The role of religion often goes missing in Canadian curricula. Until recent years, women and "ordinary life" were largely absent from most history books. I will return shortly—in my discussion of pluralism—to these sometimes overlapping, unidentified, possible cases of indoctrination.

Several participants in the indoctrination debate have noted how frequently one person positively labels a process education which someone else insists counts as indoctrination.[7] Noting this tendency certainly does not gut the latter term of its meaning for other purposes, but it should give anyone pause before levelling the criticism that someone else is indoctrinating. That the pejorative sense of indoctrination has now largely supplanted the descriptive, instructional sense of the term (dating from before World War II) may or may not be related to education's being largely a positive term, whose differentiated sense implies worthwhile learning done in acceptable ways.[8] Whatever the range of possible relationships between the two concepts, indoctrination and education, they become diametric terms only when one selects the negative meaning of the one and the positive sense of the other.

PLURALITY AND PLURALISM: FORCING A RECONSIDERATION

Plurality and Pluralism

To begin this section, I will differentiate pluralism and plurality. In common Canadian usage, pluralism tends to do two jobs which we should not only distinguish, but which we ought to assign to two separate words if we hope to maintain precision through our discussions, and eventually move those discussions forward. First, pluralism usually designates a plural situation, to which I would rather assign the term plurality. In this situation of plurality, we find more-than-oneness, the "coexistence within one political jurisdiction of people with publicly important different beliefs and ways of life," people with "incommensurate ideological" differences, who "indwell irreducibly different worlds."[9] The term commonly used for both meanings, pluralism, also implies the absolutization or advocacy of the plural situation. That is: as an "ism" it implies that the many-ness designated by the rarely used term plurality (and by the frequently used term pluralism) is worthwhile and that public policy should be directed toward its realization. Confusion attends the use of pluralism because it usually does this double duty, describing a plural state of affairs and prescribing partiality to that state of affairs. I want to restrict pluralism to the second, prescriptive meaning listed because, while I take it as given that Canada faces cultural, linguistic, and religious plurality, it is not so clear how many Canadians actually value genuine pluralism, or which kinds of plurality they wish to embrace.[10]

Thus, although I noted the typical implications of "ism" words a moment ago, my desire to restrict pluralism does not rest on morphological grounds. Still, in differentiating these two senses of pluralism, and assigning one to the separate term plurality, I think I am making morphological sense.

In graphing the range of possible responses to plurality, we may see more easily the importance of distinguishing these two common meanings of pluralism, and thus the value of assigning one of the meanings its own more descriptive word, plurality. Faced with linguistic, religious, or ethnic plurality, a society, its institutions, and individuals might respond in any of several ways:

Obviously, other words could be used instead of these five, and other intermediate points on the continuum could be identified. My suggestion here is that ordinary usage has varied from what one might expect. Words ending in "ism" usually connote a position of advocacy. Yet, recognizably, eradication and assimilation can hardly be viewed as the advocacy of plurality. Even tolerance leaves us in some doubt, despite its having become a kind of linguistic icon in multicultural, Canadian education. In light of the amount of fuzzy usage in usual discussions in these areas, I recommend to all of us the distinctive terms pluralism and plurality, and will use them as distinctive terms throughout this chapter.

History of Canadian Plurality

One comment on the prehistory of Canadian plurality is warranted. Religious wars made it clear to post-Reformation Europe and England that some common basis for public peace was required. The 1689 Act of Toleration in England was viewed by many as a legislative means to end publicly oppressive and tyrannical expressions of religious intolerance. Perceptions have shifted over three centuries so that by our own time, pluralism (in its undifferentiated sense) has achieved the status of secular doctrine, almost of cultural myth. Canadian plurality has, until recently, seemed to rest on three related, classical liberal, largely unchallenged, somewhat contradictory assumptions:

1. That we can get along only when we leave our deepest (religious) commitments in the private sphere;
2. That the public square must be reserved only for those things which we all hold in common (despite the now-so-typically Canadian use of public money to celebrate some fundamental differences); and
3. That the public school must and can be neutral.

New conditions in both Canada and the rest of the world are beginning to force all educators to consider again our understandings of both plurality and indoctrination. A "crisis of nationalism"[11] begins to tear Europe apart almost as soon as the Soviet empire dissolves. Religious violence threatens the stability of many nations. And, to the substance of this section of this chapter, people around the world ask why there is no space for their religious convictions in publicly funded schools that, they charge, are not neutral but rather thoroughly doctrinaire. In Canada, several changes now force us to reappraise plurality (and indoctrination). Immigration has brought increasing cultural, linguistic, and religious plurality to Canada. As it does elsewhere, disagreement frequently erupts in Canada regarding what topics are too divisive (language, religion, culture) or controversial (abortion, homosexuality, birth control) for treatment in Canadian schools.[12] The Council of Ministers of Education of Canada (CMEC) has recognized Canadian plurality and, in a 1992 memorandum of agreement, seemed to lean toward the acceptance/celebration end of the continuum:

> Canada is a highly diversified country in every respect. Linguistic, racial, cultural and religious differences, within and among provinces and territories, are a fundamental characteristic of its people. We view this pluralism as a source of great richness for the country, and believe that its strength lies in maintaining a profound respect for differences.[13]

Despite their undifferentiated use of pluralism, the ministers express a common Canadian sentiment. Interestingly, they include religion on their list. Multiculturalism, until now, has primarily been perceived as a cultural and linguistic matter.[14] The Canadian education ministers thus offer a more inclusive range of characteristics by including religion in their statement. With or without religion, their list points toward the respect and celebration end of the continuum that I sketched earlier. Whether Canada is pluralistic is another matter. Many Canadians point to a gulf between prose such as that in the CMEC agreement and the reality they witness in their own schools, where, they insist, some important differences between Canadians are barely tolerated, let alone accepted or celebrated.

Two other factors add to the difficulty that schools and policy-makers encounter in their work. First—a foreground factor—the public has historically come to view schools as a natural channel to bring about social change. This view has meant increasing, not decreasing, normativity in the curriculum regarding such matters as the environment, AIDS, smoking, and nutrition. Ironically, this increase in normativity comes at a time when, in the hands of schools, religious allegiances have become mere preferences, and individualism seems to have taken ethics by storm. The second is a background factor: previously central groups, such as the church, which did indoctrinate or try to assimilate and even eradicate difference, now find themselves marginalized. Here, I choose the church as an example, and the words central and marginalized specifically to echo R. I. Moore's 1990 book, *The Formation of a Persecuting Society: Power and Deviance in Western Europe, 950-1250*. Another example of this emigration from centre to margin relates to what is now roughly called "Euro-centrism" in the curriculum, a view of the world now frequently questioned by educators and others concerned with education.

What has changed to warrant my proposing that the advent of cultural and religious plurality suggests that the unsettled indoctrination debate be examined again? Little has changed within the debate itself. Rather, the social and educational landscape in Canada, like that of Britain and the United States, has undergone statistically small but politically significant alteration so that Canadian schools now serve several constituencies in ways that the members of those constituencies consider inadequate. Specifically, the epistemological assumptions underlying Western thought and science are seen to be in conflict with certain peoples' religious convictions and ways of life.

Muslims

The Canadian Muslim population remains small, but Muslims encounter great difficulty in accepting the claim to objectivity which underlies Western science.[15] I will quote representative sources to illustrate this difficulty:

> In Islam and the civilization which it created there was a veritable celebration of knowledge all...related to the sacred extending in a hierarchy from an "empirical" and rational mode of knowing to that highest form of knowledge (*al-macrifah* or *cirfan*) which is the unitive knowledge of God not by [people] as [individuals], but by the divine center of human intelligence which, at the level of *gnosis,* becomes the subject as well as object of knowledge.[16]

Many in the West consider this isolation of object from subject one of the prerequisites of knowing; knowing is viewed as an asymmetrical relation between subject and object. In fact, those who celebrate what they see as the superiority of Western science and philosophy, often point to this feature as that which, perhaps more than any other, has served to move Western science ahead.

But some cry "foul" regarding the claim that Western thought and science are neutral, objective and therefore superior. To these people, Western arrogance flows out of Western misperception of the subject/object relationship that informs the hegemonic Western view of knowledge.

Qadir puts the problem more starkly than does Nasr:

> [T]he Islamic theory of knowledge...is fundamentally different from the Western theory. One major reason for the difference is that the former is based upon the spiritual conception of [human beings] and the universe [they inhabit], while the latter is secular and devoid of the sense of the Sacred. It is precisely for this reason, according to Muslim thinkers, that the Western theory of knowledge poses one of the greatest challenges to [hu]mankind. Knowledge in the West has become problematic as it has lost its true purpose. It is ill-conceived and wrongly interpreted. It has elevated doubt and scepticism and in some cases agnosticism to the level of scientific methodology and has thereby brought chaos to all realms of human knowledge. However, it should be understood that the Western conception of knowledge is not value-free as is sometimes supposed; it is very much partial, being the product of the Western worldview.[17]

Many in the West would object that Qadir's complaints are ill-founded, that our science is value-free, and that it yields up objective knowledge. Yet, if Qadir is correct in delineating the differences between Islamic and Western views of knowledge, he makes quite plain why some people believe that allegedly neutral, publicly funded schools indoctrinate.

Now, some may object by arguing that Muslims have their epistemology wrong. But for the question of indoctrination as I mean us to reconsider it here, such an objection carries little weight. Two groups follow incompatible epistemologies, both claiming to be able to adjudge the other. In a sense, the philosophical discussion must stand aside because we live in plural Canada. Why? Because Muslims use the school system, and they are not interested in being told they simply have understood epistemology wrongly. The point is that from their point of view, Western education appears fundamentally in opposition to their at-bottom convictions about the world and their knowledge of it.[18] Qadir continues his remarks this way:

> [T]he sense of the Sacred which furnishes the ultimate ground for knowledge has to accompany and to interpenetrate the educative process at every stage. Allah not only stands at the beginning of knowledge, He also stands at the end, and He also accompanies and infuses grace into the entire process of learning. In this process the sense of the Sacred is nowhere lost sight of.[19]

I will quote just one more remark from Qadir to illustrate how deeply Muslims' difficulty with Canadian education might run: "The distinction between divine and non-divine knowledge is spurious. Knowledge is knowledge...no matter what its contents are."[20]

Given this epistemology, Muslims will not be satisfied to have a world religions class added into the curriculum somewhere in grades ten to twelve. Nor will recognition of the Islamic year satisfy them. Muslims would view these moves and others like them as unsatisfactory carrots, as insults. Religion is, in one sense, everything for them, and as the Islamic Institute at Cambridge argues continually, they believe school curriculum should reflect this. In Ontario, a few Muslim families have sent their children to Christian schools, a phenomenon already widespread in England. The parents of the Muslim children in these Christian schools reason that although Christianity may be an inferior religion, Christian schools at least recognize the hand of God on all of life. They prefer this combination to publicly funded education, which insists that the public square cannot make space for genuine religious differences and that, when religion does come to school, it must be reduced to a song-and-dance routine. The restoration of Christian religious education in British (state-funded) common schools in 1988 was, in fact, heavily supported by Muslims, who argued that religion belonged in schools. Furthermore, they argued that because Christianity—even if only nominal Christianity—was the majority religion in Britain, Christianity, rather than comparative religions, should be taught in British schools. That some Muslims in Britain still send their children to Christian schools illustrates the depth of their conviction that religious faith underlies the whole of the educational endeavour.

Canadian Aboriginal Peoples

For those from parts of Canada with minute Muslim populations, traditional Canadian Aboriginal epistemology may pose more of a challenge.[21] Like Muslims, Canadian Aboriginals protest the Western approach to knowledge that underlies and saturates Canadian school curricula. For them, an obvious point of difference with the dominant approach lies in the view of the natural world, of which they consider human life an integral, not a separate part.[22] Again, Western science and philosophy assume that subject-separateness is a strength, and even a necessary first step to the development of our science. Such a view is antithetical to the panentheism of Aboriginal spirituality. This short extract from the Thanksgiving Prayer of the Longhouse People catches some flavour of the Aboriginal view of the interrelatedness of all things:

> We have been given the duty
> To live in harmony with one another
> And with other living things.
> We give thanks that this is true.
> We give thanks to our Mother Earth.
> All that makes us strong and alive, comes from you

We are all like children as we walk upon you.
You nourish us and all living things.

Defenders of Western thought might (accurately) protest that the panentheism evident here would not move Western science ahead, or even that Canadian Aboriginal children had best learn Western ways if they want to get ahead in Canadian life. Economically, such assimilationist sentiments make sense.[23] But to express them is, in a sense, to be answering the wrong question, because Aboriginal people are concerned about a worldview inimical to their own. They argue that this worldview runs through the curriculum and that publicly funded Canadian schools (even band-controlled ones) indoctrinate. Mentioning Aboriginal history, or even worldviews, in a class here and there does not address the underlying differences between Western epistemology and an epistemology informed by traditional Aboriginal spirituality, nor does it address the problems Canadian Aboriginals thereby typically encounter in Canadian curricula.

A brief survey of Canadian curricula which give space to Aboriginal epistemology is very brief indeed. At this time, Newfoundland recognizes it only minimally.[24] In the Nova Scotia social studies curriculum, the Mi'kmaq people are studied, though not in detail.[25] New Brunswick offers a grade eleven and twelve native studies course, and two elementary schools offer Maliseet heritage programs.[26] Prince Edward Island gives 25 percent of its grade seven social studies curriculum to Aboriginal cultures.[27] In Manitoba, Aboriginal epistemology and spirituality are included throughout kindergarten to grade twelve social studies in the context of broader examination of Aboriginal culture, recognizing "that in traditional societies spirituality informs the day to day activities of the people, and that a knowledge of people's beliefs and values is essential to understanding the society."[28] According to the 1989 Indian and Métis education policy from kindergarten to grade twelve, the province of Saskatchewan requires that Aboriginal content—that is, epistemology and spirituality—be integrated into all curriculum areas. By the 1992-93 school year, Aboriginal content was being classroom tested. To their credit, officials in Saskatchewan education understood that Aboriginal spirituality was not simply a compartment of life: "When people see the term spirituality, they often assume it is a form of religion. It is not. Rather, Indigenous spirituality is a philosophy which attempts to understand human existence and relationships with nature. It is a perspective of individual and community development, human societies and the environment."[29] In Alberta, all students take Aboriginal "histories, cultures, and lifestyles" in various social studies courses "so they can benefit from the values and lifestyles of Native cultures."[30] The Native Education Project produced a Native Content Analysis Information guide in September 1989 to aid in detecting bias. While it raises several concerns, it deals little with the integrality of Aboriginal worldviews. In British

Columbia, nothing specific is required, and even in band-controlled schools, attention is varied, "depending on the convictions of the band."[31]

As one might expect, the Yukon has Aboriginal worldviews thoroughly integrated at many points (as required by the September 1990, Education Act), including permitted absences from school for religious and cultural activities. The Northwest Territories has two separate curricula specifically to address questions of Aboriginal worldviews (Dene, Kede, and Inuit). Although Canadian schools now pay a degree of attention to Canadian Aboriginal history, or to their views of environment, the epistemological foundations on which those views rest remain largely absent from Canadian education; Manitoba, Saskatchewan, and the territories being the main exceptions.[32]

So far, I have argued that Canadian publicly funded education faces a difficulty, somewhat of its own making. The indoctrination debate leaves few parties happy about what transpires in schools. Those who would dominate that debate now find themselves facing representatives of a plurality of worldviews, some, such as Islam and Aboriginal spirituality, with epistemologies utterly different from the Western rationalism that they charge shapes and controls Canadian classrooms.

SUGGESTED WAYS FORWARD

What forms or models might we use to show genuine respect for these worldviews and others like them which are fundamentally incompatible with the worldview apparently underlying most Canadian publicly funded education? Given that minority worldviews will not be satisfactorily addressed by adding a course to the school curriculum, or merely recognizing special days, foods, and music, how can we honour and implement true pluralism? If we are going to take these fundamental differences seriously, I suggest that we take a four-pronged approach. This will involve considering epistemology, the assimilationist appearance and effects of some public policies, other possible ways to structure plurality, and further exploration of some key concepts related to the indoctrination and pluralism discussions.

Reexamining Epistemological Foundations

Because we must be more cautious than we have been in the past not simply to dismiss minority worldviews with a wave of the hand, we would do well, first, to reexamine the foundations of the dominant Western epistemological paradigm. We must be more cautious than we have been in the past; we cannot simply dismiss minority worldviews with a wave of the hand.

Marginalized groups who discover a gulf between their own epistemology and that dominant in Canadian public schools gain momentum almost daily from feminist studies in philosophy as well as from other quarters. For example, Lorraine Code, philosopher at York University, notes that

> Implicit in the veneration of objectivity central to scientific practice is the conviction that objects of knowledge are separate from knowers and investigators...that they remain separate and unchanged throughout investigative, information-gathering, and knowledge construction processes.[33]

However, she argues that "knowledge is, inextricably, subjective and objective" and that "knowledge is inescapably, the product of an intermingling of subjective and objective elements."[34] Code does not go as far as many feminists in subjectifying knowledge, but she does open enough space to give a Muslim or a Canadian Aboriginal room to breathe.[35]

Richard Rorty, albeit still a confessed rationalist and liberal, has begun to speak of those finally untestable, at-bottom convictions by which we all live. He calls these our "final vocabularies" and admits to their divisive function within society, even suggesting that liberalism itself retains the power to exclude.[36] Rorty is not far from Anthony Flew on at least this matter: Flew describes at one point the "ultimacy of science" and even calls for openness "to the possibility of new, and possibly upsetting discoveries of what actually is the case."[37] Ronald Laura calls Rorty's "final vocabularies" the "epistemologically primitive" starting points of science, and he speaks of "frameworks" within which scientific and philosophical questions and answers make sense.[38] I do not know whether Muslims and Aboriginal Canadians consider people like Code and Rorty their allies. Nor do I know how many are aware that Reformed folk have been offering such criticisms of epistemology for decades. However, I do know that they are asking some of the same questions of Western science: Why did one way of viewing things gain its "epistemic privilege?" and "Is this epistemic privilege justified?"[39] In this current debate, these foundational, worldview questions are not only among the most formidable, but they are among the most important.

Rethinking Current Policies: Appearance and Effect

Besides asking rationalism to make space in the epistemological discussion for other approaches, we must review the appearance and effect of current educational policies toward minorities, especially those whose religious sensibilities are offended by what appears to them an assimilationist approach. Minority groups are now charging that indoctrination in an alien way of thinking takes place in ostensibly public schools. Members of these groups perceive an essentially religious character in publicly funded Canadian schools and they feel like they have encountered the teeth of a policy of eradication and assimilation. These encounters, ironically, occur surrounded by the language of pluralism, neutrality, and toleration—even celebration—of difference.

The defendants in the Mozert court case in the United States argued successfully through two courts that public schools essentially serve assimilationist ends, in conflict with the Christian religion.[40] While such a case has no legal bearing on Canadian education, it may have moral suasion inasmuch as this same kind of "subtle coercion"—read: indoctrination—may also characterize Canadian education.[41]

Pressure to reconsider whether publicly funded school classrooms are as neutral as their defenders claim comes from many quarters, not only from cultural and religious minorities or legal scholars. Some educational theorists as well are saying as much. For over two decades sociologists of education have argued that school classrooms further a conservative agenda. Simultaneously, voices on the right charge that classrooms promote a liberal agenda.

Reconsidering Alternative Structures for Plurality

Thus far, I have suggested that we not only scrutinize the epistemological discussion, but that we reexamine educational policies related to worldviews, to religion and to religious education. Third, I suggest that we seek ways to structure plurality other than the effectively assimilationist approach that, some people charge, presently characterizes Canadian education (even while most defenders of Canadian public education deny having assimilationist intentions). Canadians may want to attempt some kind of structural pluralism (and I mean pluralism in my own restricted sense here, where plurality is advocated). The Dutch, for example, have organized their public life in this way for most of this century.[42] Whether in broadcasting, education, or labour unions, Dutch communities based on various political ideologies and religious viewpoints have enjoyed public space (and in the case of education—public money) to pursue their goods with others of like mind.

Given how differently Dutch society is organized from our own, Canadian provinces should perhaps consider the model implemented in Quebec as a partial solution to the dissatisfaction of religious minorities. Quebec school boards are required to offer students as many as three choices as demand warrants: Roman Catholic religious education, Protestant religious education, or moral education. The first two are made available as opt-in courses, the last is required of those not desiring either of the explicitly religious options. If it wished, Quebec could extend the list to include, for example, Islamic religious education in those districts where population justified such a move. If other Canadian provinces adopted Quebec's approach, Canadians could provide legal room for minorities (and majorities) to give attention to, and expression of, their at-bottom religious commitments within some single publicly funded system. On this account, religious differences would not be ethnicized as they often are now—reduced to a song-and-dance routine for celebration days—but would be treated seriously in curriculum by people whose commitment was considered an asset rather than a liability. In making this suggestion, I assume that all religious groups with the inclination and resources to do so should be given public space and money to describe their outlook on the world.

From the point of view of some religious folk, of course, this option still suffers from one telling limitation: religion is still cordoned off in a single course, perhaps while secular materialism continues to saturate the remainder of the curriculum and the school ethos. Still, allowing representatives to make such courses available seems like the least that school boards should do if they indeed want to take worldview differences seriously.

These are only two means by which to express genuine pluralism within education, and even they come up wanting in obvious ways. There may be more, and I suggest that we must think creatively to articulate what they might be. All the creative thinking on earth, however, will be of no use, unless those who claim to be the guardians of the public square admit that all education will be informed by one set of convictions or another, and that a society concerned with fairness will see to it that parents' convictions inform their own children's education.[43]

Reopening Key Concepts

My last suggestion involves some of our key concepts. Even a cursory look at the matters I have raised here shows that we must reexamine some of the key ideas in the indoctrination and pluralism discussions.

I begin with public education. Canadians interested in education, especially philosophers of education, may need to begin asking a highly modified gloss on W. D. Hudson's question of twenty years ago, "Is Religious Education Possible?"; namely, "Is public education possible?"[44] Throughout this chapter, I have used the phrase "publicly funded" to refer to the schools most people call public schools. Without a doubt, almost all Canadians pay for these schools, and in that sense, they are public. But public, by definition, has to do with that which we do or have in common, whether meetings and parades, or transit systems and arenas. We want to recognize that the meaning of public has changed historically, and will continue to do so, but I insist that the time has come again to make the concept problematic, as did John S. Mill in *On Liberty* and John Dewey in *The Public and Its Problems*.[45] This is necessary because increasing numbers of Canadians are now saying they do not recognize the publicly funded school systems of this country as theirs; that is, they do not share the worldview underlying these school systems. For many, public schools implies neutral schools, and neutral schools do not exist.[46] In what direction must we go, or should attempt to go to make room for those groups claiming that publicly funded Canadian schools are failing either to make space for their own, openly religious, at-bottom ontological and epistemological convictions, or to recognize and admit the ontological and epistemological assumptions lying at the bottom of public education itself?

Refusal to reopen this question of how truly "public" Canadian publicly funded education actually is may indicate that defenders of publicly funded education have something to hide, albeit unconsciously. Such a refusal will serve only to increase the suspicions of those who already believe a monopoly exists and is primarily interested in protecting itself. Such a refusal may also demonstrate a shallowness of actual sentiment behind the rhetoric of pluralism so characteristic of Canadian educational discourse.

Included in this call to problematize the term "public" is the reconsideration of our definitions of "religion" as we use it with reference to education.[47] Ninian Smart has suggested that religious education courses (in the United Kingdom) consider a wide variety of ideologies when such courses treat world religions. Thus Judaism, Hinduism, Sikhism, Islam, Buddhism and Christianity would be joined by humanism, secularism, communism and whatever other "final vocabularies" or symbolic systems people ultimately employ to organize their cognitive framework. In addition to this change, Smart suggests we use the word worldviews (as I have largely done here) instead of religions.[48] Smart's suggestion would accord well with one line of opinion regarding US legal debates on separation of church and state, establishment, and free exercise. That line of opinion is that "any set of beliefs concerning a desirable way of life" functions as a religion and should be counted as such.[49] Recognizably, Smart's suggestion leads us miles away from any of the received definitions within philosophy of education, but it does lead us toward the creation of space for all Canadians to express their deepest convictions within the schools they are compelled to fund.[50]

Educational theorists also need to clarify several terms that arise in discussions of indoctrination. I include here especially neutrality and impartiality, the former because it has figured so centrally in American religion-in-education jurisprudence for over forty years and is now creeping into Canadian educational discourse, and the latter because I view it as the needed disposition among those persons committed to some worldview or other who inevitably will teach religion in Canadian public school classrooms. Those who call for neutrality in education seem to have confused something ideological or confessional, which does not exist, with something procedural and pedagogical. These people seek the former—ideologically neutral teachers—when they should be seeking the latter—those teachers capable of impartiality or some kind of procedural neutrality. That this search may necessarily be fruitless is discussed thoroughly in legal and educational literature.[51] Perhaps what drives such a search is a confusion of neutrality in public space, and secularism, which often comes cloaked as neutrality.[52]

John Valauri, in his survey of how neutrality has functioned in American establishment clause jurisprudence, notes three features of neutrality that I want to repeat here.[53] First, he notes that neutrality is a complex concept, implying both non-involvement and impartiality. For Valauri, non-involvement does not mean disinterestedness or isolation, rather it implies intentionally refraining from intervention which would reveal favouritism for one of the parties. Witness the referee in sports, who we expect to be intensely involved, yet remains impartial, by which Valauri means that one should examine and regulate one's actions to avoid giving advantage to any side.

Valauri also notes that neutrality is a formal concept, by which he means that "neutral" asserts a relationship between specified things or people. We would need specific information about each case to determine what one is neutral toward. Thus, we are never able to claim that we are absolutely neutral or neutral toward everything (unless "we" is ontologically challenged perhaps).

Third, Valauri notes that neutrality is an ambiguous term, having different meanings in different contexts, especially as it has been interpreted in the US Supreme Court, and in prescriptions for educational practice. This ambiguity may be partly related to the fact that the concept of neutrality is subject to conception building. By that I mean that a dictionary will report several meanings for neutral or neutrality, but as is the case with many central concepts in educational or social policy discussions, in actual use people begin to shape the concept according to their definitions of the good life and their visions for society.[54] I am not saying there is anything wrong when such conception-building occurs, in fact it is in some ways the lifeblood of policy-making in a democratic society, I just want us to be conscious of what we are about when we do it. That people will argue for their conceptions of neutrality in this way should catch none of us off guard. But, back to Valauri's point about the ambiguity of neutrality. Given that the concept has become so important within educational policy discussion and is thus subject to conception-building, should we not expect such ambiguity?[55]

We now ask the historical question about neutrality. Historically, have people thought schools or teachers should be neutral? The answer of course is, "for the most part, no," although we recognize that philosophers have struggled for centuries with questions of authority and neutrality in education. In fact, almost until the present century, the stated purpose of schools and the effect desired by both parents and teachers has always been to inculcate in the young specific knowledge, skills and, to our point here, values (and sometimes even "wisdom"!). And this pertains to duty, loyalty to king, and honour, democratic citizenship, good character, and the love of God, or any of several dozen other values or sets of values (depending on what century and state one examines). Neither was there any doubt historically whether school knowledge should be presented in such a way that the values in view were promoted.

Having reviewed educational history in one paragraph and concluded that neutrality has for the most part not been considered desirable, we should now ask if it has ever before this century been thought possible? Again, we boldly answer, "no." However, we must remember that because it was not considered a viable notion, it was not analyzed as such. The first religion-in-education cases began to reach US courts only in the 1880s. Now, ironically enough, a century later, many people outside the courts and the academy are becoming interested in the role of religion, and ideology in education. In fact groups from both ends of the political spectrum now say, for a variety of reasons, that schools are not neutral. Libertarians, children's rights advocates, some free-schoolers, and some home-schoolers raise complaints, especially about the effects on children of compulsory schooling and of the curriculum in place. Critical theorists and feminists observe that schools treat knowledge as if it were actually structured the way schools structure it, instead of recognizing its contingent character. In other words, all knowledge is constructed by certain people or classes of people at certain times, with certain class or gender interests in view. They argue that the received view of knowledge, in fact, perpetuates these class and gender inequalities. In short, the curriculum itself is not neutral; rather it represents a selection from among many possible contents.

This absence of neutrality in schools also concerns members of many acknowledged religions, who can cite a litany of complaints. They point to the relativisation of religious belief, indoctrination by silence about the role of religion in life, open hostility to religious belief, perceived opposition between the school curriculum and their own religiously informed views of geological origins, species development, authority, women, war, morality, sexual orientation, contraception, sex before marriage, self-authentication, the basis of self-esteem, and human perfectibility, to name only the main flashpoints.

Representatives of business interests complain that students are poorly prepared for participation in the marketplace. The missing skills themselves are not an issue of neutrality, but the dispositions toward work with which students graduate, and the failure of schools to instill skills may indeed find their roots in the same intellectual ethos.[56]

Finally, Christians in the Reformational tradition, Canadian Aboriginals, Sikhs, Muslims and many others believe that all of life is rooted in underlying, religious convictions, that it is lived in adherence to one worldview or another. Such persons also struggle with what they see as the non-neutrality of classrooms.

Within earshot of this chorus of voices, I find problematic the commonplace Canadian notion that schoolteachers should or could be neutral in matters of religion, or that such neutrality should or could be manifested by ignoring religion. Examining three non-educational situations where neutrality is used will make that problem clearer.

In a most straightforward use, we speak of a car transmission being in neutral, that is, not in gear. With the transmission in this state, the car may stand still, roll forward, or roll backward, but, by definition, cannot do so either aided or hindered by the car's engine. If the car transmission is an example of neutrality, then those who expect teachers to demonstrate neutrality regarding religion and other controversial issues must either be looking for some other kind of neutrality, or be setting themselves up for disappointment; teachers in classrooms are simply not capable of this kind of neutrality because the "engine" of one's mind is always in gear. I contend that demanding or seeking such neutrality gets us nowhere.

Moreover, we remember that during the Second World War, Switzerland adopted a policy of neutrality, which does not mean it had no concerns, wishes, or preferences. Rather, it did not actively side with either the Axis or Allies.[57] The car example digests much more easily than does the Swiss example, perhaps for this very reason. In the sphere of action, Switzerland's neutrality may be akin to that of the car transmission. But we recognize that what the Swiss felt and what they did are two separate matters. In doing so, we gain another glimpse why classroom neutrality is so difficult to achieve.

Furthermore, if we consider the referee in sports for a moment, we realize that any attempt the referee might make to act neutrally toward the two teams is bound to fail. A tight game, for example, a game played close to the rules, will inevitably favour one team over another. Allowing the game to open up—interpreting and enforcing the rules loosely—will favour the other team. So what is a referee to do? Those concerned for justice might call for just that, officiating executed in such a way that justice is done, though this stance obviously leaves great latitude and responsibility with the official as to what that means and how it is to be dispensed. This stance also implies non-neutrality—likely in more than one direction—at various points during the game. Recognizing the difficulties with neutrality in these circumstances leads us closer to the problem with classrooms. In sports officiating, we most likely define the neutrality we seek in terms of impartiality toward the two teams. Indeed, those who are calling for neutrality in the classroom are seeking this kind of neutrality.[58]

Obviously, in confessional schools, no one wants neutral teachers.[59] But for publicly funded schools, and multi-faith schools, the question remains: Is there any way to move forward in our thinking about classroom neutrality and to respond to the rather naive call for neutral teachers? I suggest that classroom neutrality on controversial issues such as religion is more akin to neutrality in sports officiating than it is to that which car transmissions achieve regularly. It is likely only the Martian teacher who is truly neutral on matters of controversy such as politics and religion. Faced with the current shortage of Martian teachers, we need to ask who can best handle education about religion in classrooms. Logically, we are faced with few choices when we look for teachers:

1.   Experts who are usually either:
     a.   insiders to religion and thus, by definition, persons who believe one religion to be true[60] or superior, or

    b. outsiders to religion who believe that religion is merely an anthropological phenomenon and not true.

2. Non-experts, with varying degrees of religious commitment, who fit roughly the two categories of expertise listed just above.

Obviously, we could fit our four classes onto a matrix, a presentation that would miss much of the nuancing necessary to discuss accurately the kinds and shades of belief we are attempting to discuss here. More accurately, we could perhaps talk about degrees of commitment and degrees of expertise by means of intersecting vertical and horizontal continua. Assuming that we expect teachers to be relative experts in the fields they teach (and thus have barred members of the second group I mentioned—non-experts—from teaching about religion), we can ask this question: Which kind of person is best qualified to teach about religion in a Canadian classroom?

In its recommendations, the 1994 Ontario document *Guidelines for Education about Religion* makes clear that religious believers are disqualified in principle because they are likely to indoctrinate.[61] In one stroke, these guidelines (which are typical) eliminate one of the two groups of experts from which one might pick teachers for courses dealing with religion. Such a recommendation rests on a misunderstanding of neutrality (one suspects among other things). Ontario Ministry of Education seems to work under the impression that ideologically/confessionally neutral teachers are out there somewhere, though they are obviously not adherents to acknowledged religions. I respond that not one of us is ideologically and confessionally neutral, that all persons carry within themselves and live by fundamental convictions about religion—I would even call them religious convictions—of one kind or another. If we all in fact do live by such at-bottom convictions, then we must ask what will be the "angle" or "cant" on acknowledged religion in Ontario publicly funded classrooms? If the teachers in those classrooms meet Ontario's preferences and are therefore not adherents to any acknowledged religious faith, we can expect that angle to be one of comparative religion, with its built-in antipathy for religious conviction. Once again, followers of acknowledged religions are given cause for complaint.

We could go at this problem of teaching about religion in publicly funded schools another way. Some people are dispositionally capable of impartially handling controversial matters in a classroom. It is these teachers, who have demonstrated that they are disposed toward and capable of such impartiality that ought to teach about religion in publicly funded classrooms. In other words, the grounds for selecting appropriate teachers are dispositional and not ideological. These grounds are related almost to skill.[62] Unfortunately, mention of the disposition toward impartiality (or the ability to teach with impartiality) is absent from Ontario's guidelines (as is usually the case in such documents and discussions of teaching religion or about religion). Instead, several university religious studies programs are recommended to prospective teachers of religion. Apparently, the twin assumptions (of Ontario's Ministry of Education) are that such programs provide the knowledge and dispositions necessary for proper instruction (or perhaps that dispositions are not an issue when one has studied comparative religion), and that what we might call "insider" education (at the Buddhist Study Centre, The Institute for Christian Studies, or The Islamic Society of North America, for example) is ill preparation for teaching in publicly funded schools.

CONCLUSION

When we proceed with commitment, we must recognize that the tolerance required in the public square should not imply indifference to real differences in the classroom.[63] Rather, teachers and students should be able to be clear about and, within certain limits, live according to their differences, even argue about those differences, albeit with civility.[64] In selecting teachers for religious education or for education about religion, we must recognize that all people possess faith commitments about religion (which I earlier called religious commitments).[65] As Niblett said more than three decades ago, "The teacher of religious knowledge who does not understand what religion is really about can no more teach the subject than a teacher of art little moved by beauty can in any real sense of the term teach art."[66]

If academics refuse to budge on their claim to privileged epistemic access, and refuse to make such terms as public, neutrality, and religion problematic, then those groups who sense their active and continued marginalization will grow increasingly impatient with the process, and with publicly funded education. Parties on all sides must show willingness to engage in dialogue. Neuhaus dismisses as impossible the notion of a naked public square, and asks instead for a hospitable public square in which all are welcomed to participate.[67] Recognizing that Canada is characterized by plurality, recognizing that annihilation and assimilation are unjust (and unworkable anyway), and recognizing that talking tolerance grants too little in some cases and too much in others, we must begin making space in Canadian schools or at least with Canadian educational dollars for the genuine expression of genuine differences.

Notes

1. The author wishes to acknowledge the editors' reading of the manuscript, as well as the thoughtful editorial work of Jan Wesselius. Also, the ICS Junior Members in the Fall 1995 Education 1513 seminar (Epistemology, Ontology, and Anthropology of Education) made very helpful criticisms and suggestions. Parts of this chapter were presented at the 1993 and 1994 meetings of the Canadian Association for Foundations of Education and the Canadian Philosophy of Education Society.
2. R. M. Hare, "Adolescents into Adults" in T. H. B. Hollins, ed., *Aims in Education*

(Manchester: Manchester University Press, 1964), pp. 47-70. (Cited as Hollins.); and John White, "Indoctrination and Intentions" in I. A. Snook, ed., *Concepts of Indoctrination* (London: RKP, 1972), pp. 117-30. (Cited as Snook.)

3.   Thomas F. Green, "Indoctrination and Beliefs" in Snook, pp. 25-46; and Patricia Smart, "The Concept of Indoctrination" in Glenn Langford and D. J. O'Conner, eds., *New Essays in the Philosophy of Education* (London: RKP, 1973), pp. 33-46.

4.   John Wilson, "Education and Indoctrination" in Hollins, pp. 24-46; and "Religious (Moral, Political, etc.) Commitment, Education and Indoctrination" in Ben Spiecker and Roger Straughan, eds., *Freedom and Indoctrination in Education: International Perspectives* (New York: Cassell, 1991), pp. 42-50.

5.   Elmer Thiessen surveys all the indoctrination arguments, explains the outcomes criterion, and outlines constructive ways for Christians to teach for commitment without indoctrinating in *Teaching for Commitment* (Montreal: McGill–Queen's University Press, 1993).

6.   Ninian Smart, "Concluding Reflections: Religious Studies in Global Perspective" in Ursula King, ed., *Turning Points in Religious Studies* (Edinburgh: T. & T. Clarke, 1992), pp. 299-306. (Cited as N. Smart.)

7.   Richard H. Gatchel, "The Evolution of the Concept" in Snook, pp. 9-16.

8.   R. S. Peters, *The Concept of Education* (London: RKP, 1967).

9.   Paul Marshall, "Toward a Unity of Taxonomy for A Plurality of Pluralities," Inter-Disciplinary Seminar paper at ICS, February 1993, p. 5; Lonnie D. Kliever, "Moral Education in a Pluralistic World," *Journal of the American Academy of Religion* 60 (Spring 1992): 117-35.

10. George O. Roberts, "The Role and Responsibility of Textbooks in Promoting Pluralism" in Edwin G. Clausen and Jack Birmingham, eds., *Pluralism, Racism and Public Policy* (Boston: G. K. Hall, 1981), p. 170; Wayne C. Booth, "Pluralism in the Classroom," *Critical Inquiry* 12 (Spring 1986): 469.

11. William Pfaff, "Reflections: The Absence of Empire," *New Yorker*, 10 August 1992: 60.

12. Brian V. Hill, "The Teaching of Values," *Journal of Christian Education* [Australia] 99 (December 1990): 49-57. (Cited as Hill.)

13. Council of Ministers of Education of Canada, "The Mission of Education and Training in Canada" (Memorandum of Agreement) (Toronto: CMEC, September 1992): 1.

14. Aminur Rahim, "Multiculturalism or Ethnic Hegemony: A Critique of Multicultural Education in Toronto," *The Journal of Ethnic Studies* 18 (Fall 1990): 34.

15. Thank you to Craig Bartholomew for bringing these authors to my attention in an interdisciplinary seminar in 1992-93.

16. Seyyed Hossein Nasr, *Knowledge and the Sacred* (Edinburgh: Edinburgh University Press, 1981), p. 12.

17. C. A. Qadir, *Philosophy and Science in the Islamic World* (London: Routledge, 1988), p. 1.

18. Syed Ali Ashraf, ed., *Faith as the Basis of Education in a Multi-Cultural Country* (Cambridge: The Islamic Academy, 1991), p. 8-15. (Cited as Ashraf.)

19. Ibid., p. 6.

20. Ibid., p. 14.

21. We differentiate traditional Aboriginal spirituality here from Christian spirituality. A majority of Canadian Aboriginals follow the Christian religion.

22. Elisabeth Tooker, ed., *Native North American Spirituality of the Eastern Woodlands* (Toronto: Paulist, 1979), pp. 31-68. (Cited as Tooker.)

23. And the sense they make illustrates how deeply economic growth is presumed to be a good within our society, that is, how far a certain Western worldview prevails.

24. Cyril McCormick, Newfoundland deputy minister of Education, letter 19 October 1992. One Newfoundland religious education textbook for grades ten to twelve attends to

traditional Aboriginal spirituality: *Worldviews: The Challenge of Choice* (Toronto: Irwin, 1995).

25. David Keenan, Nova Scotia senior education publication officer, letter 21 October 1992.
26. G. C. Keilty, New Brunswick deputy minister of Education, letter 3 December 1992.
27. Keith Wornell, Prince Edward Island deputy minister of Education, letter 4 November 1992.
28. John D. Carlyle, Manitoba deputy minister of Education and Training, letter 28 October 1992.
29. Arleen Hynd, Saskatchewan deputy minister of Education, letter 15 October 1992.
30. Lloyd E. Symyrozum, Alberta director of Curriculum, letter 23 October 1992.
31. Gerry Ensing, director of British Columbia Independent Schools Branch, letter 2 December 1992.
32. See also Tooker. Aboriginal spirituality is frequently introduced in Canadian classrooms in unwise ways, offending Aboriginals and non-Aboriginals alike, both on religious grounds.
33. Lorraine Code, *What Can She Know?: Feminist Theory and the Construction of Knowledge* (Ithaca, NY: Cornell University Press, 1991), p. 31. (Cited as Code.)
34. Ibid., pp. 27, 30.
35. See Michael Polanyi, *Personal Knowledge* (London: RKP, 1958), and his *Study of Man* (London: RKP, 1959); also Nel Noddings, *Caring: A Feminine Approach to Ethics and Moral Education* (Berkeley: University of California Press, 1984).
36. *CIS* and *ORT*.
37. Anthony Flew, *Thinking About Thinking* (Glasgow: Collins, 1975), p. 54.
38. Ronald S. Laura, "Philosophical Foundations of Religious Education," *Educational Theory* 28, 4 (Fall 1978): 313, 316.
39. Code, p. 265.
40. Nomi Maya Stolzenberg, "'He Drew a Circle that Shut Me Out': Assimilation, Indoctrination, and the Paradox of Liberal Education," *Harvard Law Review* 106 (February 1993): 581-666.
41. For example, see Carl Horn, "Secularism and Pluralism in Public Education," *Harvard Journal of Law and Public Policy* 7 (Winter 1984): 177-83. (Cited as Horn.); Michael D. Lieder, "Religious Pluralism and Education in Historical Perspective: A Critique of the Supreme Court's Establishment Clause Jurisprudence," *Wake Forest Law Review* 22 (1987): 813-89. (Cited as Lieder.); Christopher F. Mooney, *Boundaries Dimly Perceived* (Notre Dame: University of Notre Dame Press, 1990).
42. Robert C. Tash, *Dutch Pluralism: A Model in Tolerance for Developing Democracies* (New York: Peter Lang, 1991).
43. This influence should be exercised within two limits: that the education serve the public good, and that it be carried out in responsible ways.
44. W. D. Hudson, "Is Religious Education Possible?" in Glenn Langford and D. J. O'Conner, eds., *New Essays in the Philosophy of Education* (London: Routledge and Kegan Paul, 1973), pp. 167-96.
45. John Dewey, *The Public and Its Problems* (Chicago: Swallow Press, 1927), pp. 334-35.
46. The usage may, however, reflect increasing influence of American legal language and thought in Canadian educational jurisprudence.
47. Philip E. Johnson, "Concepts and Compromise in First Amendment Religious Doctrine," *California Law Review* 72 (1984): 839.
48. N. Smart, p. 303.
49. Lieder, p. 816.
50. N. Smart, pp. 23-41, 195-205.
51. Hugh J. Breyer, "Cinderella, The Horse God, and the Wizard of Oz: Mozert v. Hawkins County Public Schools," *Journal of Law and Education* 20 (1991): 63-93; G. Sydney

Buchanan, "Accommodation of Religion in the Public Schools: A Plea for Careful Balancing of Competing Constitutional Values," *UCLA Law Review* 28 (1981): 1000-48; John Remington Graham, "A Restatement of the Intended Meaning of the Establishment Clause in Relation to Education and Religion," *Brigham Young University Law Review* (1981): 333-59; Steven D. Smith, "Separation and the 'Secular': Reconstructing the Disestablishment Decision," *Texas Law Review* 67 (1989): 955-1031; Winton E. Yerby, "Toward Religious Neutrality in the Public School Curriculum," *University of Chicago Law Review* 56 (1989): 899-934.

52. Horn, pp. 177-79; Richard Norman, "The Neutral Teacher?" in S. C. Brown, ed., *Philosophers Discuss Education* (London: Macmillan, 1975), pp. 172-87.

53. John Valauri, "The Concept of Neutrality in Establishment Clause Doctrine," *University of Pittsburgh Law Review* 48 (1986): 83-151.

54. As far as I know I developed this distinction first in my dissertation at UBC in 1986. Later, I found the political philosopher Gerald Dworkin using the same distinction, in *The Theory and Practice of Autonomy* (New York: Cambridge University Press, 1988), p. 10. He notes that the "filling out of an abstract concept with the different content is what is meant by different conceptions of the same concept."

55. One further comment about neutrality is warranted in the context of noting the three elements Valauri identifies. With Robert E. Goodin and Andrew Reeve, I want to note that neutrality is usually an instrumental value; it is meant to achieve something else, e.g., achieving justice in a courtroom (for judges), or avoiding indoctrination in a classroom (for teachers). See "Liberalism and Neutrality" in Robert E. Goodin and Andrew Reeve, eds., *Liberal Neutrality* (New York: Routledge, 1989), pp. 3-4. My own observation is that this instrumentality is not always clearly in view in Canadian educational usage of neutrality.

56. We note again that some critics on the left charge that business interests have hijacked publicly funded education.

57. It would be helpful here to ask what neutral noninvolvement looks like during a war? For example, in a single, albeit important area, Switzerland could take any of several stances toward its trading partners who have gone to war with each other. It could (1) cease trading with both belligerents; (2) trade equal amounts with both belligerents; (3) trade at levels equal to prewar trade levels with both belligerents; (4) trade proportionally to the respective populations of the belligerents. Each of the last three approaches to trade would favour one or the other of the belligerents compared to the first approach (cessation with both). Even cessation arguably would hurt the belligerent most in need of whatever products the neutral nation produced. Thus, we see that all four approaches actually aid one of the belligerents more than the other. Thus, we see that strict political neutrality may be as elusive as classroom neutrality.

58. Were schools to find this kind of procedural, pedagogical neutrality, the non-neutrality embedded in the curriculum would remain. Even that embeddedness divides into two levels. The curriculum could be said to teach or to teach about one or more epistemologies, but the curriculum also found its own shape and structure within an epistemology. So we see that pedagogical neutrality, even if it were possible, would function simply as a veneer over other, deeper, commitments. The author thanks Robert Sweetman for pointing this out in an earlier draft.

59. I still want to argue that impartial teachers would serve the educative purposes of the school, while recognizing that some parents connected to confessional schools want indoctrination, not impartiality.

60. In this context, I use true intentionally and consciously.

61. Toronto: Queen's Printer, 1992. Restrictive as they are, these guidelines are more open than Memorandum #112 (Toronto: Queen's Printer, 1991) which they are meant to replace. Memorandum 112 largely proscribed treatment of religion in any way at most

times (in response to the Elgin County Decision of January 1990 which ended Religious Education in Ontario publicly funded schools). As Brian Hill points out (Hill, p. 51), to "teach certain subjects and not others declares our value judgements about the worthwhile life and the educated person" and to exclude religion is to "disvalue" it.

62. Further examination is required of the assumption that meeting ideological criteria guarantees that religion will be neither aided nor inhibited in publicly funded classrooms.

63. J. P. Powell, "Philosophical Models of Teaching," *Harvard Educational Review* 35 (1965): 494-96.

64. G. Weigel, "Achieving Disagreement: From Indifference to Pluralism," *Journal of Law and Religion* 8 (1990): 175.

65. These commitments precede and underlie any and all philosophies of education.

66. W. R. Niblett, ed., *Christian Education in a Secular Society* (London: Oxford University Press, 1960), pp. 78-79.

67. Richard John Neuhaus, *The Naked Public Square* (Grand Rapids, MI: Eerdmans, 1984).

4

"Woman" in the Plural: Negotiating Sameness and Difference in Feminist Theory[1]

JANET CATHERINA WESSELIUS

The issue of sameness and difference has long been a topic of discussion among feminists. One of its most contested features has to do with whether there is an essential similarity between women and men, or whether there is an essential difference between them. Underlying these disagreements is the assumption that all women are essentially the same (as are all men). Recently, the focus has shifted to this very assumption. Arguably, as pluralism becomes an increasingly prominent issue in our society, feminists also are becoming more aware of the implications of acknowledging the plurality of women. Perhaps it is true that women are not essentially all the same.

Often the assumption of a similarity among women has been justified by a belief that all women share the same essence, that is, something which makes us all women. As this assumption of sameness, premised on a belief in essences, was called into question, the discussion in feminist circles regarding sameness and difference began to reflect more of a concern about essentialism and constructivism. Disagreements now focus on whether sex and gender are fundamentally impervious to cultural and historical influence, or whether they are social constructs. Rather than accentuating anything we might hold in common, the emphasis has now shifted toward the difference, uniqueness, and plurality among women. Perhaps some of this shift in focus can be attributed to the intersection of feminist theory with postmodern theory.

Whereas an emphasis on sameness often leads to charges of essentialism, the focus on difference highlights the radical contingency of social constructivism. But just as there can be no easy identification of sameness with essentialism, neither can there be with difference and constructivism. Indeed, sameness could be attributed to some shared essence, and difference to contingent constructions; but sameness might also be attributed to shared constructions and difference to different essences.

This discussion seems to be particularly acute for feminists because of its vital implications for a feminist politics. Indeed, the raison d'être of feminist theory has always been politics—a politics that is directed toward the liberation of women. Historically, feminist politics have relied on this assumed sameness among women, after all, because women qua women are alike, feminism can represent the interests of all women. At the same time many women argue that their differences are not merely insignificant accidents but are in fact inextricably intertwined with their identities as women. To deny the significance of these differences is to deny the very ideals of feminism which are directed to the freedom of *all* women. If, however, there is a irreducible plurality among women, on what can we base a feminist politics? Feminism seems to require, contradictorily, that we privilege both sameness and difference.

How, then, do feminists view sameness and difference? Like the women who do the theorizing, feminist theory is not homogenous. Despite a common goal of freeing (at least) women from sexist oppression,[2] feminists choose remarkably disparate ways to achieve this goal. The oppression of women takes many different forms; and the theories of sameness and difference that feminists construct are reflective of the exigencies of misogyny. Thus, they are different depending on their particular context with particular needs at a particular time in history.[3]

When viewed from another context each theory of sameness and difference has weaknesses. Indeed, because no theory is infallibly salvific we need to be mindful of the tendency to reify a particular view. In some contexts, for example, feminists do well to emphasize differences, while on in other contexts, there needs to be an emphasis on similarities. In other words, the primary commitment must be to the emancipation of women and not to a particular theory. This does not mean, however, that all theories are equally valid. We can judge such theories by their political consequences, that is, by what they accomplish for women in a plurality of contexts. Thus, in an attempt to cover all the bases, so to speak, I suggest that we can avoid valorizing one particular theory of sex/gender similarity and difference by keeping in mind that the goal before us is the freedom of women and not the espousal of a given theory.

In this paper I shall examine the respective strengths and weaknesses of four possible feminist positions regarding sex/gender similarities and differences. For each position, I shall discuss examples from the work of several theorists from which will emerge a general tendency to view sameness and difference in a particular way. While the specific work of each feminist I discuss might otherwise have little in common with the others, I see this as evidence that feminist theory as a whole is neither amenable to totalizing categorization, nor are these otherwise useful categorizations internally homogenous.

ESSENTIAL SAMENESS

Many of the earliest feminist writers subscribed to an essential sameness between men and women. Indeed, because their political and epistemological views were often categorized as liberal, rationalist, or empiricist,[4] they argued that a distinction between sex and gender is of paramount importance. One of the earliest descriptions of this distinction is made by Ann Oakley:

> On the whole, Western society is organised around the assumption that the differences between the sexes are more important than any qualities they have in common. When people try to justify this assumption in terms of 'natural' differences, two separate processes become confused; the tendency to differentiate by sex, and the tendency to differentiate in a particular way by sex. The first is genuinely a constant feature of human society, but the second is not, and its inconstancy marks the division between 'sex' and 'gender': sex differences may be 'natural' but gender differences have their source in culture, not nature.[5]

In other words, sex is a biological given that cannot be changed because there are real anatomical differences between women and men, differences that are constant. Gender differences also exist; however, these differences are not innate, but rather, they are learned and therefore susceptible to change.

This view of sameness and difference finds its ancestry in liberal political history. As one of the proponents of this position, Mary Wollstonecraft, for example, asks: "in what does man's [humanity's] preeminence over brute creation consist? The answer is as clear as that a half is less than a whole, in Reason."[6] These feminists see women primarily as human beings who happen to have female anatomy and that their anatomy makes (or ideally should make) very little difference to their essential humanness. Since to be human is to be essentially rational, they see women as essentially rational beings. These feminists do not deny that there are sex and gender differences between women and men but these differences are accidental and contingent. For example, Kate Millet believes that "the sexes are inherently in everything alike, save reproductive systems, secondary sexual characteristics, orgasmic capacity, and genetic and morphological structure."[7] There is no essential difference between women and men; both sexes are essentially the same because both are essentially rational.

For rationalist feminists the problem of sexism is the result of two mistakes. Firstly, the differences between women and men are emphasized, and then necessity is ascribed to these differences; that is, sex and gender are confused and gender differences are reified. Secondly, sexual and gendered characteristics of women are seen as essential characteristics of women. These feminists argue that while sexual differences are ineradicable, gender differences may not be; in any case, sex is an accidental property that does not affect one's essentially human capacity for rationality. Hence, my characterization of this kind of feminism as espousing accidental difference and essential sameness.

The starkest formulation of the solution to the problem of sexism according to this view is twofold: to transform society through the elimination of sexism so that women are enabled to become fully human,[8] and to expose traditional femininity as a socially constructed, contingent property.[9] In fact, despite the apparent traditional femininity of some women (for whatever reasons, sociological or otherwise), women can be just as human (that is, rational) as men if they are given the chance to do so. Androgyny is often an implicit ideal in rationalist feminism since these feminists generally believe that most differences between women and men are learned rather than innate. Since sexual differences between women and men are merely accidental properties, they cannot justifiably be used to systematically exclude women from the rights and privileges due to all humans. Most differences between the sexes, aside from the biological, can be explained and even effaced by socialization and education.

Certainly, there is some appeal in this approach. If it can be proven that women measure up to the same standard as men (that is, rationality), their humanity cannot be denied and thus, they are entitled to the same rights and privileges. Consequently, these feminists are often hostile to any emphasis on differences between women and men, including sometimes even the biological, because difference has been used to justify the inequality of women.[10] In her description of this position, Christine Di Stefano points out that "'difference' has been used to legitimize the unequal treatment of women and therefore must be repudiated theoretically and practically in order for women to assume their rightful place in society as the non-differentiated equals of men."[11] If these feminists admit to any differences at all, they see them as inessential at best. Difference is threatening and sameness is essential because if women are the same as men then, arguably, they deserve the same treatment.

The major drawback to this approach is that it requires naively adopting rationality as a sexually neutral ideal. However, according to Genevieve Lloyd, "the obstacles to female cultivation of reason spring to a large extent from the fact that our ideals of Reason have historically incorporated an exclusion of the feminine."[12] That is, rationality as an ideal is not sexually neutral. Lloyd argues that "rationality has been conceived as transcendence of the feminine" and "women cannot be easily accommodated into a cultural ideal which has defined itself in opposition to the feminine."[13] In other words, rationality is in fact a masculine ideal. According to the view that women and men are essentially the same, one accepts the devaluing of the feminine as irrational and simply argues that women should not be identified with the devalued half of these dichotomies but should be identified with reason as are men. There is no challenge to the feminine and masculine dichotomy nor to the valorization of the rational, masculine half. Rather, the locus of disagreement lies in the identification of women with the non-rational. Such a strategy accepts (traditionally) masculine standards and values, which is again an implicit devaluing of women. If we only affirm the ability of women to be rational without challenging the valorization of reason (which excluded us in the first place), we reaffirm the masculine as norm. In this argument, women qua women are valued only insofar as they are like men. Androgyny, then, turns out to be a masculine ideal. Sameness means the same as men; difference means different from men. In many contexts, this view frees women from an essential femininity but it forces them to adopt an essential humanity (that is, masculinity) in its place. In its most extreme form, it requires women to repudiate traditionally feminine characteristics and to embrace traditionally masculine qualities. It replaces one sort of oppression with another by reinforcing traditional dichotomies and valuations. So while this position is somewhat transformative in some contexts, it never examines the purported neutrality of the androgynous ideal. All differences recede in the shadow of the truly important and humanizing sameness: rationality.

DIFFERENT ESSENTIALISM

Other feminists take an opposite view to the one of essential sameness. Not only do these feminists acknowledge differences between women and men, they emphasize the differences. In this way a distinction is still made between sex and gender. Indeed, sex and gender are perhaps the most basic aspects of human existence. The extent to which these differences are immutable is an area of great disagreement. Mary Daly holds perhaps one of the most extreme views:[14]

> Sparking is making possible Female Friendship, which is totally Other from male comradeship. Hence, the Spinster will examine male comradeship/ fraternity, in order to avoid the trap of confusing sisterhood with brotherhood, of thinking (even in some small dusty corner of the mind) of sisterhood as if it were simply a gender-correlative of brotherhood. She will come to see that the term *bonding*, as it applies to Hags/Harpies/ Furies/Crones is a thoroughly Other from "male-bonding" as Hags are Other in relation to patriarchy.... It is the opposite of brotherhood, not essentially because Self-centring women oppose and fight patriarchy in a reactive way, but because we are/act for our Selves.[15]

Not only does Daly think that women are thoroughly other than men, she revalues words that are traditionally derogatory, such as "Hags/Harpies/ Furies/Crones," and celebrates the new possibilities that this kind of revaluation opens for women. This revaluation often involves an idealization of women (for example, male comradeship depends upon women's energy). Since women are thoroughly different from men, and thoroughly innocent of the evils of patriarchy, Daly believes that "males and males only are the originators, planners, controllers, and legitimators of patriarchy."[16] Although this sort of feminism has also been called feminine anti-rationalism and radical feminism,[17] I have chosen to characterize this view as "romantic" because it involves an idealization of women's alleged difference.

Feminists of this sort see themselves as women first and foremost rather than as humans who happen to have female anatomy. Not only are there essential biological differences between women and men, there are essential gender differences as well. Nancy Chodorow, for example, attempts to "account for the reproduction within each generation of certain general and nearly universal differences that characterize masculine and feminine personality and roles" by attributing them to "the fact that women, universally, are largely responsible for early child care."[18] In her description of the extreme end of this kind of feminism, Di Stefano writes that, while gender is seen as a social convention, "these cultural artifacts are not merely arbitrary impositions. Rather, they seek to make sense out of the givens of life; in this case, they seek to make sense out of the ontological givens of reproductive sex differences."[19] Gender is seen as reflecting the sexual differences between women and men without any consideration that gender may constitute such differences.

Often these sorts of feminists also seem to accept the traditional conceptions of femininity and masculinity. They emphasize the difference between women and men while disregarding the similarities between them. At the same time, however, they emphasize the similarities among women (often, like Chodorow, the reproductive ability to bear children) while ignoring the differences between them (often race, class, and sexual orientation). Hence, I have characterized them as relying on the essential difference between women and men, and between femininity and masculinity.

The problem of sexism is not that there are differences between women and men but rather that the feminine has been devalued while the masculine has been valorized. Virginia Woolf says that "it is obvious that the values of women differ very often from the values which have been made by the other sex.... Yet it is the masculine values that prevail."[20] In this short statement, we can see two elements of romantic feminism. Women have their own set of distinctive values; yet it is masculine values that dominate. The problem of sexism, then, cannot be reduced to simple mistakes about the difference between sex and gender. For many of these feminists, patriarchy is universal and pervasive. Since patriarchy is ubiquitous, even rational activity cannot escape the contamination of sexism and is regarded with suspicion. Sometimes this mistrust of theory even leads to a mistrust of logic. Germaine Greer, for example, says that "in most situations logic is simply rationalization of an infra-logical aim. Women know...that arguments with their men-folk are disguised real-politik."[21] Consequently, many of these feminists have at least an ambivalent attitude to (even feminist) theory. Evidently, however, they continue to engage in rational activity and to theorize. But this ambivalence is at least partially reflected in the fact that few of the feminists in this group are members of traditionally male-dominated disciplines (for example, philosophy, science, etc.) and most have instead built careers in disciplines which have included a significant female presence (for example, education, social sciences, literature, etc.).

For some, the solution to the problem of sexual oppression is to revalue the feminine and to celebrate the difference of women from men. Adrienne Rich, for example, persuasively argues that "woman-identification is a source of energy, a potential springhead of female power, violently curtailed and wasted under the institution of heterosexuality."[22] Carol McMillan, also argues that "if the critical fact of womanhood...is that women bear children and men do not, then surely a new sense of the worth of women should involve, above all, a revaluation of the maternal role."[23] Sometimes, although not inevitably, the revaluation of the feminine includes the devaluation of the masculine as is seen in Daly's work.

In its refusal to accept the masculine as a norm for all humans, this kind of feminist theory certainly has its attractions. It is a turning of the sexual tables as it were: involving as it does a radical rejection of masculinity as norm, women are now able to celebrate the very qualities that have historically been used to oppress them. To be sure, these kinds of feminist theorists have made and continue to make an important contribution to feminism. Indeed, Susan Bordo credits women such as Dorothy Dinnerstein, Nancy Chodorow, and Carol Gilligan for having "cleared a space, described a new territory, which radically altered the male-normative terms of discussion about reality and experience; they forced recognition of the difference gender makes."[24] Many women are relieved to be able to openly embrace and to affirm the positive value of traditionally feminine characteristics. Sameness with men is threatening because it risks accepting the devaluation of traditionally feminine traits and the normativity of traditionally masculine traits. Difference is essential because if women are different from men, then, arguably women's values can be used to generate new and alternative insights; if women's difference from men is idealized, then women can be the agents of social transformation for a better society.

Romantic feminism does effect social transformation in some contexts by revaluing the feminine. But I suggest it is in danger of continuing to stereotype women as traditionally feminine. It posits traditional femininity as a norm without acknowledging that this femininity has itself been constituted through its exclusion from ideals of humanity. More specifically, Lloyd sees the problem in the following terms:

> The idea that women have their own distinctive kind of intellectual or moral character has itself been partly formed within the philosophical tradition to which it may now appear to be a reaction. Unless the structural features of our concepts of gender are understood, any emphasis on a supposedly

distinctive style of thought or morality is liable to be caught up in a deeper, older structure of male norms and female complementation. The affirmation of the value and importance of 'the feminine' cannot of itself be expected to shake the underlying normative structures, for, ironically, it will occur in a space already prepared for it by the intellectual tradition it seeks to reject.[25]

In other words, this revaluation does not acknowledge that traditionally conceived femininity may itself be the result of social oppression. Nor does it recognize that if there is such a thing as an essential femininity, it is likely distorted by its expression under oppression.

Moreover, femininity can become so idealized that there is almost no way to criticize any of its manifestations. Since it functions as a norm, it requires all women to conform to it insofar as they are women. Taken to an extreme, there is almost no tolerance for evidence that traditional femininity may oppress some women in some situations and almost no freedom for women who cannot or will not accept traditionally feminine roles. Unfortunately, romantic feminism may thus replace one kind of stereotype with another. Women are in danger of being forced into an essentialized (and idealized) femininity. In this way differences among women are suppressed and ignored while differences between women and men are reified. If in rationalist feminism women are discouraged from being traditionally feminine and encouraged to be more (hu)man, in romantic feminism women are dissuaded from the cultivation of traditionally masculine qualities and strongly encouraged to be traditionally feminine, regardless of individual proclivities.

ESSENTIAL DIFFERENCES

Many feminists who are familiar with postmodern theory are concerned that current feminist theory engages in its own form of totalizing discourses.[26] Judith Butler, for example, criticizes contemporary feminist politics because "the identity categories often presumed to be foundational to feminist politics, that is, deemed necessary in order to mobilize feminism as an identity politics, simultaneously work to limit and constrain in advance the very cultural possibilities that feminism is supposed to open up."[27] For these women, the problem with current feminist politics is that it is based on a purportedly shared sex/gender identity among all women. They point to the differences among women and argue that the political emphasis on sex/gender sameness has suppressed difference. Moreover, it has excluded some women by maintaining that differences among women such as race, class and sexual orientation are appurtenant to the more essential identity of gender.[28] Nancy Fraser and Linda Nicholson give a very clear statement of the problem of exclusion within feminist theory:

> While gender identity gives substance to the idea of sisterhood, it does so at the cost of repressing differences among sisters. Although...[feminist]

theory allows for some differences among women of different classes, races, and sexual orientations, and ethnic groups, it construes these as subsidiary to more basic similarities. But it is precisely as a consequence of the request to understand such differences as secondary that many women have denied an allegiance to feminism.[29]

In other words, many women who do not see sex or gender as the most basic aspect of their identity are alienated when feminism insists otherwise. Feminist politics, however, is based on the assumption that it represents the interests of all women; but if gender coherence is a regulatory fiction, it can no longer be the starting point of emancipatory politics and the very project of feminist politics is seriously undermined.

As previously noted, feminists made a distinction between sex and gender in order to dispute the biology-is-destiny argument that kept women (and men) in their place: sex might be ontologically determined but gender is a social construction and hence, susceptible to change. However, postmodern feminists point out that if feminists are right that gender is a socially constructed category, then there are more than two possible genders (for example, there are more possibilities than femininity and masculinity) and gender does not follow from sex (for example, males might manifest feminine gender). In other words, sex does not determine gender.[30] Indeed, the distinction between sex and gender seems to collapse if sex is as much a socially constructed category as gender. Since we do not have access to sex apart from gender, sex is "always already" gender. So, if sex/gender is a socially constructed category, women are not a group by virtue of having the same sex/gender.

Insofar as these postmodern theorists are also feminist, they continue to pay special attention to gender; what sets them apart is that they do not think that gender can be a privileged difference. Moreover, we cannot assume that there is gender sameness among women. Fraser and Nicholson, for example, argue that "the idea of a cross-cultural, deep sense of self, specified differently for women and men, becomes problematic when given any specific content";[31] hence, they criticize "the category of gender identity" as essentialist and ahistorical.[32]

In an effort to avoid excluding any one woman's experience by universalizing the experience of one particular group of women, these feminists wish to emphasize all difference. And since they believe that all identity is negotiable they often deny that gender identity is something constant. For example, given that Butler thinks "the feminist subject turns out to be discursively constituted by the very political system that is supposed to facilitate its emancipation," she argues that "a new sort of feminist politics is now desirable to contest the very reifications of gender and identity, one that will take the variable construction of identity as both a methodological and normative prerequisite, if not a political goal."[33]

The problem of sexism is really the problem of suppressing the differences among women. It is significant that these kinds of feminists direct most their attention to the imposition of sameness on women by feminist theory rather than to sexism. The emphasis seems to be more on the oppression caused by the suppression of difference rather than by sexism. Of course sexism can be seen as the result of eliding differences among women by imposing sameness on us. These feminists also think it is a mistake to view gender as a natural result of biology. However, unlike rationalist feminists, they do espouse the contingency of gender in order to emphasize differences rather than an essential sameness between women and men.[34]

The solution, they believe, is to celebrate differences in political alliances without theoretically privileging any particular difference.[35] According to Fraser and Nicholson, "postmodern theory" should dispense with universalizing gender claims; instead, "it would replace unitary notions of woman and feminine gender identity with plural and complexly constructed conceptions of social identity, treating gender as one relevant strand among others, attending also to class, race, ethnicity, age, and sexual orientation."[36] I characterize this kind of feminist theory as relying on essential differences because, although no specific difference may be privileged, difference (in general) is privileged over sameness.

The criticism that feminism has itself perpetrated the oppression of some women by the imposition of sameness seems to have some validity. Indeed, to the extent that feminist theory has excluded women who differ significantly from paradigmatic Western, white, heterosexual, middle-class women, postmodern criticisms are appropriate. Feminism is concerned to liberate women and it fails to do so if it remarginalizes women who do not fit the model. Sameness is threatening because it risks minimizing or even ignoring the racism, classism, heterosexism, and so on, that many women suffer. Difference is essential because it exposes universal essences as oppressive and totalizing fictions.

However, if women do not share an identity on which a political movement can be based, how can we attain solidarity to fight injustices based on sex and gender? Even if it is true that sex and gender are socially constructed categories, it is also true that the people we label "women" are categorized as a social group. Part of the oppression women qua women face may be the result of falsely universalizing women as a social group. But if we expose the category of women as a fiction without acknowledging that women nevertheless are oppressed because of their alleged sex and/or gender, we run the serious risk of "dividing and conquering" women.[37] If there is no such group of women, then anti-feminists can argue that there is no such thing as sexism. I am suspicious of a political theory that prematurely ignores the material disadvantages of women in favour of challenging feminine gender identity (Fraser and Nicholson) or challenging gender categories (Butler). This confusion regarding the constituency of feminism is a problem for any theorist who thinks that she can no longer speak about women qua women because she can no longer acknowledge that women are systematically oppressed on the basis of sex/gender. Unfortunately, it seems that a certain kind of "postmodern" feminism liberates us from the oppression of false universals and totalizing discourses but at the same time undermines attempts to free us from sex-based oppression through feminist political action.[38]

DIFFERENT SAMENESS

How can we maintain the strengths of the previous strategies while avoiding their respective weakness? I suggest that we need to recognize that women are like men in many ways without acceding to the valorization of masculinity. We also need to re-evaluate the traditionally feminine while neither reifying it nor insisting that gender conform to sex. Furthermore, we need to acknowledge differences among women without ignoring our similarities. We can argue that sex influences gender but does not determine it; gender makes an important difference (epistemically, morally, politically) but this difference cannot be determined a priori.

The fact that all three strategies can be emancipatory in particular contexts reveals that the problem of sexism can be the result of a number of ways of viewing difference and sameness. Sexism can be the result of emphasizing the difference between women and men by denying their similarity. Or it can be the result of denigrating the valuable differences of women from men. Or it can be the result of suppressing difference among women by imposing a universal sameness. It would seem that the insight to be gleaned from an examination of previous strategies is that the solution to sexism is to acknowledge *both* sameness *and* difference, *depending* on the context.

But can we successfully emphasize either sameness or difference in particular contexts without privileging one over the other—without essentializing either sameness or difference? Feminist standpoint theorist Sandra Harding argues that

> Women are, indeed, like each other by virtue of their sex and also by virtue of the otherness that men assign to women. Of course, they differ by race, class, culture, and other important social features; in important respects, they are more like men in their own race, class, culture than like women in other races, and so on. But standpoint theory does not require any kind of feminine essentialism.... It analyses the essentialism that androcentrism assigns to women, locates its historical conditions, and proposes ways to counter it.... [We] constantly call for more vigorous feminist analysis of and politics against these forms of oppression.[39]

While acknowledging diversity, Harding explains the sameness among women as the "otherness" that has been assigned to us. By beginning with our social practice of categorization, we can begin to analyze the essence attributed to women without begging the question by assuming that the essence attributed by sexism is an essence assigned to women by nature.

Even if it is true that gender identities are lived out in various ways by different women, it is still true that women are categorized as women. Many feminist philosophers argue that this categorization is built on a naive essentialism, that the category of women is "notoriously fickle and inconstant." Nevertheless, being categorized according to sex seems to be a genuinely constant feature of human experience. Perhaps this is the beginning of a solution to our dilemma: we can begin with our social practices of classification rather than with a priori generalizations about the nature of women.

In order to take account of this apparent sameness among women without essentializing it, we might take up Diana Fuss's suggestion. She says that "if we can never securely displace essentialism, then it becomes useful for analytic purposes to distinguish between *kinds* of essentialisms, as John Locke has done with his theory of 'real' versus 'nominal' essence."[40] Real essence denotes the eternal identity of something whereas nominal essence denotes our social practices of classifying and labelling something. Without jumping to conclusions about why some people are classified as women, we can recognize that some humans have been assigned a (nominal or socially constructed) essence as women. (I prefer to use the term "socially constructed" rather than nominal because it is more useful to emphasize the social aspect of assigning essences than the linguistic/grammatical aspect). That is, women are the same because—and to the extent that—they are treated the same. Women share a common categorization whether or not this is the result of a real essence. By seeing the commonality that women share as a socially constructed essence, we can account for women as a category without suppressing difference: sameness is the result of a socially constructed essence, but because it is imposed by social relations, it is not necessarily an ontological sameness. To put the point slightly differently: by seeing essences as social constructions in response to empirical states of affairs rather than as ontological givens, we can account for sameness while doing justice to difference.

While we cannot claim that sexism is the most basic form of oppression all women experience, we do need to acknowledge some commonality in order to construct a theory with any social import. And one thing that all women seem to share is marginalization on the basis of sex/gender, even though some women might also be marginalized or privileged with respect to race, class, or whatever.[41] Of course, it can be objected that marginalization is not what makes women women. But that is exactly the point: in this society at this time, the only consistent thing that women hold in common is that those people society categorizes as "women" are marginalized on the basis of purported sex/gender. Women are indeed an oppressed group but it is not nature that sorts them into a homogeneous group or marginalizes them; social conditions make them a marginalized group.   In other words, marginalization is not the real (ontological) essence of women; rather, it is a socially constructed, and hence contingent, essence.

I find marginalization a particularly powerful category because it describes not only sexism but other forms of oppression and exclusion as well. Marginalization is not a social condition that is exclusive to women. However, this fact can be seen as a strength of feminist theory because it enables us to explain how other marginalized groups can have common interests with feminists. Insofar as marginalization is justified by sex/gender, however, it is still exclusive to women. What women are, apart from this socially constructed essence assigned by androcentrism, remains an open question. Indeed, what women (and men) are remains a mystery.

It is important to note that no theory will necessarily save us from the totalizations of sameness and the suppression of difference. Susan Bordo notes that

> the dynamics of inclusion and exclusion (as history had just taught us) are played out on multiple and shifting fronts and all ideas (no matter how 'liberatory' in some contexts or for some purposes) are condemned to be haunted by a voice from the margins, already speaking (or perhaps presently muted but awaiting the conditions for speech), awakening us to what has been excluded, effaced, damaged.[42]

What we need to do, however, is, as Bordo says, to listen to others, to become aware of our own "biases, prejudices, and ignorance."[43] In other words, we will have a better chance of understanding the oppression of women in its "endless variety and monotonous similarity," to use Gayle Rubin's well-known phrase,[44] if we acknowledge the ubiquity of marginalization without absolutizing any of the forms it historically or currently takes. We must do justice to the similarity of women without riding roughshod over our differences. Harding writes that "the challenge for feminism is to reformulate theories of women's oppression without claiming to describe or explain 'woman' or 'the feminine,' and without claiming to speak on the basis of 'woman's experience' (singular) or 'feminine experience'."[45]

We need to be aware of both similarities and differences among and between women and men; indeed, considering the society in which we live, it is impossible not to be conscious of sex and gender. But the point is not to suppress either similarities or differences; rather, the point is to be conscious of the value we place on them. We live in a world with both sameness and difference, and the important aspect of this "fact" is what we make of these similarities and differences. We socially organize our empirical existence in different ways and we must acknowledge the responsibility we bear for this social organization. One thing all our disagreements over the status of essences in general, and over that of the essence of women in particular, should have taught us is that if we have an essence in common, we cannot specify it, although we continue to categorize some people as women. We should not make a priori, theoretical generalizations regarding gender differences and similarities. Instead, the commitment has to be to the liberation of women. With this in mind, we will pay attention to difference and/or sameness when it brings about justice for humanity.

Notes

1. This paper has benefited from the comments of many people. However, I must thank Robert Sweetman in particular, as not only the first, but also the most frequent reader of this paper.
2. As Jane Flax argues, "despite the lively and intense controversies among persons who identify themselves as practitioners concerning the subject matter, appropriate methodologies, and desirable outcome of feminist theorizing, it is possible to identify at least some of our underlying goals, purposes, and constituting objects" in "Postmodernism and Gender Relations in Feminist Theory" in Linda J. Nicholson, ed., *Feminism/Postmodernism* (New York: Routledge, 1990), p. 40. (Cited as *Feminism/Postmodernism*.)
3. Sandra Harding makes a similar point when she speaks of epistemology: "Important differences between the feminist science and epistemology projects and the feminist Enlightenment critiques are generated in large part by the different intellectual and social contexts in which they each explore, expand, and defend consequences of the emergence of feminist explanations of nature and social life. These tendencies have different histories, different audiences, and, therefore, different projects.... Each should be understood as an attempt to escape damaging limitations of the dominant social relations and their conceptual scheme. These projects are incomplete—we haven't yet figured out how to escape such limitations. Most likely, we are not yet in an historical era when such vision should be possible" in "Feminism, Science, and the Anti-Enlightenment Critiques" in *Feminism/Postmodernism*, p. 101.
4. For example, see Alison M. Jaggar, *Feminist Politics and Human Nature* (Totowa, NJ: Rowman and Littlefield, 1983); Christine Di Stefano, "Dilemmas of Difference: Feminism, Modernity, and Postmodernism" in *Feminism/Postmodernism*; and Sandra Harding, *The Science Question in Feminism* (Ithaca, NY: Cornell University Press, 1986).
5. *Sex, Gender and Society* (London: Maurice Temple Smith, 1972), p. 189.
6. *Vindication of the Rights of Woman* (London: Penguin, 1975), p. 91.
7. *Sexual Politics* (New York: Ballantine, 1969), p.131.
8. Janet Radcliffe Richards argues that "the aim [of feminist policy] should be to eliminate all direct social pressures which differentiate the sexes" because "although direct social pressures as such are bound to exist, when they differentiate between different groups they are inherently objectionable because they infringe the principles of justice...: they prevent people's having equal opportunity to succeed in all areas of activity" in *The Sceptical Feminist: A Philosophical Inquiry* (London: Penguin, 1980), p.180.
9. John Stuart Mill's argument can be used to further argue that traditional femininity is a social construct: "Standing on the ground of common sense and the constitution of the human mind, I deny that anyone knows, or can know, the nature of the two sexes, as long as they have only been seen in their present relation to one another.... What is now called the nature of women is an eminently artificial thing—the result of forced repression in some directions, unnatural stimulation in others. It may be asserted without scruple, that no other class of dependents have had their character so entirely distorted from its natural

proportions by their relations with their masters" in *The Subjection of Women* (Cambridge, MA: MIT Press, 1970), p. 22.

10. For example, Richards is suspicious of the "equal but different" view of differences between women and men because "it always seems to turn out that women differ from men in being *less* strong, *less* rational, *less* creative and less everything else worthwhile than men, and that these supposed deficiencies have traditionally been the excuse for excluding women from everything which men have been inclined to keep to themselves" in *The Sceptical Feminist*, p. 158.

11. "Dilemmas of Difference: Feminism, Modernity, and Postmodernism" in *Feminism/Postmodernism*, p. 67.

12. *The Man of Reason: "Male" and "Female" in Western Philosophy* (Minneapolis: University of Minnesota Press, 1984), p. x.

13. Ibid., p. 104.

14. Daly often figures as an archetype for (this type of) radical feminism: for example, see works as diverse as Jaggar's *Feminist Politics and Human Nature*, pp. 95, 104; Jean Grimshaw's *Philosophy and Feminist Thinking* (Minneapolis: University of Minnesota Press, 1986), pp. 124-27, 140-46, 155-60, 200-201; Lorraine Code's *What Can She Know?* pp. 14-15, 17; and Bat-Ami Bar On's "Marginality and Epistemic Privilege" in *Feminist Epistemologies*, p. 99 where she cites Daly as an example of "cultural" (i.e., radical) feminism.

15. *Gyn/Ecology: The Metaethics of Radical Feminism* (Boston: Beacon, 1978), p. 319.

16. Ibid., p. 28.

17. For example, Christine Di Stefano, "Dilemmas of Difference: Feminism, Modernity, and Postmodernism" in *Feminism/Postmodernism*, p. 67 and Jaggar in *Feminist Politics and Human Nature*, pp. 83-122; 249-302.

18. "Family Structure and Feminine Personality" in *Women, Culture, and Society*, M. Rosaldo and L. Lamphere, eds., (Stanford: Stanford University Press, 1974), p. 43.

19. Di Stefano, "Dilemmas of Difference" in *Feminism/Postmodernism*, p. 69.

20. *A Room of One's Own* (London: Grafton, 1929), p. 70.

21. *The Female Eunuch* (London: Grafton, 1970), p. 109.

22. "Compulsory Heterosexuality and Lesbian Existence," *Signs: Journal of Women in Culture and Society* 54 (1980): 657.

23. *Women, Reason and Nature: Some Philosophical Problems with Feminism* (Princeton, NJ: Princeton University Press, 1982), p. 102.

24. "Feminism, Postmodernism, and Gender-Scepticism" in *Feminism/Postmodernism*, p. 137.

25. *The Man of Reason*, p. 105.

26. Judith Butler argues that "by conforming to a requirement of representational politics that feminism articulate a stable subject, feminism thus opens itself to charges of gross misrepresentation" in *Gender Trouble: Feminism and the Subversion of Identity* (New York: Routledge, 1990), p. 5.

27. Ibid., p. 147.

28. Butler contends that "if one 'is' a woman, that is surely not all one is; the term fails to be exhaustive, not because a pregendered 'person' transcends the specific paraphernalia of gender, but because gender is not always constituted coherently or consistently in different historical contexts, and because gender intersects with racial, class, ethnic, sexual, and regional modalities of discursively constituted identities. As a result, it becomes impossible to separate out 'gender' from the political and cultural intersections in which it is invariably produced and maintained." Ibid., p. 3.

29. "Social Criticism without Philosophy: An Encounter between Feminism and Postmodernism" in *Feminism/Postmodernism*, p. 31.

30. For example, Butler argues that "even if the sexes appear to be unproblematically binary

in their morphology and constitution (which will become a question), there is no reason to assume that genders ought also to remain as two"; hence, "*man* and *masculine* might just as easily signify a female body as a male one, and *woman* and *feminine* a male body as easily as a female one" in *Gender Trouble*, p. 6.

31. "Social Criticism without Philosophy" in *Feminism/Postmodernism*, p. 30.

32. Ibid., pp. 31-35.

33. *Gender Trouble*, pp. 1, 5.

34. Butler criticizes feminist theory that uses the contingency of gender to appeal to an "essential humanness": "only when the mechanism of gender construction implies the contingency of that construction does 'constructedness' per se prove useful to the political project to enlarge the scope of possible gender configurations. If, however, it is the life of the body beyond the law or a recovery of the body before the law which then emerges as the normative goal of feminist theory, such a norm effectively takes the focus of feminist theory away from the concrete terms of contemporary cultural struggle." Ibid., p. 38.

35. Fraser and Nicholson contend that feminist political practice "is increasingly a matter of alliances rather than one of unity around a universally shared interest or identity.... Thus, the underlying premise of this practice is that, while some women share some common interests and face some common enemies, such commonalities are by no means universal; rather, they are interlaced with differences, even with conflicts. This, then, is a practice made up of a patchwork of overlapping alliances, not one circumscribable by an essential definition" in "Social Criticism without Philosophy" in *Feminism/Postmodernism*, p. 35. Butler also recommends a similar feminist political practice because "an open coalition... will affirm identities that are alternately instituted and relinquished according to the purposes at hand; it will be an open assemblage that permits of multiple convergences and divergences without obedience to a normative *telos* of definitional closure" in *Gender Trouble*, p. 16.

36. "Social Criticism without Philosophy" in *Feminism/Postmodernism*, pp. 34-35.

37. Diana Fuss makes a point regarding race which might just as easily pertain to sex/gender: "any critical position which deconstructs 'race' ['sex'] as an empirical fact but fails to account for its continuing political efficacy is ultimately inadequate" in *Essentially Speaking* (London: Routledge, 1989), p. 91.

38. Di Stefano contends that "the postmodern project, if seriously adopted by feminists, would make any semblance of a feminist project impossible. To the extent that feminist politics is bound up with a specific constituency or subject, namely women, the postmodernist prohibition against subject-centred inquiry and theory undermines the legitimacy of a broad-based organized movement dedicated to articulating and implementing the goals of such a constituency.... Another problem is that 'robust' solidarities of opposition [i.e., alliances or open coalition] (rather than of shared identity) may be psychologically and politically unreliable, unable to generate sufficient attachment and motivation on the part of potential activists. Can this solidarity be anything other than a local and negative solidarity, a solidarity or resistance rather than of substantive alternatives?" in "Dilemmas of Difference" in *Feminism/Postmodernism*, p. 76.

39. "Feminism, Science, and the Anti-Enlightenment Critiques" in *Feminism/Postmodernism*, p. 99.

40. *Essentially Speaking*, p. 4.

41. For example, Alison Wylie argues that "women find themselves in 'subdominant' gender-defined positions within each of these [economic, cultural, socio-political] contexts and, from these positions, they participate in activities that support the privileges of men. Despite considerable variability in what this means for particular women, this general feature of women's experience is sufficiently universal, by all anthropological and historical accounts, that it would seem to support at least a qualified conception of a

distinctive women's standpoint, one which takes into account the fact that gender is by no means the only factor shaping women's lives" in "The Philosophy of Ambivalence: Sandra Harding on The Science Question in Feminism" in Marsha Hanen and Kai Nielsen, eds., *Science, Morality and Feminist Theory* (Calgary, AB: University of Calgary Press, 1987), p. 68. As well, Bordo asserts that "all of us, as women, occupy subordinate positions, positions in which we feel ignored or denigrated"; hence, she characterizes feminism as "an 'outsider' discourse, that is, a movement born out of the experience of marginality" in "Feminism, Postmodernism, and Gender-Scepticism" in *Feminism/Postmodernism*, p. 41.

42.   "Feminism, Postmodernism, and Gender-Scepticism" in *Feminism/Postmodernism*, p. 138.

43.   Ibid.

44.   "The Traffic in Women: Notes on the 'Political Economy' of Sex" in R. R. Reiter, ed., *Toward an Anthropology of Women* (New York: Monthly Review Press, 1975), p. 160.

45.   "Ascetic Intellectual Opportunities: Reply to Alison Wylie" in *Science, Morality and Feminist Theory*, pp. 81-82.

5

Religious Conflicts, Public Policy, and Moral Authority: Reflections on Christian Faith and Homosexual Rights in a Plural Society

HENDRIK HART

INTRODUCTION

In the area of public justice, the legislator faces notorious difficulties in balancing the rights of different moral communities within a plural society. If different communities participate in public debate preceding such legislation, it is not unusual for a community to press for the universalization of its own morality. Such pressure can be particularly strong if a community considers its morality to be authorized by a religious source. A case recently before the Canadian courts concerned the human rights of a lab instructor whose dismissal from a Christian college was related to his being gay. *Faith Today* reported that in the course of the legal wrangling, an organization with intervener status "argued that to include sexual orientation in the [Canadian] Charter [of Human Rights] conflicts with other rights guaranteed there, specifically the rights of those who find homosexual conduct immoral for religious or other reasons."[1]

What do we make of this intervention? No current Canadian legislation fundamentally interferes with the right of a religious organization to hold and practise its moral views within its own community. The question therefore arises whether attempts to block universal human rights legislation may at times imply universalizing (the religious sources for) the moral authority of a community which opposes such legislation. If so, public justice might then be regarded as an opportunity to expand one's own moral boundaries so as to exclude activities of those whose moral views and practices are different. In that case we would not merely have arguments that including sexual orientation in a human rights charter would prevent the adherents of some community's morality from practising their own morality in their own community. Rather, there would now also be arguments seeking to extend the moral rights of some community to legally censor the behaviour of others. One element in such a view of rights often is an assumption that a religious organization's moral authority can be shown to be universal. If such an assumption were honoured, the organization would impose its particular moral/religious views on all members of society. Its freedom to practise its own morality would have a price, namely the freedom of any other group to honour its own morality by practising it.

A very different situation with respect to legislation in the same area can be observed in The Netherlands. Recently the Dutch parliament addressed the complexity of a moral issue such as that of homosexuality. It has particularly noted how homosexuality affects its citizens' universal access to employment. The parliament recognized that an organization or institution whose sole reason for existence is the fostering of a certain religion (like a church), cannot legally be forced to employ anyone who violates the moral boundaries taught and acknowledged by the religion in question. But parliament recognized as well that an organization or institution which, though it has a religious basis, also engages in activities in addition to the promotion of religion (for example, a Christian school, hospital, or home for the aged), cannot legally refuse employment to anyone for "the sole fact" of that person's sexual orientation. And parliament has included in the notion of sexual orientation any action that can reasonably be expected to be integral to it, such as being in a same-sex relationship. If other factors also present themselves, for example the obvious and open spurning of the religious character or the moral practices of the organization, employment may possibly be legally denied. But difficulties experienced in fundraising among supporters, just because a loyal employee is gay and in a relationship, would not be a sufficient ground for dismissal.

A culture in which the attitudes just sketched exist side by side is in conflict. People such as those in the first example often are strongly convinced that God (or a universal law of Reason, or the good of humanity) authoritatively and universally compels us to assess the morality of same-sex intimacy with some simple, unambiguously clear, and abiding principles of right and wrong. These people expect governments to promote public justice by passing legislation based on this compelling final authority in matters of morality. They are convinced that governments, in the name of their higher authority, must share their moral outrage against any homosexual acts and make these acts illegal. The second example shows a very different attitude. Here a government legally protects a basic right to employment from being unduly undermined by an employer's morality which in some significant way differs from that of the employee, without being insensitive to either the impact of moral issues or the compelling nature of the deeper issue of religious authority. These examples of conflict are typical of modern pluralist societies. Such societies are often so deeply and widely fractured in dealing with issues in which people's differences in religion, morality, and public justice intersect, that the divided approaches create clashes.

Since the clashes often touch on important economic concerns, the law in a modern society will often guarantee minimal employment rights in the public interest. Unavoidable public conflict must not endanger basic access to fundamental means of existence.[2] This may include religious/moral conflict. Hence many modern societies have enacted legislation which ensures access to employment for people whose morality is questioned by others, perhaps even by the majority of a society. In a number of societies such access to employment is guaranteed to people regardless of sexual orientation, including the enactment of such orientation within moral (widely defined) and legal boundaries. Not only must homosexuals be granted employment despite disapproval by an employer of their sexual orientation, but homosexuals living in same-sex relationships must have access to such employment as well.

All Western jurisdictions, however, no matter how liberal, grant religious institutions some privilege in relation to anti-employment discrimination. But the extent of such privilege differs. No Dutch church is obliged by law to employ a minister who is a homosexual, even if that person is celibate. In Canada as well, religious authority, via constitutionally guaranteed freedom of religion, provides some immunity from anti-discrimination laws in the workplace.[3] Canadian law, in fact, seems to tolerate wider discrimination than in The Netherlands. However, a recent article in the *Christian Legal Journal*,[4] shows that Canada does also place limits on lawful discrimination otherwise permitted on religious grounds. The authors draw attention to a recent judgment in which a Board of Inquiry dealt with lawful religious discrimination. The Board introduced the following factor in evaluating employment qualifications stipulated by a religious employer: "The qualification is a reasonable and bona fide qualification because of the nature of the employment" (12). It is clear that this factor bears a close resemblance to "the sole fact" clause in the Dutch legislation. One might interpret the Board as saying: "The mere fact of not meeting a certain qualification is not an absolute; there must be an integral connection to the nature of the job." This interpretation seems plausible, because in analyzing this factor, the Board applied the so-called BFOQ test stipulated in the Supreme Court of Canada (13). This test includes the following two criteria: 1) "Is the aptitude or qualification rationally connected to the employment concerned?" and 2) "Is the rule properly designed to ensure that the aptitude or qualification is met without placing an undue burden on those to whom the rule applies?" (14). By applying these criteria, the Board found against a Christian employer who had dismissed employees for departing —by living together out of wedlock—from the expected lifestyle of employees.

The above examples show that the issue of homosexual orientation is not limited to questions of religion or morality, but touches on significant matters of livelihood. The extent to which having a job of some kind is largely unavoidable to survive in our culture, combined with the extent to which religious authority is said to demand employment discrimination towards people of a particular sexual orientation, makes the interconnection of religion, morality, and public justice a very important issue. In this context I will reflect on the fact that, contrary to what is often thought, religious authority in these matters is seldom straightforward. Even within a broad religious community (such as Christianity) it is seldom simply clear that certain moral behaviours are prohibited by the religious source of authority observed in that community. An employer may appeal to the Bible to justify refusing employment to some person for immoral behaviour. But that person may appeal to the same Bible to justify this behaviour. This is a plausible scenario in our society. In my view this requires that governments intent on doing public justice by legally limiting moral freedom should create such limits only in the interest of preserving moral freedom and preventing uncontrollable moral harm. The examples of legislation I have cited show how fragile and subtle this issue is in modern Western society. Forbidding all discrimination can itself be discriminatory. But indiscriminate discrimination in religious institutions constitutes an intolerable threat to some people's livelihood.

In this chapter I will reflect on that approach to morality and religion in which the two are both related to one another and remain distinct from one another. This is not the only view of the matter, but it is one well known in the literature, and it is the one I support here. In this view morality and religion are related to the extent that in given cases they may be mutually supportive. They are distinct both in the sense that morality and religion are irreducibly different and in the sense that a specific position in one domain cannot be logically and necessarily linked to the other. I will apply all this to the appropriateness, especially in the case of homosexual orientation, of a single-minded and authoritative attitude toward public justice in our pluralist culture if that attitude universalizes a particular source of moral authority. In doing so I want to make clear that in public debate about moral issues, the relation between religious or ideological authority linked to sacred texts on the one hand, and the authority of the law on the other hand, is, at least in significant and controversial cases, an ambiguous relation at best. Indeed, a revealing example in our culture is the utterly confusing relation between religion, morality, and the law in the widespread public and ecclesiastical debate about homosexuality. In exploring single-minded and authoritative linkages of religion, morality, and the law I will first describe some structural elements of fundamental conflicts in a pluralist society. I hope to show that religious conflict about moral authority is an integral component of our society's pursuit of public justice. After that I will discuss a specific example of the difficulty in establishing the religious authority of a moral approach to homosexuality. Religious people often insist that they are authorized only to apply their particular moral approach as a universal one. In my example theologian Richard Hays makes a case for the clarity of such universally authoritative moral principles regarding homosexuality in the Christian religion. The example is significant both because it concerns a crucial discussion of our time and because it vividly illustrates the lack of clarity in the relation between the Bible and homosexuality. I will therefore examine it in detail and I will try to show that Hays's attempt to establish clear moral authority is overstated. In the closing section I will then try to set out how deeply held moral convictions rooted in religious authority can be related to public justice more inclusively, while simultaneously preserving religious and moral integrity.

SOCIETIES IN CONFLICT

Collisions and conflicts in modern pluralist societies occur in part because issues of religion, morality, and public justice cannot be separated, even though they are clearly different. In the Enlightenment's classic liberal approach such separation is actually promoted. Irreconcilable religious conflict is kept out of public life by being characterized as private. Public issues can then be pursued with appeals to universal principles of reason, unprejudiced by divisive and private religious beliefs. Today, however, this separation of private religion and public reason appears unsuccessful. So-called private religious conflicts surface time and again in public arenas as significant ingredients in political strife. Bosnia and Ireland provide only the more dramatic illustrations of this. So the question arises: why are conflicts in religion, morality, and public justice so intertwined? I will mention four factors among others.

First of all "religion" has a public dimension. It cannot be confined or reduced to private denominational or cultic ritual practices, acts of worship, and doctrinal beliefs. Such a narrow meaning of "religion" hides its relationship to the largely inarticulate depths of human conviction and concern associated with ideologies, worldviews, final vocabularies (Richard Rorty), the spirituality of moral sources (Charles Taylor), our indwelling in commitments underlying tacit knowing (Michael Polanyi), life's existential boundary issues (Karl Jaspers), ultimate human concerns (Paul Tillich), or fiduciary attitudes to certitudes (Ludwig Wittgenstein). All of these, just like "religion," give direction and foundation to our most important actions, choices, and attitudes.[5] Though these fundamental directions are not fully articulate in their meaning, we nevertheless tacitly rely on them for guidance. They are deeper-than-rational beacons, symbolic points of orientation, trusted epiphanies of hope for the future.[6] Participation in the struggle for local, national, and global justice is more than sharing, debating, and criticizing certain rational beliefs in order that these beliefs may become a common basis for action. In public deliberations deeper-than-rational reliances are at work as well.[7]

The inarticulable depth of religious convictions makes it impossible to deal with them adequately on the level of the rational beliefs they inspire.[8] Beliefs, as broadly referred to in Western culture, are a species of rational-intellectual behaviour. They are articulated conceptual understandings to which we give assent. But religious conviction, though incorporating beliefs, is more than merely beliefs. If religion were merely a matter of belief, it would be a strange sort of belief indeed, because it does not seem to be susceptible to a settling of differences by means of public discussion. John Locke rightly observed that a law or an argument do not suffice to make citizens share the same religion. But he wrongly concluded that therefore religious convictions are simply private. Nevertheless, religion continued to be characterized as a kind of belief. Public beliefs allegedly subject to objective reason were therefore separated from private beliefs purported to originate in subjective faith. But it does not follow that religion, which is more than mere belief, was successfully separated from our public actions. Rather, it meant that in the depth of their interwovenness with public actions, religious convictions were placed beyond awareness of their role in rational persuasion or public debate. In time the public forgot that these convictions, though not the result of rational discussion, function as a pre-condition for such discussion.[9] They provide the basic directives which help people decide what is rational in such a discussion.

Secondly, these depths of conviction are especially experienced as authority-inspiring foundations. On them people build their concrete and actual moral positions, public as well as private. Morality in its depth concerns people's active respect for others as fellow humans, the nurturing of human mutuality, equal dignity, ability to count on one another's support in being and maintaining oneself in the fullest possible sense of being human. Genuine morality respects difference and welcomes the other. Genuine morality therefore also transcends its articulation and the striving for agreement in moral beliefs.

Moral codes, the actually articulated rules, attitudes, and expectations of morality, vary widely. Moral positions, as expressed in moral codes, fundamentally structure people's experience of the limits and possibilities of humanity in interhuman relations. They help foster the humanity people look for, respect, and support in their relationships. When challenged in their actual moral codes, people usually point to what they experience as their deeper foundations rooted in what I have called religious convictions.

In a recent book the complexity of the relation of religion to morality is submitted to careful scrutiny. The authors take widely divergent positions. But all agree that there is an unavoidable relation between religion and morality.[10] Religious people nourish, develop, and sustain the religious sources of their morality in ritual practices of worship, while so-called non-religious or secular people nourish them in, for example, philosophy, literature, and the arts. Both an appeal to St. Paul in a Christian community and an appeal to Aristotle in a secular tradition often function in the same way.[11] The point of these appeals, in both cases, is to lend the weight of authority to a moral position.

Thirdly, if we bring together the above two considerations (that public life is rooted in a pervasive, yet not fully articulated depth-dimension; and that morality derives its authority from this dimension) in their relation to public justice, the unavoidability of religious influence in politics will become more clear.[12] To make this clear I will first explain the notion of public justice and then show some differences and relationships between justice and morality.

Public justice is the space in which unavoidable human conflicts of (legitimate) interest are legislatively regulated. It enables people to lawfully exercise their responsibilities as freely as possible. It especially prevents, eliminates, or minimizes the potential injury inherent in the unavoidable conflicts. The element of unavoidability is important here. All of us engage in unavoidable actions—breathing, moving through space, taking in food—with equally unavoidable consequences. I can only breathe air present in the space through which I have to move. There is no other air. If part of my moving through space unavoidably requires my use of mechanized transportation, which unavoidably affects the air I must breathe, the environment becomes a space in which my need to breathe and the transport authority's need to keep a fleet of buses going will conflict to some extent. A complex society like ours creates a complexity of unavoidables: unavoidable actions and their unavoidable consequences create unavoidable conflicts, originating in lack of control over how unavoidable consequences of unavoidable actions unavoidably affect others.

The space in which conflicts of interaction are unavoidable is what I, following John Dewey, refer to as public space. Public justice is, in this context, an enabling function of society; a spacemaker for responsible agency. It provides legal channels that regulate the otherwise unavoidable conflicts. Public justice enshrines and protects rights and freedoms by legislating public space. The control over that public space is in the hands of governments. The government will try to enact legislation protecting my lungs without paralyzing the transport system. Governments serve public justice via political discussion which issues in legislation for all inhabitants of the public space. Public justice is, for that reason, essentially a form of justice which in its very structure must be justice for all; for whomever inhabits the public space.[13]

Justice is not morality. But the two are closely related. The same can be said about religion and morality, as I will soon show. An example will make clear what I mean. Many people regard the sale of banned Western foods and drugs to developing nations as immoral. However, there is often nothing illegal about these sales. And since justice is regulated with laws, we have an example here of something immoral which legislation does not consider unjust. What is clearly unjust will, hopefully, be made illegal. But, barring some unavoidable exceptions I will later mention, most citizens of a liberal democracy do not want their personal morality legislated, do not want legislation to interfere with personal moral freedom and responsibility. In our culture, again barring some exceptions, people do not want laws about how to make love. In former Canadian prime minister Pierre Trudeau's words: the state has no business in the bedrooms of the nation. Legislation is for areas in which unavoidable consequences of unavoidable actions create unavoidable conflicts with the result that some people may be crushed except for legislation which restores them to justice.

The borderlines between justice and morality are sensitive. Euthanasia is illegal in Canada, but the discussion of it is not, because on the morality of euthanasia people differ. Similarly, Toronto professor Gerald Hannon is forbidden by law to engage in sex with children. But discussing the morality of such relationships in his classes is protected by academic freedom, in spite of the deep and widespread public revulsion toward even such discussion. Another example: few people want to tolerate religions or moral codes that require ritual mutilation or human sacrifice. Yet many Western public authorities experience difficulty in dealing with the Somali ritual practice of female genital mutilation. Public justice is in part aimed at creating maximum legal protection of a maximally free moral space. Yet the legislator cannot, in the name of rights and freedoms, legally tolerate just any morality simply because it calls itself moral. The moral space is bound by what is called public morality, the vague boundary of "community standards."[14] How do we move here?

Formally, the relationship between justice and morality could be stated as follows: morality transcends justice and justice is one of the conditions for morality. Morality transcends justice at least in its crucial dimensions of personal freedom and responsibility, which in their core cannot be legislated. And justice is a foundation for morality in providing the free space in which morality can responsibly remain a matter of personal freedom. This close relation between morality and justice is crucial. It means that morality is impossible without justice, because justice opens up, serves as foundation for, possibilities for moral choices. It also means that justice must be complemented by morality, because a full enhancement of our humanity by one another is a moral issue which can never be adequately achieved by legislation alone. Our moral sensibilities always prompt us to survey the arena of public justice, both to make sure that the public authority does not force our morality, and to watch out for a lack of justice that would similarly interfere with moral freedom and responsibility.

Political debate will therefore always be surrounded by issues of morality in its broadest sense. People expect justice to support our culture's ability to grow in people's respecting one another in their basic humanity. Nevertheless, the legislator will generally not provide legal boundaries which interfere with moral freedom. The legal boundaries will only provide external limits within which moral freedom can be lawfully practised. In this way morality itself will internally be bound only by moral limits. Legal limits may determine that having sex with a person under a certain age will be against the law. This limit is appropriate, because here, in society's judgment (officially registered in, for example, court decisions), unavoidable injury in unequal power relations is at stake. Public justice as the foundation on which alone a morally alive culture can grow in freedom will be partially measured by its ability to play this morally enabling role. But no amount of legality will by itself constitute a sex act as moral.

In the public debates relevant to these issues, sharp differences in moral outlook regularly emerge. And usually it becomes apparent that these differences point to deeper convictions which I have earlier characterized as "religious." Arguments will be heard that some move is immoral because freedom is the highest good, or because hurting others is the greatest evil, or because goodwill toward others should direct all of our actions. All of these arguments appeal to some deeper source of authority, which is sometimes, though not always, linked to an overtly religious tradition. Achieving public justice is impossible without public discussions of morality, in which "religious" differences cannot remain hidden and should therefore not be ignored. If public justice is intimately related to morality and if moral authority cannot be reduced to rational-moral beliefs shared through purely rational procedures, religious issues deeply implicated in moral positions must be on the table in the arena of debates about public justice.[15]

A fourth structural dimension of the interrelation between religion, morality, and public justice now comes to the fore. In discussions of morality and public justice the position I follow here holds that differences in moral and political visions, as well as in religious commitments which support these visions, show no simple and direct correspondences. The undeniably real relations between religion, morality, and public justice turn out to be highly complex. From the fact that a community is Christian, one cannot predict how its members will vote, for example. And from the fact that a moral position is gay-positive, one cannot conclude that this position is necessarily secular and atheist. Different moralities are present within the same religious tradition and the same moral stance in different religious communities. Nevertheless, even though uniform links between religion and morality are not logically necessary, or simple and singular, people who reflectively enter a public discussion in which moral issues are at stake in relation to intended public legislation will normally base their moral visions on deeper than moral foundations. Even more, they will experience the claim of their deeper convictions on their moral pronouncements as authoritative, despite the lack of logical rigour. This results in the bewildering experience that someone who argues against legislation from a moral point of view with Christian roots can be opposed by someone with a different moral vision who nevertheless appeals to the same Christian roots.

This fourth structural relation is crucial to the next section of this chapter. I want to stress that the bewildering experience of identical moral positions defended from different religious vantage points, coupled with different moral positions defended with appeals to the same religious authority, is unavoidable in a pluralistic society. There are many reasons for this. One is the need for concrete cultural orientation in the linkage of religion and morality. Another is that the embodiment of religious orientation in relation to the encoding of a moral position is a fruit of the free and responsible engagement of human agency. Further, moral and religious positions derive their longevity precisely from their ability to inspire a flexible variety of specifications. All major religions know what Christians call denominations. This is not an accidental or even undesirable deformation of religion. It is a direct result of religions being experienced as the source of life-giving spirits, which must be able to inspire an almost immeasurably rich diversity of forms of life. Each concrete form of life limits the life-giving force which takes on that form. Because in our culture religion and morality have become concentrated in religious and moral beliefs and because beliefs are taken as conceptual phenomena which, to be true, must ideally move toward rational agreement, the idea is strong that true religion would essentially require fundamental agreement. In fact, however, the roots of religious orientation are varied, multi-layered, and capable of immeasurably rich complexities of interpretation. It is not at all surprising that among Christians we have not only conservative and liberal, traditional and progressive positions, but also Marxist, existentialist, rationalist, Enlightenment liberal, and many other interpretations, all discussing the relative validity of one another's stances.

Given the nature of the intertwinement of religion, morality, and public justice and given the plurality of religious and moral positions in our culture, a pursuit of public justice in which a particular religious authority and a specific moral position are privileged, will, given the moral requirement of respect for difference and the inclusivity of public justice, most likely tend toward being both immoral and unjust. This serious conclusion should have considerable moral persuasion to avoid authoritarian religious stances in public debates on issues such as homosexuality in plural societies. It should not be overlooked, however, that one important ingredient in this complexity is the ambiguity of the relation between religion and morality. But the ambiguity is often denied. Many Christians will claim that the religious authority on which they base their universal claims with respect to homosexuality is established with utmost clarity in their tradition as well as in the Bible. In the next section I will therefore discuss an important example of the ambiguous relation between the Bible and a universal position on homosexuality for Christians. This example will hopefully lead to an appreciation of the need for legislated public justice, because the ambiguity in question is incapable by itself to prevent moral injury, as is clear from the prevalence of Christians using the Bible as an excuse for even extreme cases of homophobic behaviour.

AMBIGUITY

The previous section included the observation that there is no logically clear or compelling relation between a given religion and a specific moral position. They are related. But the relation is not such that one can expect all people of a given religious persuasion, say all Christians, to have a single shared attitude towards especially controversial moral issues, say the issue of same-sex relationships. It is therefore not surprising that people in fact do differ on the morality of same-sex relationships and that this difference is not only between religious and secular people, but also between religious people from fairly homogeneous backgrounds. Moral positions generally have ambiguous relations to world-views or religions which provide them with their authority.

This ambiguity becomes quite evident in discussions among people who share (in some significant sense) a worldview or religion, but who disagree about the moral positions they take within the context of that worldview or religion. I will illustrate how this ambiguity is at work in a discussion of homosexuality in the Christian community, in spite of the author's claims to the contrary. Homosexuality is widely acknowledged as a crucial moral issue and is intensely controversial in all of society. Christians frequently disagree with one another about the morality of homosexuality for what they claim are religious reasons alone. And they also often conflate the protection of their right to hold moral convictions about homosexuality with the right to demand legislated universal imposition of their convictions. Hence, Christian discussion of homosexuality is especially instructive to illustrate the reality of moral differences in relation to public policy in pluralist societies.

As a representative example of Christian discussion I have chosen Richard B. Hays's response to John Boswell's well-known book *Christianity, Social Tolerance, and Homosexuality.*[16] I will not be primarily interested in who is right, Hays or Boswell. I also do not intend to defend the one or attack the other. My primary interest is to show that when Hays claims that Christians have access to an unambiguously authoritative text on which to base their moral position in regard to same-sex relationships, he overstates his case. Given the intensely partisan and prejudiced attitudes which Christians on all sides of this discussion display, I will make my case as strong as I can by going into great detail. For if I would not be successful in showing Hays to have an unwarranted optimism with regard to the clarity of the Bible in relation to homosexuality, my entire discussion would lose its basis.

Boswell's book is widely noted for its socio-historical analysis of the early relation between Christianity and homosexuality. Its main purpose is to show that early Christianity cannot be held accountable as the single or most important cause of intolerance toward homosexuals in modern Western society (6). Boswell's strategy is not so much to concentrate his analysis on theological treatises, but rather in addition to these also to interpret the social and non-theological literary history of early Christianity (22 ff.). He cautiously (39) concludes that early Christians were far more tolerant of homosexuals and homosexual behaviour than a reading of exclusively theological writings has made us believe. His book is both widely known and respected, as well as fiercely contested and dismissed. Gay-positive Christians frequently appeal to it as an authoritative source for their arguments, while Christians who disapprove of same-sex relationships often have little good to say about Boswell's book.

Hays acknowledges the "authoritative place in theological discussions of homosexuality" Boswell's work has acquired (184). At the same time, his own response to Boswell has acquired a similar place.[17] Hays, however, does not significantly take into account the socio-cultural and literary history with which Boswell tried to deal. Instead, he presents a mainly theological (hermeneutical/exegetical) analysis of primarily one biblical text, namely Romans 1:16-32, to show that Boswell mistakenly relativizes Christian rejection of homosexuality, especially in the light of the Bible's clear teaching.

This is excellent material to illustrate the issue of ambiguity. Not only because both Boswell and Hays admit that the issue of homosexuality is a complex and difficult one. Even more because it will be clear to a careful reader familiar with the Christian discussion of homosexuality that Boswell's historical thesis will fail to convince Christians who have a theologically oriented, negative attitude to homosexuality, while Hays's exegetical conclusions will not put to rest the misgivings of Christians who have questions about Romans 1:16-32 as the sole authority for a contemporary Christian ethic of same-sex relations.

I also choose Hays's discussion of Boswell because the text allows us to examine closely how Hays, as a reputable and orthodox New Testament scholar, comes to regard his position as beyond dispute and because it is centred on the relation of hermeneutics to exegesis.[18] Further, certain crucial features are not in question in the discussion, such as the importance of both authors belonging to the Christian community, their scholarly reputation and personal integrity, and the crucial interest both display in "setting the record straight" about some aspect of the relation between Christian faith and the morality of homosexuality. Thus the discussion is to a significant extent intramural. Both authors could easily have functioned as "expert" witnesses before a legislative committee seeking clarity in the Christian debate about homosexuality. Finally, the most crucial text in Christian discussion about homosexuality is Romans 1, which is precisely the focus of Hays's discussion. His article is recognized as a classical presentation of the traditional Christian argument for the authority of the Bible in taking a gay-negative position. Hence it seems important to discuss this piece in some depth.

Further, Hays's critical discussion of Boswell is not just a private discussion among scholars, but has its origin in Hays's "deep concern about the impact of Boswell's exegesis upon the church" (185). This concern does not, however, prevent him from expressing gratitude for Boswell's "insistence on discussing these vexed issues with scholarly care and charity" (185). What concerns Hays is the real possibility that Boswell may succeed in persuading the church that (at least some form of) same-sex relationships are biblically acceptable. This concern focusses on Boswell's construal of "the Romans text" (185), because Hays offers the thesis that this "single major New Testament text [Romans 1:16-32]...unambiguously portrays homosexual practice as a sign of humanity's alienation from God the creator" (186). For Hays the clear authority of this text for the church is so crucial that if Boswell can successfully argue for his different interpretation of this text, Hays fears "there is no New Testament justification for rejecting homosexual practice as a legitimate moral option for Christians" (186). However, Hays is convinced here that Boswell "fosters...confusion between exegesis and hermeneutics" (186, see also 199, 201, 204, 210, 211). Consequently, Hays concludes that the justification for rejecting same-sex relations retains a firm anchor in the unambiguous authority of the New Testament.

Finally, the discussion is important because even Hays, after having established the clarity of the Romans text and having stressed its authority, cannot avoid admitting that after all that, we still have decisions to make that are painfully difficult, a choice is left (211). There are "questions that we must grapple with as we seek to assess the place of Romans 1:16-32 in shaping normative judgments about sexual ethics" (209).

Contrary to Hays, Boswell opts for ambiguity (37). He does not as such focus on the debate about whether or not the Christian faith and the Bible support or reject homosexual behaviour (xv). His concern is to show that our intolerance of homosexuality does not necessarily find its roots in early Christianity (6). He is provisional and careful about the validity of his material (31, 37, 39, 333-34). Hays, to the contrary, enters into the discussion of the permissibility of homosexual behaviour and often is definite and final in his language. He uses terms such as "unambiguously" (186), "unmistakably clear" (192), "incontrovertible clarity" (196), and "clear condemnation" (204) in demonstrating his main claim (Boswell's confusion of exegesis and hermeneutics) and avers that "Boswell's treatment of Romans must be most vigorously challenged" (199).

Understandably, then, Hays's language from time to time betrays a strong emotional investment in his safeguarding the church from Boswell's work. He indeed writes as one who is sure of his case. He suggests at one point that "Boswell's enthusiasm for his case has apparently overcome his better judgment" (198). He talks about "a textbook case of 'eisegesis,' the fallacy of reading one's own agenda into a text" (201). At one point he is "left wondering what an ancient writer could possibly have said to avoid being coopted in the service of Boswell's hypothesis" (202). He sees Boswell "gagging his sources" (204) and committing "a foolish anachronism" (210). Clearly Hays is both aware of the pitfalls of interpretation in this sort of discussion and convinced that a "correct reading" can be established.

All in all, therefore, Hays's analysis of Boswell enables me to illustrate an important aspect of the problem I earlier said policy-makers encounter, namely the lack of clarity we experience in trying to establish direct links between religion and morality.

In order to provide sufficient depth to my discussion of Hays's important article, I will first evaluate his assessment of Boswell's reading of Romans 1 (Hermeneutics 1). Next I will discuss Hays's own reading of the Romans text (Hermeneutics 2). I will then make observations about Hays's reading of Boswell as a historian (History). I will also briefly discuss Hays's reading of biblical authority in our contemporary ethical context (Biblical Authority). I will end with briefly summing up how my reading relates to the main issue of this chapter (Summing Up).

Hermeneutics 1

Hays in one place formulates his objections to Boswell's treatment of Romans 1:26-27 as follows: Boswell "scrutinizes the text through the hermeneutical lenses of modern categories alien to the first-century historical setting" (204). Elsewhere he remarks that "part of the dispute centres precisely on the question of whether contemporary homosexual relationships really are analogous to those that Paul knew about" (206). These two remarks characterize a crucial element of the context for Hays's reading of Boswell, "the point at which Boswell...must be most vigorously challenged" (199). Hays is worried that Boswell takes modern categories such as "sexual orientation" and naively reads Romans as though Paul knew about such categories. He reads Boswell as imposing contemporary criteria on an ancient discussion. Hays says this should not be done. So he rejects what he takes to be Boswell's conclusion, namely that Paul should not be read as condemning in his day what we know today as same-sex relations.

The weight of this objection is not clear. Robin Scroggs, whose work is also briefly discussed by Hays, explicitly distinguishes Paul's context from ours.[19] But Scroggs comes to the same conclusion as Boswell: Paul cannot be read as obviously and simply condemning the same-sex relations contemporary gay-positive Christians have in mind. Scroggs concludes that, since Paul did not have in mind what we have in mind today, Paul should not be read as addressing our concerns. But when Hays considers Scroggs, he wonders whether "there is a radical qualitative difference between homosexual practices ancient and modern" (210). So in reading Boswell, Hays seems to say that Paul's situation and ours are too different, while in reading Scroggs, he seems to say there may well be no difference between Paul's situation and ours. Here we may see a tension in Hays himself. On the one hand he seems to refer to our modern situation as very different, as "alien" to Paul's time. On the other hand he questions significant differences between Paul and modernity. I realize that in the former case the difference concerns categories of interpretation (the concepts gay and straight), while in the latter Hays is concerned about the matter being interpreted (same-sex or heterosexual behaviour). Nevertheless, it may be helpful to be aware of the possibility that Hays's evaluation of continuities and discontinuities depends on the consequences we attach to them. There may be a hint here that Hays is suspicious of any reading that diminishes Paul's condemnation. How do we assess such possible suspicion?

It may be fair to accept that our categories "homosexual" and "sexual orientation" are recent. But does this mean that in Paul's Rome there was no reality to which we could apply the terms "heterosexual" and "homosexual"? Might Hays believe the "difference between homosexual practices ancient and modern" (210) is possibly not significant because he doubts the reality of a homosexual orientation even today? He wonders whether "there are studies" (209) to show a significant difference in orientation.[20] In Boswell's view, the answer is clearly "yes," both in our time and in Paul's. He thinks there were sexually active gay people in Rome, as well as straight people who had same-sex relations. This reading of the Roman situation is not universally accepted, even among non-religious pro-gay writers. The Roman situation is a matter of discussion. But Boswell was well at home in this discussion and, on the basis of the evidence as he saw and presented it, he drew his own conclusions: the reality of what we call same-sex orientation was known in ancient times, and trothful unions similar to marriages existed among people of this orientation (43-44, 49-50, 55).[21]

To disagree with Boswell's views on sexual orientation both now and in history and to give evidence for the legitimacy of such disagreement is fair. Hays, however, does little more than dismiss Boswell as obviously confused, and then spends his time showing to what disastrous consequences the alleged confusion leads. Is it fair for Hays, without reference to the literature on sexual orientation, to summarily dismiss Boswell's conclusions? Boswell's treatment of homosexuality in history in the introduction of his book (the book Hays discusses) is worth reading in this context. Boswell's advice to be "extremely cautious about projecting onto historical data ideas about gay people inferred from modern samples" (24) might have warned Hays that Boswell was not naive about historical distance.

What in fact does Boswell do? He tries to imagine, based on Paul's language and on what Boswell himself concluded about the situation in Rome, whether Paul took into account the reality of being gay. Being gay was apparently, as far as we now know, not discussed by the ancients with a specific terminology. Nevertheless, in Boswell's view, it was both real and known in Paul's times. Having considered this matter, Boswell then reads Paul's text as addressing what we would call a typically heterosexual context. He observes that Paul must be taken to disapprove of "homosexual acts committed by apparently heterosexual persons" (109). In Boswell's view, Paul referred to same-sex acts that were a departure from (all) people's "normal" heterosexuality. And this observation does not in principle differ from what Hays himself says. For Boswell here makes no claim that Paul knew of any distinction in orientation, but only that he refers to same-sex behaviour as a departure from the heterosexual norm.

Boswell's views—that Paul's attitudes to same-sex relationships in Romans 1 must be limited to how he understood these relationships—have found resonance. Given subsequent discussions and twists in the debates, Boswell's language when he launched his views was less precise than we might wish today. However, his central claim remains clear: on the basis of what he knows about Rome in Paul's time, Paul's condemnation could not have been intended for what we call homosexual orientation, because Paul either did not know of this orientation or, if he did, Paul did not specifically identify gay people as such. The Romans text is clearly limited to references to behaviours and acts. It does not have in view a special kind of people (gay people) who might engage in such acts. And that, according to Boswell, as well as many others, could be a ground for assuming that Paul cannot be taken to have condemned homosexual acts between people who are what we call gay. Paul may just not have been aware of this sort of same-sex behaviour. Even then, it is quite possible, as Hays (perhaps rightly) suggests, that Paul would have regarded even what we call homosexual orientation as evidence of sin (208). But since it is not clear that Paul knew of such orientation, it is speculative to assume that he would indeed condemn it. We would need much more evidence than Hays's very hermeneutical analysis of the Romans 1 text.

In the course of discussing Boswell, Hays appeals to Victor P. Furnish and D. Sherwin Bailey (200, 201). He does not report, however, that their observations actually support Boswell. They, like Boswell, claim that Paul did not have in mind what we talk about today as monogamous same-sex relations between people of homosexual orientation. They conclude, as did Boswell, that Paul can't be read to condemn what he did not talk about. The Boswell phrase quoted by Hays (199) that Paul "was not discussing persons who were by inclination gay" means to do no more than what Furnish and Bailey do: observe the distance between Paul's time and ours. And all three conclude, as does Scroggs, that since there is this distance, Paul's condemnation of his present cannot simply be taken as a condemnation of our present.

There is a major difference between Boswell and others who also believe that Paul cannot be read as condemning, for example, contemporary faithful and monogamous same-sex relations in Christ. The difference is that Boswell, quite uniquely, has a reading of Roman culture in which the gay/straight difference was known, and in which there also were gay Christians who entered into marriage-like relationships with one another.[22] On this crucial point, Hays interprets Boswell in a curious manner. He observes that Boswell "writes a muddled and equivocal paragraph which first hedges but then reasserts his stance" (201). In this paragraph Boswell writes (1) that it is not clear whether either Paul or other Jews distinguished between same-sex behaviour among gays and among straights, and (2) that this issue is not all that important, because Paul wrote about behaviour and not about personality types (109). What is "muddled" for Hays?

Apparently Hays does not take Boswell's reading of the Roman situation seriously and does not carefully exegete Boswell's text to discover its subtleties. Hays accuses Boswell of anachronistically introducing an irrelevant distinction. I think one might also say: Boswell only observes that the distinction did not function for Paul. When Hays says that according to Boswell "the distinction is fundamental to Paul's position" (201), it is important to realize that this can only be fairly said if we read Boswell as saying: "the distinction is fundamental, so the fact that Paul probably did not make it is important."

Let me briefly recapitulate. Boswell is not sure Paul made the distinction we in modern times name the homo/heterosexual distinction. Furnish, Baily, Scroggs, and others are sure Paul did not make it. They think there was no such distinction made at all in Paul's time. On grounds he considers valid, Boswell is more careful and says he does not know whether Paul was aware of the distinction, even though he thinks a writer closer to Paul's time, such as Chrysostom (see below, History), knew the distinction and implies that Paul clearly had a heterosexual context in mind. Boswell then goes on to say that it doesn't matter so much anyway, because Paul did not discuss personal sexual identity, but sexual types of behaviour. Boswell explicitly affirms what Hays claims Boswell does not see at all, namely that Paul talks about a behavioural condition, and not about individual persons or sexual orientation. Taking together the two passages from Boswell which Hays discusses (199, 201), it appears Boswell simply does not make the points Hays criticizes. Hays overreads Boswell as suggesting "that Paul *intends* to condemn homosexual acts *only* when they are committed by persons who are constitutionally heterosexual" (200-201, my italics). Boswell only suggests that Paul's condemnation does not specifically target what we refer to as homosexual orientation. That suggestion remains valid even today and even after Smith's important 1996 article in the *Journal of the American Academy of Religion*.

From the discussion so far I surmise that Hays's reading of Boswell is skewed because he does not take seriously enough the possibility that Boswell may be right in his reading of the Roman situation.[23] Such a possibility would indeed impact on both the hermeneutical and the exegetical issues Hays raises. For it would then perhaps become hermeneutically necessary to take into account just what specific situation Paul referred to in Rome. Then Hays could no longer ignore this issue. In addition, meanings Hays now considers to be straightforwardly exegetical, such as the dominant role of the creation connection in Romans 1, might be more hermeneutically loaded than Hays surmises.

If these varied and considered possibilities have a legitimate role in the discussion of Romans 1, it will likely be less easy to identify a unified, clear, and direct linking of a universal position on homosexuality with Christianity. For the disputed elements that make up the various possible readings all have more than one exegetical and hermeneutical possibility. On the face of it there would seem to be some naïveté in the idea that the Bible, yielding a plethora of approaches to most issues of significant debate among Christians,[24] would for all time be unambiguous in its authority on the issue of homosexuality. I will not, however, rest my case at this point. I will also explore the claims Hays makes about Boswell's confusion of hermeneutics with exegesis in relation to Hays's own reading of Romans 1 (Hermeneutics 2).

Hermeneutics 2

So far my reading of Hays has raised issues concerning his interpretation of Boswell's text. I have suggested that the hermeneutical problems Hays found in Boswell are less obvious than Hays portrays them. But there is an additional issue, namely Hays's own exegetical approach to the Romans text without explicitly declaring his own hermeneutical moves and without signalling his awareness that these moves are not simply common sense. If Hays's claims were merely exegetical, we might be more inclined to view his findings as unambiguous. But what if his exegesis in fact assumes discussable hermeneutical moves?

Quite unexceptionally, Hays reads Romans 1:16-17 as crucial not only to Romans 1, but to the whole letter (188). More exceptionally, he identifies one important characteristic of this text—and its sequel to the end of the chapter—as a piece of theodicy, a human justification of the justice and integrity of God's ways. The meaning of this justice and integrity comes to light in the gospel, which reveals God's righteousness as well as God's saving power. The righteousness is revealed as God's wrath against unrighteous humanity, the saving power as God's saving grace for all who are in bondage (188-89).

Two hermeneutical/exegetical issues surface here, namely the issue of theodicy, and the issue of God's justice as manifest in wrath. The first issue concerns the legitimacy of reading Romans 1 as theodicy. If such a reading is necessary, much of Hays's exegesis may follow. But whether or not the passage is theodicy is a matter of hermeneutics. On a different hermeneutical view, Hays's exegesis doesn't follow as easily. In much of the Reformed theological tradition, for example, the idea of Scripture containing theodicy at all has traditionally been problematic. Reformed theologians such as John Calvin, Karl Barth, Gerrit Berkouwer, or Hendrikus Berkhof consider the human expectation that God's ways be justified at all, a matter of impiety. They base their objection to theodicy in large measure on their reading of this very letter to the Romans, where in 9:21 Paul rhetorically implies that our status before God makes theodicy inappropriate.[25]

The second issue is the distinction between, on the one hand, God's justice as including justified wrath against injustice, and on the other hand, God's saving grace. How Hays understands this distinction is poignantly clarified when he says that God's wrath is part of God's justice: God's righteousness includes God's wrath. But Hays then adds in brackets that the righteous God is a "righteous merciful God whose righteousness is revealed preeminently in his act of deliverance through Jesus Christ" (207). I read Hays here as saying that justice and mercy are to be distinguished, since justice is revealed both in wrath and in mercy, though mercy is preeminent. I suspect Hays's mention of preeminent mercy is in brackets because he sees the mercy theme "developed at length elsewhere in Romans" (207). In Romans 1, as read by Hays, Paul is concerned with theodicy related to God's justice as wrath, not with justice as mercy.

Because I am partial to the Reformed theological tradition and thus read Romans 1 in the light of Romans 9, I do not evaluate theodicy in Romans 1 the way Hays does. Rather, right here in the beginning of Romans, in my view, Paul is already concerned with making manifest the "preeminent" (Hays) sense of the power of God for salvation. Those who have faith are those who trust God's justice as it was made manifest most clearly in the gospel, that is, they trust God's justice as mercy. Gospel for Paul, as I read him, means: God's justice in Christ is mercy, the gospel of justice always is a gospel of mercy (see Romans 3:24-25).[26] But because of these two different hermeneutical moves, that is, within the setting of two large interpretive frameworks that differ from those of Hays (relativizing theodicy and reading Romans 1's justice together with Romans 3's mercy), I now make different exegetical moves. Hays's exegesis is clothed with a different hermeneutical framework than mine. Yet in an essay which is deeply concerned with this very distinction, he does not declare the distinction between his exegetical and his hermeneutical moves.

Does it make any difference to declare hermeneutical moves such as I indicated? I think it does. The reading of Scripture is never just an exegetical reading, certainly not in the case of key passages. Hermeneutics always plays a background role. So in the context of, for example, a Reformed hermeneutic which evaluates theodicy differently, it becomes possible to read Romans 1:18-32, clamped between 1:16-17 and 2:1, as saying something about a particular Jewish mindset of Paul's day. From that point of view I can make more than Hays does of Paul's "rhetorical trap in 2:1" (195). That Jewish mindset strongly emphasized God's wrath. But Paul, as I read him, wants to make clear that the gospel proclaims God's justice as mercy and that, hence, the proclamation of wrath disembowels the gospel for both Jew and Greek. And this in turn could imply that the reference to homosexuality comes in a section which not only, as Hays agrees, is not intended "to provide moral instruction" (195), but which might even be intended to repudiate a moral mindset among some of Paul's fellow Jews.[27] New Testament scholars have raised the possibility that 1:18-32 is not intended to give us Paul's own thinking,[28] and this possibility is by no means raised just to get away from condemnation of homosexual acts.[29]

A final observation on the hermeneutics of Romans 1 concerns Hays's confidence that Paul uses Genesis 2 in Romans 1 to provide a ground for knowing what is sexually natural. Genesis is then taken to establish the heterosexual male-female order as God's permanent created order. There are two difficulties here. One is the assumption that Genesis can be "ontologically" or "philosophically" read as establishing such a permanent creation order. That assumption needs more explicit discussion, since the very notion of reading our concept of creation order as present in the Genesis text may well be a reading influenced by Greek metaphysics.[30]

The other difficulty is: how do we relate a permanent order to Paul's strongly intended weakening of certain orders (Jew/Greek, free/slave, male/female) in Galatians 3:28? The unusual language of the Galatians passage suggests that Paul not only deemphasizes the ethnic or social orders of his time but also a dimension of what Hays and others read as creation order. For whereas the usual construction of the "pairs" in the text is that of a "neither/nor" (neither Jew nor Greek, neither slave nor free), the reference to male and female has the unusual "neither/and."[31] This unusual construction is very likely a reference to the "male and female" of Genesis 2. Richard Longenecker sees nothing particularly important in such a reference for the meaning of the "male and female." But I submit that Paul's implicit reference to Genesis could be read as his "relativizing" of the "order" of Genesis. However, this is the very order Hays thinks Paul would press as a creational ground in Romans 1. This tension between possible readings of Romans 1 and Galatians 3 with reference to order and creation makes a simple exegetical appeal to creation order controversial and introduces an (unavoidable?) element of hermeneutical ambiguity into the discussion.

In the preceding two sections on hermeneutics I have tried to show that Hays's claim about Boswell's confusion between hermeneutics and exegesis is made in the context of an essay in which Hays himself shows problems on this score. Admittedly Boswell is weak as a reader of the Bible and Hays is commendably reliable. But in this particular case Hays does not simply establish an undeniable point of exegesis, untainted by his agendas or hermeneutics. "Having an agenda" is not peculiar to Boswell, as Hays seems to indicate, but is unavoidably the case whenever we deal with controversial moral interpretations, whether of Scripture or of any other authoritative religious source.[32] Hays's own agenda in his discussion with Boswell makes his readings (of Boswell as well as of Paul) ambiguous as soon as we introduce other hermeneutical perspectives. Sacred literature is read in commitment. Such commitment is related to a pre-articulate sense of the message of the text as a whole. In our commitment to the sacred text, both commitment and text depend on our relationship to the organic unity of the deeper meaning to be found in each. And the historical movement of our articulations of this deeper meaning provides the ambiguity with which each interpretation of an important text comes to us, as well as the "agenda" which is present behind all of our exegesis and hermeneutics. Over time, and between communities, a religious text lacks analytic propositional clarity and instead provides the interpretive space for keeping alive an ongoing tradition.[33]

History

So far I have pointed to problems in Hays's reading of Boswell's interpretation of Paul, and in his own reading of Paul. But he does not rest his case with the reading of the New Testament, his own expertise. He also questions Boswell's expertise, social history. Hays makes several criticisms. He quotes Boswell to the effect that there "appears to have been no general prejudice against gay people among early Christians" (202) and then expresses his incredulity about this in the face of the "unremittingly negative judgment of homosexual practice" (202). But Boswell knows about this negative judgment. In his view, however, that historical information is based on limited sources. Did it escape Hays that Boswell does not limit his discussions to theological/philosophical writings directly commenting on homosexuality, but includes non-theological literary documents and cultural artifacts (22)? Boswell wants to access an often untapped source of knowledge precisely because, in his view, the knowledge Hays depends on presents a one-sided picture. And Boswell is also aware of the serious problems involved in opening up the "unexplored" area of "social topography" (38/39).

Hays's judgment is that "the evidence that does exist suggests that they [ancient Christians] regarded...[same-sex behaviour] as so self-evidently loathsome as hardly to require discussion" (203). Perhaps so. But Boswell suggests there is more evidence than what Hays regards as evidence. Hays concentrates on Boswell's "strategy...to discredit the logical validity of early Christian polemics" (203). But I see no evidence in Hays that he has actually considered that special dimension of a strategy Boswell announces as his own, namely interpreting letters, poetry, and other literary and cultural sources. Assuming Boswell's strategy, are Hays's criticisms on the point at issue valid?

Precisely in the reading of Boswell, Hays seems to fall short. The historical problem Boswell especially addresses is not, as Hays believes, that of "the rise of massive social intolerance of homosexuality in the early Medieval period" (185). Boswell is concerned with social tolerance over a wider period, and indeed also writes about the early period. But the rise of massive intolerance does not concern him until the late Middle Ages, in part four of the book. Hays presents as "Boswell's basic historical thesis" something Boswell expressly denies, namely "that social intolerance of homosexuality was a function of the triumph of 'rural' cultural patterns over 'urban' culture" (185). Though Boswell does pay some attention to rural-cultural relationships earlier in Western history, he explicitly says that they are "irrelevant to (if not contradicted by) the social changes" Hays has in mind (31, 37).

In this historical context Hays's interpretation of Boswell's reading of Chrysostom is instructive. Boswell claims that Chrysostom knew the distinction between what we call homo- and heterosexual behaviour (109). Boswell also claims that, according to Chrysostom, Paul's condemnation of homosexual acts was limited to heterosexuals motivated by lust rather than by love (117). Hays makes hard and fast negative judgments about Boswell's carefully phrased, plausible interpretations. But does he take into account that Chrysostom was trained in the pagan Greek academy and could therefore plausibly have been influenced more by a Greek than a Roman view of homoerotic activity, even when he rejected it? Boswell's interpretation may not be fully convincing, but neither is Hays's. Hays does not seem to accept, for example, that Chrysostom's warning against homoerotic behaviour as cited by Boswell (131-32, 362-63) is in part the warning of a Christian monastic against the behaviour of ordinary Christians. And that underscores precisely Boswell's point, namely, that apart from some preserved and clear indictments by theologians, everyday society, including Christian society, was quite accepting of homoerotic behaviour in the time of Chrysostom.[34]

It seems possible that Hays is unaware that some so-called condemnations of homosexual practice in the ancient world, if carefully studied, may be less universal and categorical than appears at first sight. G. K. Dover's by-now classic *Greek Homosexuality* presents much evidence that Greek condemnations of homosexual acts were aimed only at the person who is passive in the relationship.[35] Only that person acts against nature. A male who allowed himself to be anally penetrated was very widely regarded as perverse in the ancient Greek world, simply because being penetrated was considered a feminine thing. I give this example in order to point out that Hays is correct in urging us to be careful about taking ancient authors seriously in their time. But I think Hays then also needs to be more aware of the possibility that apparently "universal" condemnations in the Bible may turn out to be restricted to the specific contexts ancient authors had in mind, and that current and contemporary practices should not simply be read as the target of these ancient condemnations.

Biblical Authority

Whatever Hays may think of Boswell's work, he does acknowledge that none of his own disagreement directly affects the question "concerning the appropriation of the biblical teachings in later historical settings" (205). He observes that the Bible's teachings related to morality do not automatically have authority for today (206). What then are we to make of Hays's claim that in

Romans, homoerotic acts are "explicitly and without qualification" characterized as distortions of the created order (207)? Is that not begging the question when the issue is whether or not Paul's words are unavoidably (Paul might say "by nature") qualified by whatever the context of his situation allowed him to know? Does Hays see things in Paul's ancient text which require us to read it, in the case of homoerotic behaviour, without qualification? Does Paul's appeal to creation constitute such a requirement? But Paul also appeals to Genesis and creation to establish his view of order in relation to male and female. We no longer read all of Paul's views as directly valid for our male/female relationships today, even within the church. Perhaps Hays does read Paul in such a way with regard to homosexuality. Perhaps in his view faithful readers must conclude that any and all same-sex acts, whatever form they take on today, are already intended to be included in Paul's strictures. But how would Hays avoid the argument that any of Paul's references to human acts (in spite of Hays's qualification: "however they may be interpreted" [207]) would be restricted by the interpretive boundaries of Paul's statements? How could Paul effectively be interpreted to be referring to realities of which he was unaware?

If Isaiah read the drift of the Old Testament gospel as more inclusive than the letter of the law would allow,[36] might we not read Paul in the light of the gospel of Jesus and conclude that the drift of Jesus' life as God's word incarnate was more inclusive than Paul literally realized in his day? Why would it necessarily be inappropriate for us to point to understandings of same-sex love of which Paul may not have been aware and to which he may not, therefore, have been pointing? True, Paul's language seems universal. But that language was, by Hays's own admission, largely borrowed from contemporary Jewish sources (194-95). Then why would the universality of that language have authority beyond the universality within the reach of these sources? It is quite possible to understand the Hellenic-Jewish rejection of "all" homoerotic behaviour known to them or even imaginable to them as by them intended to be universal, without thereby obliging us to include all such behaviour known and imaginable to us. Up to this very moment it remains unclear that Paul could be read as condemning faithful and monogamous same-sex relationships related to what we understand as homosexual orientation.

A similar observation may be made with reference to Hays's claim that "the witness of Scripture is univocal" (210). Is that not saying too much? It certainly appears that whenever Scripture explicitly speaks of same-sex activity, it does so negatively. But does that not, again, require us to ask just what these passages were speaking of? And must we not also ask why, once we know their concrete reference, they were speaking negatively? If, for example, the passages always had conception, fertility, or fruitbearing as part of their meaning we, who no longer always take procreation as essential to marriage, would no longer be included in the precise "world" of the Bible's negativity.

For Hays all this seems simple and straightforward. But is it? And if so, is that perhaps itself related to a less straightforward hermeneutic "world" in which Hays makes his exegetical decisions?

Hays, however, does seem to leave some room for an open discussion of the issue of homosexuality, in spite of what I take to be his somewhat oversimplified approach to biblical authority. He leaves the most room for the possibility of a contemporary approach that differs from Paul's by considering the legitimate relevance of our own contemporary experience. Although Hays considers our struggle with the authority of experience "notoriously difficult" (209), he does nevertheless acknowledge that there are "questions that we must grapple with" in assessing Paul (209). But how serious is he? For example, Hays doubts Scroggs's suggestion that "mutual, non-exploitative, faithful homosexual relationships" are not targeted by Paul (210). This is a crucial issue and Hays provides no evidence of having made careful study of it. Is Hays well informed in this area? When he asks: "Are there studies that purport to show that homosexual preference is the result of involuntary 'orientation' rather than of free choice?" (209), I surmise this is not only a rhetorical question designed to show that to Paul such studies would not mean much, but also a rhetorical questioning of the existence of such studies. If the latter is indeed the case, Hays is entering into a discussion of a sensitive moral issue apparently under-informed about studies on sexual orientation, as well as about literature discussing long-term and monogamous gay and lesbian couples.

The issues of involuntary orientation, sexual fidelity, and long-term relationships in the homosexual community may not be important for Hays. He reads Paul to say that all sin is an involuntary dimension of our human condition, which drives all of us to do evil things for which we are all nevertheless culpable (209). Whether one is heterosexual and so driven or homosexual and so driven makes little difference, it is all sin. But that observation does not seem helpful in the present discussion. It contains no hints on how to distinguish homosexuality from unchosen physical handicaps which are also the result of living in a fallen world and toward which we are not only tolerant, but with which we help people as much as possible, in order to make life livable for them with their handicap. Even though Tourette's syndrome can lead to undesirable ethical consequences, we treat people with this syndrome respectfully. The issue is one of whether manifest immorality, that is, behaviour injurious to the humanity of our neighbour, is unavoidably tied in with the behaviour in question. The fact that Paul was clear on this in relation to same-sex behaviour as known to him says almost nothing about those contemporary same-sex relationships in which Christian morality is a self-consciously pursued standard by the couple in question.

Hays's concluding suggestion regarding a possible way forward for pro-gay Christians is an exploration in the area of "empirical investigations and... contemporary experience" (211). But is that a serious suggestion, when Hays can see the value of such exploration only if we can confer upon it "an authority greater than the direct authority of Scripture and tradition" (211)? If he is unaware of such greater authority, how can Hays seriously suggest these other explorations? In spite of his apparent openness toward experience, he does little to encourage us in that direction. But why? Tom Wright, a New Testament scholar in Hays's own tradition for whom Hays has great respect (and vice versa) claims that, with Scripture as our authoritative orientation, we have great freedom to spell out the norms for modern living.[37] Jesus' parable about the Messianic banquet (Luke 14) includes invitations to those who were originally declared unfit to serve God in the temple (Leviticus 21:16-23).[38] If for some reason the freedom to spell out norms is unavailable in the case of homosexuality, such a reason should be carefully unfolded. The freedom we have is indeed not licence. But where there are constraints, they are more likely to be explicit in Scripture itself. The fact that Scripture itself does not make our freedom in a specific area explicit would seem to be a rather weak constraint (Hays 211).

Scripture itself shows that earlier strictures can be removed at later times, if a deeper spirit of inclusive redemption found in the Scriptures points beyond the Scriptural letter and moves people to give more adequate expression to that deeper spirit. Scripture, that is, knows of experience of God's fundamental intent in Scripture itself deeper than what is articulated in any of Scripture's literally concrete details. This not only occurs in the move from Old to New Testament, but also within either Testament.[39] The deep spiritual intent of biblical revelation, though clearer to a later generation, may on some point not be as clearly spelled out earlier. Yet life with God according to the Scriptures may reveal more clearly to a later generation what God is up to. The mystery hidden for ages but revealed in Christ (1 Corinthians 2:7, Ephesians 1:9, Colossians 1:26) becomes ever clearer (2 Peter 1:19). God's full intent is not totally spelled out in the Bible. Bible-directed experience may access this intent more fully than it is spelled out in the Bible.[40]

It seems that, for Hays, going beyond Paul must be supported by evidence that Paul's indictment is "explicitly counterbalanced by anything in Scripture or in Christian tradition" (211). My question is: where is that requirement itself formulated in Scripture or in Christian tradition? How did Isaiah (56) go beyond "the law"? How did we decide that women no longer need to cover their heads in church? I would say Isaiah and we did that by interpreting Scripture in ways that are continually said to be impermissible when it comes to reinterpreting Scripture on homosexuality. But this exception for homosexuality seems to have no explicit Scriptural warrant. What does seem to have warrant in Scripture, though less clearly in Christian tradition, is the radical inclusiveness of the gospel.

Summing Up

Hays's article makes the claim that at their biblical core the matters he writes about are clear and unambiguous. He concludes by admonishing us to "forthrightly recognize" that same-sex relationships are portrayed by Paul in Romans 1 as "a vivid and shameful sign of humanity's confusion and rebellion against God" and that, therefore, "we must form our moral choices soberly in light of that portrayal" (211). I hope to have shown that Hays's argument concerns matters considerably more complicated and open to other approaches than he portrays. More importantly, I want to claim that it could not be otherwise. Given our distance from the sources, our distance from the cultures in which the sources originated, our distance from the complex conflicts in those cultures and in their Christian communities, given also our contemporary distance from one another in the conflicting approaches we have to the Bible, its authority, and its interpretation, and given the distance we have to one another in the moral interpretation of same-sex relationships, any claim to clarity, universality, and unambiguous authority must be a tour de force.

LEGISLATING JUSTICE

In the first section of this chapter I argued that, in spite of a close and necessary relation between public justice, morality, and religion, a religion is not necessarily or historically connected with one single, specific morality and a particular morality cannot be the sole possible context for specific legislation in a pluralist society. Though legislation intended to serve public justice will generally be enacted only in the context of moral discussion, the discussion will always remain somewhat inconclusive, that is, without consensus. Nevertheless, participants in the moral discussions will often feel strongly justified in their own moral position because, in their experience, their position is backed by a "higher" authority, which in this chapter I have called religious. In spite of the strong feelings about this higher authority, however, moral discussion in a pluralist society does not lead to establishing any such higher authority as the unambiguous, single, and universal authority for all members of that society. Hence the inconclusive results of, and the lack of consensus in, the moral debates which contextualize discussions of controversial issues of public justice in Western culture.

In the second section of this chapter I discussed in detail one particular example of an attempt to show that some higher authority (the Bible) requires an unambiguous moral position with regard to same-sex behaviour. The example itself is authoritative, because it involves a scholar with a high reputation, trained to pursue and bring to light clarity and distinctness in thought and articulation, and intending to argue against ambiguity. If settlement of a dispute concerning unambiguous religious authority related to a controversial issue such as homosexuality is possible at all, it certainly would have had every opportunity to come about in this case. I tried to show, however, that Richard Hays, who claimed to be able to show on primarily exegetical grounds that the Bible's relevance to a given moral position on homosexuality is unambiguous, was unconvincing. Hays, by and large, did not consider that a significant position on the religious authority of the Bible for any given issue of importance is itself usually not a matter of mere exegesis, but requires taking a hermeneutical stance. He uncritically took the hermeneutical approach of a particular hermeneutical tradition, the Anglican or Episcopal tradition, namely, that matters of faith derive their authority from Scripture, church tradition, reason, and experience. And within that tradition he then made particular moves whose hermeneutical significance for exegetical issues was not discussed. It was possible to show, however, that if another hermeneutical tradition was chosen as context, Hays's exegetical moves seemed less convincing, let alone unambiguous.

In the course of my discussion I pointed out that the force of an argument involving religious authority is not first of all its logic or lack of ambiguity, but its religious conviction. This conviction has deeper roots than can be read off the surface of articulations found in a religious text and can therefore not simply be forced on someone with a different conviction by the logic of rational argument. A genuine confessional tradition, though having an authoritative literature (the Bible, confessions, dogmas), must nevertheless always remain open, fluid, and adaptable to ways of expression that lend themselves to the historical movement of time. If faith is reduced to conceptual belief, as it often is in our culture, faith becomes fixated in clear propositions (beliefs). Faith then closes itself down in a search for truth as indisputably universal agreement. Such faith will be prone to lose touch with its time.

Given the above, it is not surprising that Christians with strongly held convictions who participate in scholarly discussions of homosexuality show that the issue is far from settled. Hays's discussion of Boswell is no exception. Christians are divided precisely about the clarity of the Bible's teachings and the authority of those teachings concerning the contemporary moral validity of same-sex relations. For the moment consensus seems impossible, whether in a (divided) religious community such as Christianity, or in an (even more divided) open society such as Western pluralist democracy. What does this imply for the drafting of legislation relevant to rights and freedoms?

It would be a mistake to think that more expert witness will result in a resolution. The problems Hays finds in Boswell do not decisively undermine the reputation or authority of the latter, nor do my findings in Hays have that effect for him. In discussing any complex matter such as homosexuality, what may be called "agenda blindness" enters in at every point for every scholar. We read and write as we are. The texts speak to us inside our own worlds of expectations. In the present situation there is, and can be, no such thing as the one Christian or biblical position on homosexuality; especially not plainly, simply, and straightforwardly. Even small textual details legitimately remain open to ongoing discussion. But discussion remains meaningful, especially when we come to realize that the demand for agreement in beliefs as a test of our confessional integrity is too costly a concession to the Enlightenment. Though once upon a time rational agreement was the test for toleration, today the insistence on this test is better recognized as a form of intolerance.[41]

In this context no legislator can act justly or morally by basing public justice on the argument that Christian morality clearly, uniformly, and univocally proscribes homosexual acts. Nor do Marxist morality, Enlightenment morality, feminist morality, or even gay morality offer a single and unambiguous moral position on this issue. Specific moral positions on specific controversial moral issues in a morally plural society cannot lay claim to universal, unambiguous, uniform authority and expect to be acknowledged by all.

As I noted earlier, those who actually hold a moral position will often do so with universal intent. They experience their position as the one all of us should hold. But they are not in a position to subject others to their position. In addition to the deeper diversity of religious or higher authority which backs up the various moral positions, education, prejudice, personality, class, personal/family background, political correctness, and other factors affect persons within the same religious or ideological community differently. These factors are not always sufficiently taken into account explicitly in discussions of the religious/ideological roots of moral positions. And for those who hold these positions, these factors are not on the surface of their awareness. But in reality Marxism, humanism, liberalism, Christianity, and naturalism are not sufficiently homogeneous to provide resources for unambiguous, morally specific, or detailed moral agreement on significant and controversial issues. Hence all we can expect is moral solidarity in subcommunities, subcultures, groups, or families within a larger religious tradition. In such narrower confines a homogeneous and unfractured position on homosexuality often does exist. But the legislator who wishes to do public justice, who wishes to protect and promote rights and freedoms for all in a given society, would perpetrate injustice precisely by allowing one of the existing moral outlooks to be legislatively prescribed for all. In addition, precisely because of the moral significance of respect for difference, a legislator who ignored such difference would, in addition to being unjust because of being exclusive, be immoral because of the erasure of difference. I already noted this at the end of the first section of this chapter. Given this background, is there a way forward in achieving public justice in relation to plural moralities rooted in plural religious positions?

The difficulties experienced in these situations are complex and perplexing. Some societies, Dutch society for example, are far more tolerant of homosexuality than North American society. This, too, will play a role in what justice a legislator can be expected to enact. What is legislated must somehow be positively related to what is perceived to be legislated. In recent Western history it is very difficult to perceive as moral what is taken to be normative only by some. Against this background it is hard for some community to consider as truly moral some action by others which blatantly deviates from that community's moral standards. In part this is because many traditions have too often confined the meaning of "moral" to specific "content." In certain areas, at any rate, people tend to consider actions immoral (same-sex behaviour, for example) without considering what constitutes the immorality, that is, in what way such action constitutes moral injury to the people engaged in the action. As a result it becomes difficult to acknowledge truly "universal" moral principles in moralities that significantly differ from one's own in detail. Many Christians are unable to consider the possibility that homosexuality and morality could go together. At least in part this is likely due to the circumstance that the proscription of same-sex behaviour in the Bible gives no insight into the moral principles that are trespassed in such behaviour. The moral authority of the example is carried over from the religious authority of the source, but without any insight into the moral nature of the issue.

What is immoral about same sex relations? Would we not expect the immorality of such relations to have to do with their immoral qualities, that is, qualities which constitute a moral violation of another person? But is gender a moral quality in and of itself, such that it necessarily constitutes moral injury if someone sexually relates to someone of the same gender? Such a construction is arguable if, for example, the possibility of genetic fruitfulness were necessarily part of the sex act. In the past this has been argued. But today not many people believe that sexual intimacy without the possibility of pregnancy is immoral. We focus more closely on the building up or breaking down of a partner's human dignity as a key to what is or is not moral. This leaves room for a morality of concrete behaviours that is more varied and inclusive than if, for example, fruitfulness were to be a constitutive moral component of sexual intimacy. In contemporary sexual ethics monogamy, faithfulness, respect, and mutuality would seem more appropriate moral norms for sexual intimacy. And many argue that same-sex couples are as ready to meet these moral norms as heterosexual couples.

If we neglect these background issues, we can very easily speak of sexual morality as limited to two-partnered heterosexual monogamy for life and with the possibility for progeny. But where are the moral norms here? Why could we not accept as moral all loving, mutual, respectful, trothful, mature, monogamous, and equal sexually intimate relationships in which the humanity of the partners is enhanced, supported, promoted, and protected?[42] All these arguably are specifically moral categories. If we were to accept such more universally articulated norms for sexual intimacy, we could imagine many more different arrangements as moral than in our present frameworks. In fact, when our present framework is seen not as one particular way in which to shape a more universal norm, but as the norm itself, then a different kind of behaviour not fitting within this specific framework is already by definition anti-normative. If only marriage as we define it today is moral, domestic partnerships could by definition, no matter how conducted, never be moral. In this situation, however, conflict with the morally normative call to respect difference is bound to occur. Here, I think, is a clear situation of an unavoidable conflict with great potential for injury.

In such a difficult situation of unavoidable conflict it becomes the task of the legislator who seeks to serve public justice to provide space for all to live morally. That means: space for all citizens to be moral, to have moral freedom within limits not imposed by the morality of others.[43] Such a course of action is itself inspired in part by a certain moral stance. This moral stance, that is, this stance which enables people to honour and support the humanity of other persons as persons, morally obliges a plural society to make legal space for others to exercise their own different morality. Taking a moral position is itself a moral act, which therefore itself needs to respect moral difference, because respect for difference is crucial to morality. At the same time, the public legal requirement that a plural society legally make public space for the morality of others does not commit people to morally endorsing or condoning what they perceive as the immorality of those others. The need for legal widening of moral space springs forth from the unavoidable political circumstance that in a modern democracy with its plural moralities, a politics of unnecessary legal strictures on people's morality amounts to disrespectful behaviour toward persons as persons, that is, amounts to immoral politics. Moral choices are choices for persons-in-communities that cannot be enforced by the legislator. Legal strictures are permitted only, for example, to prevent moral harm to persons involved in immoral relationships within which they lack moral freedom because they lack power or equality. In this way our society has legal strictures on the adult practice of sex with minors, because we perceive this as harmful in view of the inequal relationship. Nevertheless, Gerald Hannon is legally free to discuss the morality of such behaviour. The only acceptable boundaries are those that are publicly perceived to interfere with the public moral good beyond our control. In a discussion moral injury is largely avoidable, while in a practice such injury is too probable to leave it to the freedom of individual moral judgment.

The legislator in this situation is called to administer public justice, justice for all. In our pluralist society this calls for legal protection of a space within which some will behave in ways that others perceive as immoral. In this situation the legislator is sometimes faced with a demand for putting legal limits on immoral behaviour. Certain immoral economic practices, for example, in which people are injured by manipulations they can neither avoid nor control, may demand legal protection for the innocent and unwilling victims. In our culture a just acceptance by the public legislator of the judgment that some immoral behaviour requires such legislation needs to be morally supported by a widely shared public consensus. Such public consensus will differ from society to society, embracing a wide variety of moral positions found in that society. But public legal limits cannot be provided if they are clearly out of touch with this public consensus. Such consensus is present, for example, in cases where the elderly are conned out of their life savings. The behaviour on which, with widespread public support, legal limits are placed in this case arguably leads to unavoidable moral harm to people who do not wish to be so harmed. If, however, a society harbours wide moral support for racism or homophobia, legislation will not be able to change this situation. In fact, legislation may not even be possible. If an out-of-touch elite imposes a legal regime not morally supported by the public, widespread disregard for the law will result. In such situations the elites who reject racism and homophobia need to create prior access to publically effective education and discussion for those who exhibit the unacceptable behaviour.

Neither rational arguments nor legal limits are fully adequate for setting moral boundaries. So long as people are free to protect themselves from moral harm resulting from unavoidable consequences of actions they cannot avoid, moral conflicts need to be settled in morally acceptable ways. For instance, a morally acceptable repudiation of perceived immorality can be provided by moral example, which may be authoritative in its persuasive promotion of human dignity, while not interfering with the freedom of individual-communal moral responsibility. This is powerfully illustrated in the case of safe sex as a moral practice which saves lives, as against promiscuity which costs lives. Most of the helpful persuasion toward safe sex has come from example, whether the example of peers or that of educational advertising. It is not obvious that the use of condoms can be enforced in the same way as the use of seatbelts.

In these situations the legal protection of the moral integrity of moral minorities is essential. This protection must extend, so far as possible, to moralities not morally acceptable to the public majority. For that reason morally generous ideas of morality need to guide the legislator. These ideas should not be expected to be characterized by rationally supportable clarity, univocity, and unanimity. If within moral/religious communities such singular ideas are in practice not achievable, as Hays's discussion of Boswell illustrates, a plural society can *a fortiori* not be expected to respect talk about agreement on what is moral when in fact such an agreement does not exist. Rather, the ideas of morality entertained by the legislator should be characterized by a moral generosity which embraces as many component communities in that society as seems possible. Thus, the rights of both pro-gay and anti-gay moralities need to be so protected that adherents of both can find living space in the same culture. A moral concept of public moral space must, for a public accepting this space, include the conviction that the legislated expulsion of a morality merely because it differs from ours will be immoral and certainly not legally supportable. The public-legal exclusion of moral minorities is possible only if toleration of such minorities would constitute an unavoidable and demonstrable public harm to public morality.

The point I have been trying to make is that "living space in a culture" cannot be limited to so-called private spaces such as homes, families, or churches. In our culture all citizens need equal, just access to an almost limitless complex of goods and services, rights and privileges. And these, of course, have as their flip side a host of obligations and responsibilities. Just as we cannot limit morality to the private sphere for religious groups, so religious groups cannot limit access to our culture's privileges only within their moral boundaries. The discussions over how to settle our differences are bound to go on for a while yet. But we need a clearer awareness that controversial moral positions based on religious convictions cannot hope to claim universal authority. If widely shared, such awareness may contribute to a more sensitive handling of our moral conflicts.

Though within the Christian tradition objections to the approach I have outlined are easily anticipated, it is equally easy to point to elements of the gospel which support my approach. Most important among these is the central role played by the language of Isaiah in the articulation of the gospel. In this language, especially in Luke, the image of widening our boundaries, of enlarging our spaces, of making room for those who are now outside is prominent. Given this kind of space, it is not surprising that the apostle Paul declines to be a moral judge of people outside of the Christian community (1 Corinthians 5:9-13). The issue I have wanted to address in this essay is not one of whether people are entitled to condoning or not condoning certain actions from a moral point of view. Rather, I have wanted to focus on the issue of public justice in a plural society in which moral positions are in conflict. In that context it seems clear to me that demanding of citizens that they observe Christian moral practices, and of legislators that they enshrine Christian standards in public legislation, goes against the grain of the New Testament. St. Paul's moral discourses in 1 Corinthians, though clearly advocating firmness and unity within the community, also respect difference within that community (8:9) and acknowledge unavoidable plurality in a public context (5:10). It is remarkable that the latter acknowledgement supports social relationships with people regarded as being immoral.

Notes

1.   *Faith Today*, July/August 1995, p. 42.
2.   For the meaning of "unavoidable" see below.
3.   Economic discrimination reaches farther than employment practices. Entitlements and

benefits such as spousal pensions, bereavement leave, and many other economic matters can be affected by unfair discrimination. But since the employment of people with a homosexual orientation in religiously oriented institutions is such an integral part of the discrimination discussion, I will limit my brief observations to this issue.

4. John R. Sutherland and Kevin G. Sawatsky, "Community Standards and the Christian College Employee," *Christian Legal Journal* 4, 1 (Fall 1994): 7-15.

5. Henceforth I will use "religion" to refer to what the just-mentioned authors have referred to with different names. Religion best expresses the one function all of these differently named attitudes display, namely, being a respected, trusted, and not fully articulate source of fundamental direction in central concerns of human life. The relevant writings of the various authors mentioned are: Richard Rorty, "Private Irony and Liberal Hope" in *CIS*, especially p. 73; Charles Taylor, *Sources of the Self: The Making of the Modern Identity* (Cambridge, MA: Harvard University Press, 1989), p. 1ff. (Cited as Taylor); Michael Polanyi, *Personal Knowledge: Towards a Post-Critical Philosophy* (New York: Harper and Row, 1958). See especially chapter 10; Karl Jaspers, *Der Philosophische Glaube angesichts der Offenbarung* (Munich: Piper, 1962); Paul Tillich, *Systematic Theology* (Digwell Place: James Nisbet, 3 vols., 1953, 1957, 1964); Ludwig Wittgenstein, *On Certainty* (Oxford: Basil Blackwell, 1969).

6. Taylor, especially pp. 53-90.

7. Ibid., pp. 403, 413, 491.

8. The real does not coincide with what can be rationally articulated. Physicians and psycho-therapists are well aware that many of the realities which are really experienced by patients are often notoriously difficult to "put into words."

9. On the function of convictions which condition our judgments (pre-judgments or "prejudices") see Hans-Georg Gadamer, *Truth and Method* (New York: Crossroad, 1984), pp. 235-40.

10. See Bert Musschenga, ed., *Does Religion Matter Morally? A Critical Reappraisal of the Thesis of Morality's Independence from Religion* (Kampen, Holland: Kok Pharos, 1995).

11. Some might observe a decisive difference here, in that the one is said to appeal to revelation in blind trust and the other to a tradition of reason open to public examination. But such an observation hides a reluctance to come to terms with what postmoderns may call the theologic of a logocentric ontologic hidden in the tradition of reason. In that tradition Plato and Aristotle are authoritative founding texts similar to the Bible in Christianity. In addition, appeals to reason are not without trust, while appeals to revelation are not without openness.

12. Religion, morality, and political justice are only some of the many distinct domains of human experience. Other such domains are social, economic, emotional, and cognitive. One author who frequently draws attention to the need for distinguishing these and other domains in discussions of morality is Mark Johnson in *Moral Imagination: Implications of Cognitive Science for Ethics* (Chicago: University of Chicago Press, 1993). His point is that the cognitive frameworks we employ to recognize and adjudicate claims in these domains differ from one to another. A very elaborate theory of such distinct domains, by him called irreducible modes of experience, is found in Herman Dooyeweerd's three-volume *A New Critique of Theoretical Thought* (Amsterdam and Philadelphia: H.J. Paris and the Presbyterian and Reformed Publishing Company, 1953-1959). The theory of modality is found in Part I of Volume II, pp. 3-426.

13. The public and the private are not, in my view, separate and divisible domains, creating a public/private split. Rather, all of our actions, all human relationships, and all of society have public as well as private dimensions. Religion is a private matter, for example, in so far as people adopt a religion as a matter of personal responsibility. But religion is a public concern in so far as building safety and other such matters come into the picture.

14. For wide areas of agreement in our culture, see Taylor, p. 515. Courts that are called

upon to adjudicate disputes about censorship often appeal to "community standards," which are, in the present context, a widely agreed upon space within moral boundaries.

15. Robert Audi and Nicholaus Wolterstorff, *Religion in the Public Square: The Place of Religious Conviction in Political Debate* (Lanham, MD: Rowman & Littlefield, 1997). For two additional titles addressing the same range of issues from a similar perspective, though not necessarily reaching the same conclusions, see James W. Skillen, *Recharging the American Experiment: Principled Pluralism for Genuine Civic Community* (Grand Rapids, MI: Baker Book House, 1994) and Richard Mouw and Sander Griffioen, *Pluralisms and Horizons: An Essay in Christian Public Philosophy* (Grand Rapids, MI: William B. Eerdman's Publishing Company, 1993). (Cited as Mouw and Griffioen.) See also Paul Marshall's "Liberalism, Pluralism and Christianity" in Jonathan Chaplin and Paul Marshall, eds., *Political Theory and Christian Vision* (New York: University Press of America, 1994).

16. (Chicago: University of Chicago Press, 1980). References to this book will be by bracketed page numbers in the body of my text.

17. In "Relations Natural and Unnatural: A Response to John Boswell's Exegesis of Romans 1," *The Journal of Religious Ethics* 14 (1986): 184-215. References to this article will be by bracketed page numbers in the body of my text.

18. Hermeneutics and exegesis might, for the purpose of this essay, be compared to the testimony of expert witnesses at a trial (exegesis) and the interpretation of the total picture by the prosecutor for later presentation to the jury (hermeneutics). *Exegesis* is the skill of *expert analysis of technical issues* in a text, usually issues of the meaning and structure of language, grammar, lexicography, and the like. *Hermeneutics* is the broader *skill of interpreting* the text. Especially in postmodern times, however, the distinction between exegesis and hermeneutics is becoming more and more blurred. It is at least clear that the two influence and depend on one another in important ways. Fortunately, Hays's piece self-consciously places exegetical "matters of fact" within the broader context of a hermeneutic perspective. Hays, therefore, faces rather than avoids the problems of interpretation which arise as soon as we realize that "facts in context" are frequently prone to conflicting readings.

19. *The New Testament and Homosexuality* (Philadelphia: Fortress Press, 1983).

20. Though it seems to matter little to Hays if there are such studies, because to his mind Paul would take them as a confirmation of the reality of deviant behaviour (208-209).

21. Also see his recent *Same-Sex Unions in Premodern Europe* (New York: Villard Books, 1994). On the latter point Boswell seems to have the support of Mark D. Smith in his 1996 article "Ancient Bisexuality and the Interpretation of Romans 1:26-27," *Journal of the American Academy of Religion* 64, 2 (1996): 223-56.

22. See the immediately preceding note. Smith writes that sexual orientation was unknown in antiquity, but that lifelong unions did exist.

23. Hays may have reasons for not taking Boswell seriously, but we are not made aware of those. Smith's 1996 *American Academy of Religion* article also does not settle the issue, for it clearly claims only that Paul's condemnation covers the Kinseyan waterfront, but excludes sexual orientation.

24. Christians accept or have accepted hotly debated diversity on war and peace, usury, divorce and remarriage, celibacy, abortion, women's roles in the church, and many other issues.

25. I will not discuss the legitimacy of reading theodicy in Romans, a complex issue. It is possible that the traditional Reformed view lags behind contemporary readings of all of Romans as concerned with the justice of God's relation to Israel, more than with salvation by grace. In addition there is a difficulty with the very notion of theodicy. Is it rational justification of what appears as divine injustice? Or is it rather a human pleading for the justice of God by way of understanding the gospel in faith? I am concerned merely to

point out that much more than simple exegesis is at stake here.

26. For a more developed account of this see Hendrik Hart, "The Just Shall Live: Reformational Reflections on Public Justice and Racist Attitudes," *Christian Scholar's Review* 16, 3 (1987): especially 268-77. I do not believe that the view of God's justice as mercy needs to be developed in classical Reformed ways, nor do I believe that the "justice as mercy" theme is incompatible with reading God's justice in relation to the question about Israel and the Gentiles.

27. A moral mindset, that is, concentrated on judgment, punishment, and condemnation rather than on mercy. For more on this and on how Paul might have interpreted this in the light of the gospel, see J. Richard Middleton and Brian J. Walsh, *Truth Is Stranger Than It Used to Be: Biblical Faith in a Postmodern Age* (Downer's Grove, IL: InterVarsity Press, 1995), p. 103. (Cited as *Truth Is Stranger*.)

28. See Martin Hengel, *The Pre-Christian Paul* (Philadelphia: Trinity Press International, 1991), p. 143 n. 238; E. P. Sanders, *Paul, The Law, And The Jewish People* (Philadelphia: Fortress Press, 1983) p.131; Alan F. Segal, *Paul The Convert: The Apostolate and Apostacy of Saul the Pharisee* (New Haven, CT: Yale University Press, 1990), p. 259 n. 6.

29. This is evident, for example, in Calvin L. Porter's "Romans 1:18-32: Its Role in the Developing Argument," *New Testament Studies* 40 (1994): 210-28.

30. See various discussions in Brian J. Walsh, Hendrik Hart, and Robert E. Vander Vennen, *An Ethos of Compassion and the Integrity of Creation* (Lanham, MD: University Press of America, 1995).

31. See Richard Longenecker's *New Testament Social Ethics for Today* (Grand Rapids, MI: Eerdmans, 1984) p. 75 n. 6.

32. Not every conceivable agenda is legitimate. Truly unavoidable agendas may be interpreted as necessary dimensions of interpreting sacred texts when in such agendas our confessional commitments behind the surface-meaning of the text urge themselves upon our interpretations. In the context of the church's current debate on homosexuality the idea that only gay-positive readers of the Bible have agendas at best betrays a certain naïveté on the part of gay-negative readers.

33. The reality of this context allowed Isaiah, in chapter 56, to read past the law of Leviticus and Deuteronomy and enabled Jeremiah, in chapter 7, to declare the literal text of the law (in relation to its deeper meaning) as not given by God. In these two texts the prophets call attention to the legitimacy of reading the deeper meaning of a text as having priority over the surface meaning of that text. For an interpretation of the Bible which is both loyal to it as canonical authority and open to being in critical continuity with it, see chapters 5 and 8 in *Truth Is Stranger*.

34. That Chrysostom's ideals were out of synch with his generation's practices also appears from Peter Brown's *The Body and Society: Men, Women, and Sexual Renunciation in Early Christianity* (New York: Columbia University Press, 1988). See especially the chapter "Sexuality and the City: John Chrysostom," pp. 305-22. To use a modern example, official Vatican pronouncements on human sexuality tell us very little about views and practices of Roman Catholic believers in, for example, the United States.

35. (Cambridge: Cambridge University Press, 1979).

36. See note 32, above.

37. In "How Can the Bible Be Authoritative," *Vox Evangelica* (1991): 27-32. For a brief summary see *Truth Is Stranger*, pp. 181-83.

38. In so doing he follows the example of Isaiah 56, who treated unambigious legislation against the sexually deformed and against strangers (Deuteronomy 23:1-8) as slated to disappear in Christ. See also note 32, above.

39. See notes 32 and 37, above, concerning Isaiah 56 in relation to Deuteronomy 21. Also see Romans 14 in relation to the end of Acts 15.

40. John 1:16-18 is an example.
41. On the relation between tolerance and reason see my other essay in this volume.
42. Monogamy does have at least potential moral significance for relational issues such as jealousy, longevity of the relationship, the growth of intimacy, and others.
43. See Taylor's description of wide moral agreement in our culture, p. 515.

6

Rethinking the Family:
Belonging, Respecting, and Connecting

JAMES H. OLTHUIS

The study of the family used to seem to many one of the dullest of endeavours. Now it appears as one of the most provocative and involving.
ANTHONY GIDDENS

All happy families are alike; every unhappy family is unhappy in its own way.
LEO TOLSTOY

All happy families are more or less dissimilar; all unhappy ones are more or less alike.
VLADIMIR NABOKOV

The ache for home lives in all of us, the safe place where we can go and not be questioned.
MAYA ANGELOU

Contemporary sociology of the family and the field of family therapy are both undergoing great upheavals in the nature of theorizing about the family. Reflecting the increased variety in family life and in family forms, and especially concerned with high levels of violence in families,[1] feminist and postmodern theorists are calling for new conceptualizations of the family.

As part of this kind of rethinking, I initiated a three-year research project in search of relevant correlations between family forms and levels of violence in families. Is there an increased propensity to injury and abuse in families organized along the lines of an authoritarian model as compared to those organized along lines of a permissive model? Are rule-oriented families more disposed to harm, or are non-rule-oriented families more likely to incite turbulence? Is the make-up of the family—patriarchal, single-parent, same-sex, ethnically diverse, mixed faith—a significant indicator of potential abuse? Finally, recognizing that families in transition due to immigration, divorce, remarriage, serious accidents, terminal illness, death, economic deprivation, unemployment are high-stress families, is it possible to locate other variables which help explain why the incidence of violence in some of these families is very high while in others it is very low? Concomitantly, are there feasible explanations for situations when violence erupts in families when external stressors are relatively minimal?

To give the study an empirical focus I invited Catharine Crawford to conduct qualitative research interviews with street youth at Yonge Street Mission-Evergreen where she had previously worked. Through the interviews of fifty youth, as well as eight discussion groups with five participants each, she heard from the street youth themselves not only about the reasons they left home, but also about what the street family provides, and what they believed makes families "good enough." Catharine's project[2] dramatically backed up the need to rethink the philosophy of the family. For the results, when viewed in the light of the precipitating questions with which we began, were most ambiguous, inconclusive, and puzzling. According to the interviewees, extreme abuse, both physical and emotional, occurred almost equally in both authoritarian and permissive homes. In most cases both family models—rigid control and chaotic boundaries—existed together in competition with each other and with mother as likely to be authoritarian as father. However, although the great majority (84 per cent) reported experiences of physical violence at home, when asked to name unmet needs, safety placed only sixth out of seven. Socio-economically, more than a third of the street youth reported that their families were middle or upper class.

At the same time, the street youth listed "listening, understanding, and assurance of worth in the family" as the top three unmet needs. According to their report, authentic experiences of belonging and intimacy in their families were very uncommon. Crawford's conclusion is striking: the street youth interviewed were on the street, "not centrally because of rules or bodily violations, but fundamentally because they have not been welcomed, recognized, embraced, blessed, or shown mercy."

As Catharine and I read and reflected on the interviews, it became clear that the common feature in all the situations predisposing to violence and eventually the street was neither authoritarian control nor permissive non-control, but the presence or absence of intimacy, a sense of belonging, respect, and sharing—of good connections and mutuality. Words that I had written more than twenty years ago came to mind.

> The authoritarian and permissive types of families are not only each other's opposites, they are also each other's complements.... What children require most—living along in troth—is missing. Both ways are methods of avoiding intimacy. The importance of this underlying, overarching, lived-in troth for the family cannot be over-exaggerated.

> With intimacy in action families are basically on the right track
> whether or not they tend to be authoritarian or permissive.... The
> answer to the authoritarian-permissive dilemma is not just carefully
> balancing the two family styles, but in a third alternative.... The family
> is a we-situation in which parents and children develop and grow into
> full persons through open and mutual sharing.[3]

At that moment, the seeds of this paper were planted: it is the quality of the relational interactions in the family that fosters genuine intimacy or generates violence. Our research, we concluded, was suggesting a move from a traditional functional approach to family dynamics to one based on a relational model of mutuality in troth—mutual commitment, mutual recognition, mutual trust. It is on this basis that I attempt in this essay to reframe a relational model of family and family therapy in which the development of healthy (and unhealthy) families relates, fundamentally and most directly, not to traditional concerns about roles, functions, and types, but to the degree of mutuality in troth established (or not established) between parents and children. Describing the core focus of the family as trothful relating contrasts with the typical functionalist structural concern in terms of rules, control, and hierarchy. However, the emphasis on quality of relation and connection fits very well with the concerns of the feminist theorists of the Stone Center at Wellesley College in their ongoing development of a new relational model of growth and development.[4]

To heighten the awareness of what a relational troth perspective involves in understanding both the nature of family dynamics and irruptions of domestic violence, it is important to first attend to traditional, modernist sociological theories of the family and family therapy.

"STANDARD THEORY OF THE FAMILY"

In North America, sociologists such as Talcott Parsons and William Goode developed in the fifties and sixties the "standard theory of the family"[5] in which the family is an adaptive unit mediating the needs of individual and society. Since the family's failure to fulfill its social functions (reproduction, maintenance, social placement, and socialization) "means that the goals of the larger society may not be attained effectively,"[6] smooth functioning of the families is vital for success of society. For Parsons the "isolated nuclear family" (with husband/father as "instrumental leader" and wife/mother as "expressive leader") is the only family type that does not conflict with the demands of an industrial economy. Such families—termed "private domestic zones"—would create (male) breadwinners and incubate good workers and good consumers for the economy of the marketplace. In what has become known as the liberal ethos in which the individual is the primary unit of social experience, the (private, individualized) family and the (public, contractarian) market were symbiotically intertwined—supposedly for the good of both.

As is becoming increasingly clear, it is families and especially children that have suffered most grievously when the family is interpreted as a "control" unit in the quest of economic imperatives. For this places the focus on "efficiency," "use," and "function" (rather than on committed caring and belonging), and in the process leaves family well-being to the vagaries of the individualistic market. "A society that privatizes responsibility for the well-being of children treats families as social adversaries in a competition for the polarized rewards of a market society."[7]   The result has been the wrong kind of attention to children and the breakdown of the family with which we are currently struggling.

Although Salvador Minuchin and other major family therapists did not buy into Parsons's own sexist views on the division of labour, their basic categories of "structure" and "functions" involving "contracting"and "role negotiations" come from Parsons's structural functionalism.[8]   Since, for example, family problems are for Minuchin indications of imbalance in family organization, structural family therapy focuses on clarity of boundaries and restoring hierarchy. The family-systems approach in which the family is a social system of interacting parts has become, after the Second World War, the "most successful expression of the standard sociological theory."[9]

In systems theory healthy families maintain both boundaries and hierarchical control. Broderick and Smith understand the structure of the family as a hierarchy of control involving family rules, goals, and policies.[10]   The maintenance of control requires that the family have clear boundaries separating it from its environment, in a scheme wherein extremely closed and extremely open systems are conceived as unhealthy. Thus, sexual abuse can be seen as a typical result of a very closed, rigid system which develops the rule that all needs are to be met within the family.[11]   In this theory, unduly open family models are thought to give rise to a variety of other pathologies.

In tension with theories concerned to maintain family stability are the so-called conflict theories with their focus on individual identity development. Exchange theory (perhaps the most individualistic of social theories) sees individuals engaging in interaction only when beneficial.[12]   On this model, the family becomes a venue for the exchange of goods and services. On the one side, there are familistic ideologies emphasizing control, and on the other side ideologies stressing individual freedom and choice.

In the modern West these contrasting theories dialectically relate, usually in terms of the social contract model pioneered by Hobbes, Locke, Rousseau, and Kant. On this view individuals who are free and independent agree to form mutually advantageous societies to secure their fundamental rights. Consent creates social bonds which are morally legitimate. Although the family has never quite fit into this model—it is a kind of moral anomaly: a non-voluntary social unit—it has nevertheless by and large been dealt with in terms of this social contract model. The significant factor in all of this is that the family is seen fundamentally as a necessary control unit, with its members intrinsically resisting such control.

In modern family therapy, the dialectic manifests itself in the dominant role of the separation/individuation theme. Instead of seeing the family as a cradle for identity formation from which there is no need to separate/individuate (to be a self is to be a connected self) as in a relational model, the family is set up as a necessary regime of control from which, since it restricts and represses, one must, qua individual, separate oneself.

When this polar dialectic is identified, it becomes clear that the permissive (non-rule) model in its anti-authoritarianism lives off the patriarchal model without fundamentally providing an alternative. Operative in both models are power-over metaphors which oscillate between control (domination) and freedom-from-control (do-as-you-like). In both, the we-situation of mutual intimacy, interaction, and support—the matrix which allows the deep needs of the children to be met—is missing.

While the control motif is obvious in so-called authoritarian families, the children in such families are often left to their own devices in all areas not covered by the rules. Similarly, while the freedom-from motif marks permissive families, often the do-as-you-will ethos is a veneer covering over powerful parental wishes and demands. Problematic in both kinds of situations is the manipulative power games which act to erode the support and unconditional love and belonging needed to develop a grounded sense of self-identity. When a child grows up in a context where pleasing mom and dad is the central concern, the child is not given the respect and affirming space needed to find his/her legs, make mistakes, and become response-able as well as responsible. In reaction, such children easily develop a built-in antipathy to authority. Likewise, when a child grows up in a context in which anything goes, the child may feel abandoned to his/her own devices, effectively robbed of the support and guidance needed to develop enough self-esteem to make a difference in the world. In reaction, such children often seek solace in authoritarian causes to escape the isolation and insecurity of being "free."

In both scenarios, however—despite their obvious differences—at a deeper level children are often left feeling not respected, without honour, insecure and unsupported in becoming persons with a sense of entitlement and agency, persons at-home-with themselves able to give of self and internally connect with others. Sociologists of the family, thus, have largely assumed a rule-governed (or non-rule-governed) perspective focussing on functions, roles, and types, and see the family as a control unit for the purposes of enculturation. Concomitantly, in family therapy parental roles have been labelled "distant," "peripherally involved," "engulfing," "invasive," "depressed," and the dysfunctionality of the families has been typed as "alcoholic," "schizophrenic," "enmeshed," "codependent," etc.   Children, in such models, typically "triangulate," and have difficulty in "differentiating."

I was adopted at nine months to the only parents I have ever had. I always remember my mother being really outgoing but now she keeps to herself and is dealing with a number of health problems. My parents split up when I was seven years old. As far as I can tell, they broke up over him always being sick and worn out. They had a very hip, egalitarian marriage—they talked things out together and were tender to each other. I was proud of how they got along. Dad died when I was eight. He was a stern but well-tempered man who ran a busy family business. I grew up around a lot of money. I believe he was loving, but just not an affectionate man. My sisters hated me for his death—"It's all his fault" they would say.

There was trouble with my sisters from the beginning. I was the boy, the youngest, was always getting into trouble, and I think this made them intensely jealous. I was a strange child—weird and hyper and I couldn't focus. While my sisters were filled with resentment about my "uniqueness," my parents never turned off the welcome: I was their precious, special adopted one. Do I feel that I belonged there? To be honest, my special status outcasted me.

As I child I believe I was disciplined fairly, but sometimes maybe I got off too easy. When I was about twelve or thirteen there was a lot of pressure to succeed but then they gave up on the idea of me succeeding. At first they used to say, "It doesn't matter what you do, you'll be successful," but I proved that they could actually fall out of love with me. If I had a problem with my parents they'd just say "I don't know, Doug," maybe because I spoke unclearly out of not wanting to hurt them emotionally.

Even when my sisters would tease me saying, "You're just the pet Mom and Dad brought in," I couldn't tell my parents—I didn't want to insult them. You see, my parents kind of left the growing up to me, for better and for worse I guess. They trusted my decisions to be level-headed. I was given a lot of leeway and now I'm too open with others. My moods are diverse. I think I have psychological trouble and I'm very flirtatious. I was given my first book on sex written by Shere Hite when I was eleven. There were no limits to anything in my family— no taboos. Except maybe to say that I wondered if I belonged there.

I first came to the streets at fourteen. I was asked to leave home due to my drinking problem. I have been on and off for eight years and the longest I've had an apartment is two months. Now the tables have turned with my one sister and she wants all the advice from me since I've survived the streets. The streets are still my family though.

What I notice as missing from my childhood is that I'm not comfortable with my feelings and how to relate to people. When I was a kid I loved my folks by keeping the hard stuff back. I was concerned that I was too much for them. They needed to understand me better. I'm more complex than they know.[13]

POSTMODERN CRITIQUE

In the mid-seventies, family sociology with its modernist paradigm of rational order, normality, universality, ahistoricity, and uniformity was hit by the postmodernist attention to disorder, fragmentation, individuality, historicity, and plurality—and the terrain has never been the same since. The hitherto standard assumption of "the family" as a universal institution with a universal core has been challenged. The standard model is considered to be only one family form, an ideological construct called patriarchy. The result of the discussion is exemplified in Canada, for example, by the publications of The Vanier Institute of the Family which, since 1981, has been calling for acknowledgement of multiple constellations of family life.

Thus, the postmodern sociologist Margrit Eichler pleads for a multi-dimensional model of family interaction in which the convergence or correlation of activities in a monolithic approach such as emotional involvement, procreation, socialization and economic support is no longer assumed.[14] High interaction in one area, i.e., procreation, may be accompanied by low interaction in another, i.e., socialization. To make clear the fluid boundaries of contemporary families, she—tongue-in-cheek—defines the family: "A family is a social group which may or may not include adults of both sexes, may or may not include one or more children, who may or may not have born in their wedlock."[15] Similarly, Norman Denzin describes a new type of family in the postmodern period: "It is a single-parent family, headed by a teenage mother, who may be drawn to drug abuse and alcoholism. She and her children live in a household that is prone to be violent."[16]

Theorists have begun to "deconstruct" the concept of the family itself by insisting that sex/gender structures underlying the family receive focussed attention. Feminist theory critiques family system approaches (I think rightly) for their neglect of "differences in power, resources, needs and interests among family members,"[17] particularly women and children, and for developing a model in which there are no agents or originating causes but only the infinite recursive connections of feedback loops. Luepnitz expresses concern that systems theory values "the continued functioning of the whole as opposed to emphasizing the conflicting interests of the constituent parts."[18] In a similar vein, Virginia Goldner is concerned that explaining wife beating in terms of feedback loops may be a sophisticated way of blaming the victim.[19] That is to say, we cannot ignore the reality that the commitment of wives to stay in abusive situations is not simply a matter of internal systemic interactions, but is aided and abetted by social constructions regarding the nature of marriage, the place of women, and, historically, the relative legitimacy of violence in culture at large.[20]

In other words, the postmodern emphasis on alterity and multiplicity has opened up family studies not only to the diversity and variance of family forms, but to explorations of how, in the "standard theory of the family," the family became a pawn in the economic game of market relations, often at the cost of the health of all family members, in particular women, children—and, not to be forgotten, grandparents and single adults. The important theoretical question now is: with all the diversity and variation, what does it mean to talk of a family and of healthy families? Is there anything non-variable, anything distinctive— or, is there any "core"—to families?

AN INTERSUBJECTIVE RELATIONAL MODEL

In this context I want to suggest that focussing, not on family function, role, or type, but on the *quality of relationship*—the presence or lack of intimate connecting—provides a new angle of approach. Instead of seeing people as free and independent individuals who begrudgingly acknowledge each other's equality in order to arrange a just social contract, we begin with human interconnectedness (intersubjectivity). To be(come) human is to be in connection with self, other selves, creation, and God. This impetus to connection is the eros of love. To be born is to be gifted with love (I was loved, therefore I am) and to be called to love (I love, therefore I am).

In this view, equality is not presupposed, nor is impartiality privileged, what is central, rather, is differences among all of the creatures with which our lives our inextricably interwoven. Difference (with its inequalities) is the central moral reality that we must honour, but without breaking community. Indeed, genuine community begins with the acknowledgement of difference. This is in contrast to the tenets of modernity in which sameness equals equality equals morality, and inequality equals difference equals immorality. Whereas modernism begins with persons as isolated, autonomous, self-interested, Cartesian egos or Leibnizian monads called to compete with others and control nature, a relational view begins with selves-in-relation, gifted and called to love and care for each other and creation in responsibility. In contrast to control models that hallow power-over and freedom-from in an attempt to mediate individual freedom and group control, a relational approach advocates mutuality models that cherish power-with and freedom-to in which individual identity and empowerment is generated, nourished, and enriched in connection.

Indications that attention to intimacy and belonging may help us rethink the philosophy of the family are emerging in contemporary postmodern research. Through the study of the practical use of the term in various cultures, David Cheal advocates the use of the term "family" as broadly applicable to people involved in "enduring intimate relations."[21] Froma Walsh highlights Arlene

Skolnick's description of the family as "a place of enduring bonds and fragile relationships, of the deepest love and the most intractable conflicts, of the most intense passions and the routine tedium of everyday life."[22] In surveying the major clinical and research-based models of the family, Walsh concludes that "connectedness and commitment of members as a caring, mutually supportive relationship unit ('we are family')"[23] is one key indication of healthy family functioning.

At the same time, attention to diversity, historicity, and gender concerns is leading feminist family therapists to argue (again I think rightly) that speaking of "families' pain, darkness, and pleasure in terms of 'functional effectiveness' and 'dysfunction' dehumanizes our work."[24] Luepnitz complains: "Families were discussed in terms of organization and hierarchy, not in terms of intimacy."[25] In reaction, she strives for a new language in psychotherapy that speaks "not of 'dyads,' 'executives,' and 'dysfunction,' but of mothers and fathers, of history, memory, pain and desire."[26]

Developing a new language of intimacy along these lines will help, I am suggesting, not only in rethinking the idea of family health, but also with re-visioning the flourishing of children as an intergenerational affair with families as agents of cultural transmission and commitment.

FAMILY: BELONGING-TO AND BEING-WITH

Since it is in a family that children are brought into the world, nursed, and loved into life, it is a place of particular vulnerability and intimacy. Since it is in the family that we first learn (or fail to learn) our most deeply ingrained lessons about love and care, belonging-to and being-with, connection and disconnection, sacrifice and promise, violence and forgiveness, any model that emphasizes relationships needs to give pride of place to families and their flourishing. God gives us the family as a special place of unconditional belonging, mutual caring, and deep sharing. Being cared for within the family, we experience belonging, trust, empowerment, connection—and learn to be at ease in the world. It is in the family that compassion begins to root in our souls.

On the other hand, when we do not experience good enough caring, we feel lost in the world, develop mistrust, disempowerment and disconnection—and learn to be at dis-ease in the world. The seeds of violence—isolation, inadequacy, fear, and anger—rather than compassion begin to germinate in our souls. When parents—grandparents, aunts and uncles, friends, childcare workers, teachers, all caregivers—employ their power with deep respect for a child's dignity and integrity (power-with as opposed to power-over), the child develops self-esteem and a healthy sense of self. Here a haven of troth, trust, and mutuality takes shape in which openness is encouraged and acceptance is guaranteed, where children are valued for who they are rather than what they do. It is in such holding environs of safety, respect, and belonging that children are empowered not only to be themselves, but to be themselves-in-relation to others.

Troth nurturance bespeaks a certain kind of relationship: "a relationship that entails affection and love, that is based on cooperation as opposed to competition, that is enduring rather than temporary, that is non-contingent rather than contingent upon performance, and that is governed by feeling and morality instead of law and contract."[27] According to a relational model, the optimal conditions for healthy development occur in families which create and sustain a high degree of mutuality-in-troth between parents as well as between parents and children. It is the dynamic of recognition, respect, and connection —mutuality—that engenders a sense of self-confidence, enhances the ability to bond, and promotes harmonious relations.

Moreover, envisioning families as fundamentally grounded in relations of troth—an intergenerational base community of trust, nurturance, and mutual honour among grandparents, parents, and children—allows such betrothed relations to show up in various configurations without, on the one hand, disfiguring and losing the family, and on the other hand, without unrealistically and unhistorically restricting a family to one ideal family type. Focussing on relationships and intimacy rather than on organization and role also opens up conceptual space to treat directly the matters of parental (un)availability, trust/betrayal, emotional presence/absence, esteem/shame, privacy/secrecy, empowerment/helplessness—issues essential in any discussion of family dynamics and domestic violence.

Violence in the family violates bodily integrity, shattering the developing core self-structure of the children, subverting and paralyzing the ability to bond with others, replacing it with intense fear, mistrust, and a deep sense of powerlessness. Thereafter, a sense of disconnection, of alienation, permeates every relationship, including the child's relationship to self. Disconnection rather than connection (with self, others, creation, and God) becomes the pervasive reality. And it is isolation which deepens feelings of helplessness and powerlessness, which are the very breeding grounds for more violence whether motivated by need for compensation, denial, or escape.

> Between the ages of four months and eight years I was in four different foster homes. My mom couldn't cope when my dad cheated on her and she wasn't able to take me back until I was eleven. I had to be removed anyway from the last foster family due to sexual abuse. My dad died of an overdose during that time but when he'd get visitation with me he'd tell me he loved me and would do anything for me. He'd hold me and tell me I was his little girl. I felt good with him.
>
> My mom resented me and despised me, would push me aside, call me dirty names and say "I wish I didn't have you." We didn't have

much when we were growing up (I was always filthy) and Mom was always looking for money to spend on booze. When I came back to live with her she found that I could be useful if I slept with her boyfriends for money. She didn't care anyway when I said I had been raped the year before by someone on our street. The prostitution lasted five years, and when I got pregnant she told me to get an abortion. I took off for the streets then because I was tired of being blamed for dad's death and of not being wanted.

Saying what I felt made my mom cry and she said she didn't want to hear it. When she tried to commit suicide I took her pills away. She would give me the time of day when I needed advice about boyfriends, and then when my daughter was born she brought a rattle. But Mom just couldn't be there for me when I needed it. It was like she didn't want me alive. Even though she rejects me, I try to say that I love her, but I have big doubts. I wish I could be with my father. He wouldn't hurt or beat me.

Now I've been on and off the streets for six years—I just keep coming back. Sure there are abusive relationships here but it's the same at home. The big reason I'm on the street is because I was exploited and unloved. Even now when I loan my mom money she won't pay me back. I try, but she won't acknowledge me and has no respect for who I am.

RELATIONAL DISCONNECTION

Most everyone will agree that not-good-enough parenting is the cradle of violence. However, reconceptualizing the problem of violence as fundamentally a problem of relational disconnection has yet to receive the attention it deserves in family therapy, and especially in family studies. I am suggesting that the more usual explanations for violence in the family, although they no doubt delineate contributing factors, need to be reframed within a focus on the relational dynamics of connection and disconnection.

Social scientific studies of violence in the family point to a multiplicity of interacting preconditions to explain violence: individual characterology and genetic makeup, family structure (microsystems), immediate family environments such as families of origin, jobs, friends, small communities (exosystems), and the larger macrosystems of cultural beliefs and attitudes.

There is little doubt that characterological shortcomings contribute to family violence. But since not everyone suffering from certain character deficits or defects engages in physical and sexual violence, much more needs be said. Perpetrators are not limited to a particular character type. Even if it were possible to locate a gene (or genes) predisposing certain persons to violence (which in my view is most implausible!) we would still need to demonstrate that this predisposition in itself causes violent behaviour. Again, although it is true that psychological stress is often a contributing factor, it is highly unlikely that it by itself causes violence. If stress causes violence, we would, for example, also expect a high incidence of violence in other situations of extreme stress, such as the workplace. That, however, is not the case. Alcohol, drug abuse, and poverty are also considered explanations for violent behaviour. While alcohol, drugs, and poverty are often connected with incidents of violence, it is not at all clear that they are the causes. People just as often drink or smoke up to excuse the behaviour or to numb themselves to it. And many people who are addicted or who are poor do not perpetrate any kind of physical violence.

It is also regrettably true that the use of violence has too often been encouraged in the past by the widespread assumption in society that physical force, or at least the threat of such force, is a legitimate and acceptable way to control behaviour, maintain authority, and solve disagreements. When this is combined with socialization practices in which masculinity bespeaks dominance, physical power, and prowess while femininity is equated with submission, powerlessness, and helplessness, it becomes clearer not only why women and children are most often the victims of abuse, but also why such violence in families, neither recent nor rare, has been implicitly condoned or kept in the shadows for so long. It also becomes exceedingly clear that "[t]he silence on men's violence must be permanently broken."[28]

However, pointing to hierarchical structure as if it is the dominant and sufficient condition for violence overlooks the fact that, historically as well as presently, there were/are countless hierarchically ordered male-dominated families in which violence, at least physical or sexual violence, did/does not take place. In other words, hierarchy as such—as flawed as it is—does not necessarily lead to violence. There must be something more.

That something more comes into focus in terms of what Alice Miller has called "poisonous pedagogy," which "crushes spontaneous feelings,"[29] degrading and humiliating children. When spontaneous feelings are forbidden and unexpressed, especially anger, they do not disappear, but, over time, are transmuted, hardening into a hatred against self or others, generating an intense drive for release and discharge. This emotional abuse—John Bradshaw aptly calls it "soul-murder"[30]—often erupts into outright physical and sexual violence when it is re-enacted in a vicious cycle of violence as these children grow older and become adults, and look for victims of their own. The problem of violence is the problem of "the lost world of feelings." Covered over, denied, unowned, unworked-through feelings are the seeds which erupt into the weeds of violence.

The emotional havoc done to all through the deprivation of feelings is colossal. In our culture, the toll exacted on men has been particularly damaging because it is little boys, more than little girls, who were/are taught to keep their true feelings under wraps ("big boys don't cry"). Socialized by "the media, the military, male peer groups, sport, and pornography,"[31] men were/are taught that a successful man is independent, externally oriented, competitive, brazen, and in control. Faced with this impossible image of macho masculinity, suffocating in an emotional vacuum, deprived of human tears, many men lash out violently at women and children to quash their feelings of being hopeless and powerless. "After listening to the stories of countless women in shelters, and after sitting in on several treatment groups for violent men," Joy M. K. Bussert testifies, "*I can only conclude that battering—at least in part—is a substitute for tears.*"[32]

RESPECT: BEING SEEN AND HEARD

A reframing of our understanding of violence in the family begins with a recognition of the human need to be seen and heard as unique persons. When, as an infant, I see you seeing me in an affirming (or non-affirming) way, I begin to see myself in affirming (or non-affirming) ways. My self begins to fill and stretch, my spirit begins to hum, I come alive as a person, at-home-with myself —I become. If I make a difference or have an impact on you, I experience a profound sense of empowerment. If I am able to share my feelings, including my painful ones, and you receive me not defensively, not evasively, not in attack mode, but kindly and tenderly, I develop a sense of empathy and connection with both myself and with you.

When, however, I do not experience being seen and heard as the person I am, I begin to feel not-at-home, empty, powerless, worthless, shamed, fearful. When I feel that I make no difference, when I am hurt, fearful, and lonely, and when I do not feel free to share my feelings of anger and pain, I am devastated, beside myself, and my heart closes. "No one sees me." "No one hears me." "No one likes me." "No one shares with me." I must be "invisible," "stupid," "bad," "worthless." Deep feelings of resentment and anger begin to burrow deep in my soul. It is too much, the wounding is intolerable, I can only run. Attempting to dull the pain, I abandon myself.

As the inner self is forced into hiding, it simultaneously constructs an adaptive sense of self that covers over the hurt, an armour to shield against further wounding. I try to motor on—often with a big smile on the out-side—and cover over the aching emptiness and the gnawing fear. I compensate: maybe becoming what I intuit my caregivers want me to be, e.g., a "pleaser" (the family hero); perhaps posturing as "indifferent" (the family clown); possibly entrenching as a "resister" (the family scapegoat).[33] In the process I become disassociated, emotionally numb, spiritually vacant. Control—protection against pain and fear—becomes the be-all and end-all of life.

Often the control turns into an obsession or compulsion to hold down or cordon off the pain of my heart. Such control builds up the pressure, and I seek release, either to numb myself further to the pain that I can never quite keep down, or to give a sense of feeling to a numbed life. Here we have the cycle of addiction—whether to work, causes, superficial relationships, substances, or distracting obsessions and compulsions—which acts to divert me from the reality that my inner self is imprisoned, missing in action. These illusions of connection, simulations of presence, veil inner disconnection and absence.

Many of us may cover over the pain and powerlessness with feelings of grandiosity or escape in indifferent, aggressive, or paranoid behaviour. We become walking time bombs of hate, or smouldering cauldrons, nursing our resentments. In either case, denied or nursed, anger often breaks out in violence. According to the Hincks Centre for Children's Mental Health 71 per cent of children called violent at age six turn into "violent adults."

When we discover that our parents are not emotionally available to us, we soon learn to repress our feelings to avoid the despair of not being met, or the humiliation at having our feelings discredited or taken away. We get the message strong and clear: emotions are dangerous, do not trust them, they only get you into trouble. Our best strategy is to close the doors on our inner life and pretend it does not exist. We may fall into silence. And our spirit begins to die little by little. For once we have lost touch with our feelings, we begin to lose touch with our inner self. If we cannot have our feelings, if our thoughts do not count, if our needs do not matter, then we must not matter. Something must be wrong with us. If our parents do not respect us, we must be unworthy of respect. If we feel left out of the family, we must be odd, missing something, flawed. This is internalized shame.

In other families mom and dad are absent one moment and present the next. That too takes a big emotional toll on children for they never know if the horizon is safe for them to be themselves. The emotional anxiety of the parents terrorizes the children. Did I upset Mom? What did I do wrong? Is it safe now? Can I feel good today? Or is better to hide my feelings and pretend? Confusion creeps in like a fog. Often children begin to feel unconsciously and sometimes consciously that they need to take care of the parents or meet their every need. There is a secret trap in this for children, for when children begin to take up and fulfill the parental role, they learn to relate to others in a certain way, but since their heart's desire to be what they are, children, and their entitlement to care remains unmet, their connections to others are superficial or only apparent. Children learn very early—too early—in these situations to put aside their own needs and to find themselves in doing for others. But since they are not really emotionally able to handle parental responsibilities, these responsibilities begin to weigh as unwelcome but unavoidable burdens. The usual result is a numbing of feelings towards others and towards self, a flight from self in order to maintain the semblance of a life. Some children may gain their identity as super-responsible, as ten year olds going on sixty. Since underneath they feel alone, insecure, overwhelmed, and frightened, when complimented for their maturity, they begin to feel themselves as frauds—and their internal isolation deepens. Other children, sensing the weight of such burdens, will seek their identity in rebellion, for in that way they get at least some attention. In other situations, when the relationship between parents is emotionally shallow or non-existent, a parent may develop a special relationship of intimacy in which the child becomes the "lover."

It is in the process of genuine connection with others that children learn to connect authentically with themselves, becoming aware of their own needs, their gifts, and their limits. Without this mutual process a person struggles for the rest of his/her life to have a proper sense of one's own boundaries, one's own needs, and one's own gifts. Not feeling cared for, we do not learn how to care for others. Not feeling heard by others, we cannot really hear others. In attempting to become insensitive to my own pain, I simultaneously desensitize myself to the pain of others. The need to keep emotional distance from our own sufferings does not allow us to be emotionally open and present to the sufferings of others.

On the other hand, openness to feelings opens the space for both myself and others to develop mutual empathy, respect and esteem. If a young child suffering hurt is able to give voice to the pain and anger, and if that child feels received and heard in the pain, the child develops the ability to integrate anger into life without denial or without getting lost in it. When the child experiences openness from the parents—that is, when the parents do not defensively see the child as a challenge or a threat and are emotionally available—the child feels free to express her/his deepest feelings unmonitored. When feelings can be expressed and are received, the walls of defensive silence are broken and the curtains of separation are breached—belonging happens, connections form, mutuality develops. In this context, it is worth noting that recent research points to "relational variables" (close bond with caregiver, few prolonged absences from primary caregiver in first year of life, positive attention from family members) as the "major factors contributing to resiliency in children growing up in families characterized by poverty, marital discord, desertion, divorce, parental alcoholism, and mental illness."[34]

"A person who can understand and integrate his anger as part of himself will not become violent."[35] Or, as I like to put it: if we do not own our anger, our anger will own us—sooner or later. Especially difficult circumstances, stresses and transitions of whatever kind—all the factors customarily fingered as the causes of violence—often become the occasions for, or triggers of, the violence. Thus, it is not atypical for an adolescent to be suddenly surprised and troubled by disquieting feelings that they have held down for most of their lives. If there is nowhere for the teenager to turn, drugs can serve to quiet the turmoil and the diversion of violence can serve as a shortcut to respect.

Similarly, when adolescents and adults out of touch with their feelings find themselves in intimate situations calling for vulnerability, they are internally confused, terrified—at loose ends, powerless. To regain the missing sense of pride, power, and respect, they will sometimes extract it from someone weaker through intimidation, and often physical or sexual violence. Likewise, having children evokes in parents their own unmet needs which, if they are not worked through, incites them to exploit their children in order to have these needs satisfied. When children resist, parents, often under the guise of parental authority, will force compliance through emotional (if not physical) manipulation (more often boys) and sexual abuse (more often girls). In the process parents re-enact their own trauma, projecting it onto their children. The victim has become persecutor, in turn setting the stage for the creation of a persecutor in the next generation. "The way we were treated as small children is the way we treat ourselves the rest of our lives" and the way we treat others.[36] The sins of the parents are passed on unto the third and fourth generation—unless.... Unless we work to break the cycle—in the grace of God who "shows mercy unto thousands of them that love God" (Deut. 5:9,10), "to a thousand generations" (Deut. 7:9).

DENIAL AND SECRECY

Denial and secrecy are two common ways in which families undermine intimacy. It is not that secrets in and of themselves are such a serious problem. We all have secrets, and every family has its share. The problem comes when a pall of secrecy is cast over some crucial events or persons in the family history—with its concomitant pretending that there is no secret. Family members often collude in avoiding facing reality and take flight in denial. When children, for example, experience the reality of alcoholism or abuse, and family life goes on as if nothing out of the ordinary is happening, they begin to accept it as normal, perhaps see it as punishment for their wickedness—or learn not to see it at all. Or a daughter may sense that something important is going on or has gone on, but is stonewalled, sidetracked, teased, or shamed every time she voices her intuition. In such instances, the family member experiences isolation and dis-ease in the very community designed for belonging and ease. At the same time, the holders of the secret are themselves isolated.

Families that have experienced the tragic loss of a loved one may also collude with each other to avoid talking about it in order to protect each other from pain and agony. However, in so doing the family members are deprived of opportunities to mourn, grieve the loss, and reclaim their lives. Thus, although family silence can serve a variety of functions, when family members are not able to fully acknowledge what they see, hear, and feel, there is a short-circuiting of the relational interaction which is essential to a deepened connection with others and increased sense of esteem for self. Indeed, family secrecy isolates members not only from each other, but from the larger world. They then lack the empowerment and support necessary to go out into the world with a sense of confidence. The result is a facade of connections covering over a serious impairment in the ability to bond with others.

From a relational perspective, such denials are uttered and conspiracies entered and maintained so that on some level—albeit superficial and illusory—a family connection can survive. This is of extreme significance, for it helps explain the exceptional strength of such bonds of secrecy. Often family members years later, even as they discover the healing relief of divulging the secret, are surprised by the deep feelings of betrayal of the family that well up within them. Often they need to battle the fear that their betrayal will destroy the family, and that they will be left without a family. Even those who choose to cut off all connection with their families need to go through a deep sense of mourning. Or they will take their family scripts and worries with them, and likely will either be too burdened to have the energy for healthy relations, or too involved in relationships which play out the family script.

The fact that people will do almost anything to stay in connection despite everything is perhaps best illustrated in people who develop multiple personalities. In that way, they creatively split off horrific aspects or facets of their experience and yet maintain, via distinct personalities, some level of interpersonal connection. A "pleasing" personality can develop typically some kind of life in more or less complete isolation from a "rebellious" one.

> I lived with my birth parents all my life—until I ran at fifteen. My relatives were involved in my "upbringing," you could say from when I was six till I left home. My dad was mainly an angry alcoholic, in and out of my life. Sometimes he drove truck for a living. My mom had a rough life and did not show her emotions, except anger through violence. She worked at a bank.
>
> I'm the youngest of four kids and all my older siblings would hit me when I was young. Mom said we were all mistakes and that she was disappointed I survived. I somehow never got taken by the CAS [Children's Aid Society], but my one sister did and she did really well there. A foster home would have been ideal! Other brothers and sisters went to live with relatives but I was never sent anywhere. I was the quiet one who stayed and watched all the violence happen. When I ran, it was to get away from the arguing and the violence. My parents would always try to make it up to me with toys and money but I would always give my stuff away to the welfare kids on my street. Now I'm on welfare and the street is my home. I grew up in a highrise only a stone's throw from downtown...only a stone's throw to a different life.
>
> Dad was hardly ever in the home, and if he was, generally, he would be drinking and throw us out in the traffic to play. I was always good but they'd still say if I do not do what I'm told I'll get the stick, or "wait till your father is home" and I'd get beaten. I made my own rules and I knew what to do to keep myself out of trouble. But if I had

a good time at something I'd get yelled at too. I kept to myself, fed myself, did my chores, and I would hear from them, "You're going to end up sleeping in the gutter and doing nothing all your life." I did not start to get into trouble or do drugs till I hit the streets, but now I'm worried that what they said about me is true.

The worst was being threatened about telling what they did to me. My aunts used me sexually and my uncle told me when I was little they'd leave me hanging over the stairwell overnight if I ever told. If you ask me today I'd still probably say sex is the way to show closeness. They'd torture me sometimes to show me they were serious, like, by making me hold a phonebook over my head for three hours. There was also everyday physical abuse from my mom, but everything fell apart after Dad committed suicide when I was twelve. The last time after Dad beat me up he killed himself in front of me screaming, "I'm sorry" and "I cannot handle this." Things got so much worse after that because they say I drove him to it.

As a kid I felt insecure when I'd be locked in the closet. Now when I sit in my little corner of the rooming house I feel safe. My family hurt me and there was no understanding, but I'm happy the way I am. I can give to other people and they can't take that away from me.

CREATING HEALTHY FAMILIES

Violence, rather than compassion, begins to take root in any of us when we do not feel embraced, respected, and connected in our families of origin. The above stories of Doug, Maggie, and Tan—drenched in betrayal, abandonment, disenfranchisement, unheard pleas, broken bodies, and abused spirits—give voice to deep pain and raise a haunting cry: What can we do to make our families healthier, safer, and more nourishing?

As the importance of that daunting question is more and more becoming central in our public consciousness, I end this essay by suggesting three guidelines for the shaping of public policy, and by describing the kind of initiatives which need to be instigated in every community.

1.   Family flourishing needs to be recognized more clearly as the pre-eminent public concern that it is, not only in remedial programs, but especially in proactive, preventive programming.

Benefit: Only when the emphasis is on prevention is there the realistic possibility of lessening violence in families, certainly in the long run. Because of the stark realities of family violence, governments are tempted to enact policies which are largely or exclusively remedial in nature. However, since violence results from feelings of alienation, powerlessness, and isolation, as important and necessary as remedial measures are, prevention-focussed programs of family and community education and support are indispensable and equally imperative. Good shelter, good food, good bonding, good feelings (including clean anger)—the key ingredients in a healthy family—are the major antidotes to violence. Advocacy for, and promotion of, caring, committed, and emotionally healthy families needs to be a top legislative priority.

2.   Policies need to recognize the uniqueness of the family as a particular troth-bonded group for belonging, caring and commitment which is adaptable for various socializing purposes rather than merely an aggregate of individuals contracted for certain variable functions.

   Benefit: When the focus on the family is on the quality of its relational processes rather than on form or function, the promotion and protection of family health can be fully supported even as a diversity of family forms can be fully honoured. With this emphasis on the quality of relational process, it also becomes clear that the so-called nuclear family is not necessarily any healthier than blended families or single-parent or same-sex partnerships—nor any worse. It all depends on the quality of the life together. Thus, the fact that the family as an institution is undergoing diversification and change in no way means that the family is dying.
   This is of strategic importance because it is the fear of the loss of the family that fuels conservative resistance to diversification under the banner of "family values." Instead of nostalgia for the privatized nuclear family which was always more a myth than reality, a better pro-family policy would be a support of efforts that support all families—irrespective of form or kind—as places of enduring belonging.

3.   Schools, churches, other social agencies, and cultural organizations need to focus more effort on the development—in concert with governments and perhaps at the invitation of government—of a coordinated multi-programmed "family support network" for the explicit purpose of fostering good parenting and healthy emotional development. Although it has the ring of a cliché, its truth remains unchallenged: a society can only be as healthy as its families. When anyone—regardless of age, sex, or race—is at risk in our society, we are all at risk.

   Benefit: If the role and influence of intermediate institutions—religious, cultural, voluntary, corporate, etc.—was dramatically increased through co-ordination of their vast resources, the untapped wealth of the various cultural traditions could be made more readily available both for the support of families and for help in resolving family problems. This becomes all the more crucial when we realize that persons do not heal very well in isolation. Recovery happens best in relationship. A sense of robust identity and the basic capacities for trust and intimacy are optimally engendered, fostered, and rejuvenated in contexts where one is surrounded by people with whom one feels at-home.

Both factors point in the direction of community-directed and -based approaches in which bridges are constructed between governmental services and the specialized services of various interest groups, faith organizations, and cultural groupings. In North America, the rich resources of the various cultural and religious traditions are an underused and underacknowledged resource because there has been not only a well-developed tendency in the discussion of family values to act as if individuals and governments are the two major influences on families, but also because governments, in their laudable concern to be non-discriminatory, have habitually insisted on and enacted least-common-denominator policies and agencies that must remain "neutral" about important value (including faith) questions. Both this perception, and this practice, need to change.

INITIATIVES

It is clear from our study and research that communities and schools can help in the detection, and even more in the prevention, of violence by setting up what could be called "bridge programs" in which front-line community service providers, counsellors, and therapists could explore particular issues of family life, identity, and self-esteem development, and friendship formation for the general benefit of the community's children and parents.

Schools in particular have the opportunity to introduce prevention programs with courses beginning in kindergarten and continued through to adolescence. Such programs would deal not only with issues such as racism, sexism, prejudice, healthy sexuality, dealing with difference, attitudes to the marginalized, but would also include courses on "developing self-esteem," "expressing feelings," "making friends," "handling conflict," and "bullying." Children would benefit from exploring themes such as what to look for and trust in friends, how to deal with feelings of rejection, negotiating power in the school yard, communicating boundaries in relationships—any or all of these typical family and peer problems.[37] It is particularly important that such courses move beyond the "talking about" stage and include participant involvement in anger-management exercises, healthy ways of coping with fear, disappointment, and frustration.[38] Therapy possibilities for those who require more individualized attention also need to be available.[39]

Religious institutions such as churches, synagogues, and mosques need to be encouraged—perhaps supported by government grants—to take an even higher profile in family education and programming. Many faith communities have already produced excellent resource materials on the detection and prevention of sexual abuse. For example, The Church Council on Justice and Corrections has produced the impressive "Child Sexual Abuse Prevention: A Resource Kit." They have also spawned a family violence awareness-raising project for local churches called "Fire in the Rose." Fire in the Rose equips a congregation to spend eighteen months learning about, and reflecting upon, the violence as it exists in church and community. The project also provides guidance for outreach strategies, and needed internal changes.

Woodbine Heights Baptist Church, a Toronto congregation which participated in the pilot version of Fire in the Rose, has launched a series of projects in response to their involvement, including a support group series for the community entitled "Confident Kids®." Parents come together weekly and receive support and education in their respective groups about family life and the importance of sharing and respecting feelings. Children and parents with a wide range of experience of the impact of violence have participated in this outreach project. It has been this church's experience that every family, regardless of degree of impact, can be strengthened by this anti-violent approach.

The message is clear: if we are serious about confronting the problem of family violence, we need to foster families of belonging, respect, and connection with a spirit of open-heartedness which affirms other people regardless of economic status, sex, race, creed, or family form. What is urgently required is a commitment to what O'Neill calls a "covenant of care"[40] in which a solid and compassionate mantle of care for our children is woven from the threads of concern and commitment from individuals, families, communities, and governments. Only then have we begun to see and hear Doug, Maggie, and Tan—all our children.

Notes

1. In the words of sociologists Jane Collier, Michelle Rosalto, and Sylvia Yanagisake: "we are faced with the irony that in our society the place where nurturance and non-contingent affection are supposed to be located is simultaneously the place where violence is most tolerated," in Bonnie Fox, ed., *Family Bonds and Gender Divisions* (Toronto: Canadian Scholars Press Inc., 1988), p. 43. (Cited as Fox.)
2. Catherine Crawford Thompson, *Reading Between The Lines: No Place, No Comfort, No Honour* (Toronto: World Vision Canada, 1994).
3. James H. Olthuis, *I Pledge You My Troth* (San Francisco: Harper & Row, 1975), pp. 89-91, 104.
4. Judith V. Jordan, Alexandra G. Kaplan, Jean Baker Miller, Irene P. Stiver, and Janet L. Surrey, *Women's Growth in Connection* (New York: Guilford Press, 1991).
5. David Cheal, *Family and The State of Theory* (Toronto: Harvester/Wheatsheaf, 1990), pp. 4, 5.
6. William Goode, *The Family* (Englewood Cliffs, NJ: Prentice-Hall, 1964), p. 5.
7. Marvyn Novick in John O'Neill, *The Missing Child in Liberal Theory* (Toronto: University of Toronto Press, 1994), p. x.
8. Deborah Anna Luepnitz, *The Family Interpreted* (New York: Basic Books, 1988), p. 65. (Cited as Leupnitz.)
9. Cheal, *Family*, p. 67.
10. C. Broderick and J. Smith, "The general systems approach to the family" in

Contemporary Theories About the Family, vol. 2, W. Burr, R. Hill, F. I. Nye and I. Reiss, eds., (New York: Free Press, 1979), p. 125. For Reuben Hill the family system has six functions: "physical maintenance for family members of food, shelter, and clothing; addition of new members through reproduction; socialization of children for adult roles; *maintenance of order*; maintenance of morale and motivation; production of goods and services," Cheal, *Family*, p. 65 (italics mine).

11. J. Maddock, "Healthy family Sexuality," *Family Relations* 38 (1989): 134.

12. F. I. Nye, ed., "The basic theory" in *Family Relationships* (Beverly Hills: Sage, 1982).

13. Permission and full release has been granted for the use of the stories of Doug, Maggie, and Tan presented in this essay from selected interviewees from qualitative research interviews with street youth, 1992-93, conducted by Catharine M. Crawford in a research project under my supervision.

14. Margrit Eichler, *Families in Canada Today* (Toronto: Gage, 1988), p. 10.

15. Ibid., p. 4.

16. Norman Denzin, "Postmodern children," *Society* 24 (1987): 33.

17. R. Hare-Mustin, "The Problem of Gender in Family Therapy," *Family Process* 26 (1987): 21.

18. Luepnitz, p. 66.

19. Virgina Goldner, "Feminism and Family Therapy," *Family Process* 24 (1985): 53.

20. *"Women do participate in their own abuse, but not as equals,"* Luepnitz, p. 163.

21. Cheal, *Family*, p. 130.

22. Froma Walsh, ed., *Normal Family Processes* (New York: Guilford Press, 1993), p. 23.

23. Ibid., p. 58. She also points to "respect for individual differences," "equitable sharing of power and responsibilities" for couples, "nurturance, protection and socilization," "organizational stability," "adaptability," "open communication," "effective problem solving," "shared belief system," "adequate resources for basic economic security," pp. 58-59.

24. Luepnitz, p. 67.

25. Ibid., p. 6.

26. Ibid., p. 24.

27. Diana Gittins, "What is the Family? Is it Universal?" in Fox, pp. 41-42.

28. Ron Thorne-Finch, *Ending the Silence* (Toronto: University of Toronto Press, 1992), p. 249.

29. Alice Miller, *For Your Own Good* (New York: Farrar, Straus, Giroux, 1990), pp. 3-102. (Cited as Miller.)

30. John Bradshaw, *Bradshaw On: The Family* (Deerfield Beach, FL: Health Communications, Inc., 1988), p. 20.

31. Thorne-Finch, *Ending*, p. 250.

32. Joy M. K. Bussert, *Battered Women: From a Theology of Suffering to an Ethic of Empowerment* (New York: Lutheran Church in America, 1986), p. 29. Quoted in James B. Nelson, *The Intimate Connection* (Philadelphia: The Westminster Press, 1988), p. 71.

33. James H. Olthuis, *Keeping Our Troth* (San Francisco: Harper & Row, 1986), pp. 39-43.

34. Irene P. Stiver, "Dysfunctional Families and Wounded Relationships—Part I," Paper published by Stone Center, Wellesley College, 1990, p. 5.

35. Miller, p. 65.

36. Ibid., p. 135.

37. For discussion of programs of this type, see Peter Jaffee, et al., "An Evaluation of a Secondary School Primary Prevention Program on Violence in Intimate Relationships," *Violence and Victims* 7, 2 (1992); Jeanne Khol, "School-Based Child Sexual Abuse Prevention Programs," *Journal of Family Violence* 8, 2 (1993); and Steven Schinke et al., "Stress-Management Intervention to Prevent Family Violence," *Journal of Family Violence* 1, 1 (1986).

38. My thanks to Catharine M. Crawford, not only for her research and insights, but also for sharing from her experience in conducting such prevention programs in some Toronto schools in 1994 with twelve- to fourteen-year-old students.

39. Some boards of education are experimenting with the development of early intervention curriculum, including life skills or "personal life management." "Men for Change," Halifax, have developed a course called "Healthy Relationships: A Violence Prevention Curriculum" for grades seven, eight, and nine. (Available from Men for Change, P.O. Box 33005, Quinpool Postal Outlet, Halifax, NS B3L 4T6.)

40. O'Neil, *Missing Child*, pp. 74-85.

Part II

Negotiations of Difference

7

Female Genital Mutilation: An Examination of a Harmful Traditional Practice in a Canadian Context

LISA CHISHOLM-SMITH

We did not know that on the morning we arrived in the village one of Tashi's sisters had died. Her name was Dura, and she had bled to death. That was all Tashi had been told; all she knew....
Years later, in the United States, she would begin to remember some of the things she'd told me over the years of our growing up. That Dura had been her favourite sister. That she had been headstrong and boisterous and liked honey in her porridge so much she'd sometimes stolen a portion of Tashi's share. That she had been very excited during the period leading up to her death. Suddenly she had become the centre of everyone's attention; every day there were gifts. Decorative items mainly: beads, bracelets, a bundle of dried henna for reddening hair and palms, but the odd pencil and tablet as well. Bright remnants of cloth for a head-scarf and dress. The promise of shoes!
ALICE WALKER, Possessing the Secret of Joy[1]

This puberty rite is a girl's initiation into womanhood. It enables her to accomplish the transition from a state of irresponsibility to one of responsibility.... Circumcision makes women clean, promotes virginity and chastity and guards young girls from sexual frustration by deadening their sexual appetite. If all women were circumcised we would not be burdened with AIDS.
MAMA PHILOMENA NJERI, a Kenyan FGM practitioner[2]

A child cannot consent to be mutilated and a parent cannot provide consent for a child to be mutilated.
RICHARD MOSLEY, of the Federal Justice Department interpreting Canada's criminal code in relation to female genital mutilation[3]

FEMALE GENITAL MUTILATION

Although the practice of female circumcision (FC) attracted significant international attention in the 1930s when the British first tried to abolish it in Kenya, and although the World Health Organization has considered it a major health concern for nearly two decades, until recently few North Americans were aware that over eighty million females worldwide have been subjected to some form of ritual genital mutilation.[4] The fact that some recent immigrants to Canada (and other Western nations) plan to continue this practice in their new homes has sparked outrage, confusion, and controversy. This traditional practice, which involves cutting away part or all of the external female genitalia, and has serious health consequences for women, tests the limits of Canadian tolerance. Health professionals, policy-makers, and citizens find themselves in the difficult position of wanting to respect the cultural traditions of immigrant groups while at the same time ensuring that girls and women are protected from the "unnecessary pain, health complications, permanent bodily damage, and even death"[5] which can result from this practice. As Anne Moon, former spokesperson for the Toronto Public Health Department explains, "It is a real cultural dilemma for everyone.... We do not want to offend 'immigrants' or appear culturally arrogant. Nor do we want to drive...[the practice of female genital mutilation] underground."[6]

Even naming this practice is controversial. To Westerners the use of the term female circumcision is misleading since it suggests that this practice is similar to male circumcision, a relatively harmless operation in which the foreskin of the penis is removed.[7] Indeed, with respect to this ritual the more appropriate male analogy is castration since it involves the partial or total removal of the external female reproductive organs.[8] In 1990 a conference sponsored by the Inter-Africa Committee decided that the term female genital mutilation more accurately described "the cruel and radical operation suffered" by millions of women worldwide.[9] For the purposes of this discussion I use the latter terminology which presupposes an ethical decision regarding the status of this ritual which the more neutral English term, female circumcision, does not.

What follows is an examination of the issue of female genital mutilation (FGM) in a Canadian context and the efforts to combat this practice which have been initiated to date. Since a basic understanding of how and why this ritual is practised in its traditional settings is a necessary prerequisite to any consideration of this issue in Canada, I will begin with a general overview of the practice of FGM in Africa. Next, I will examine the pluralist dilemma which FGM creates for Canadians and will argue that despite the many cultural sensitivities which surround this issue, it is not only legitimate, but vital, that Canadians implement policies which will prevent and—to the extent that it already exists—eliminate the practice of FGM among immigrant groups in Canada. Finally, I will examine the ways in which Canadian physicians have already responded to FGM and, with reference to the approaches taken by several other Western nations, most notably Great Britain, will highlight some of the advantages and disadvantages of passing a specific law prohibiting this practice in Canada.

Although I make use of sources from a number of different countries, my analysis is focussed to some degree on the Somali community in Canada. There are several reasons for this. First, although "the practice of female circumcision is nearly global in its distribution,"[10] Somalia together with Ethiopia and Sudan has one of the highest incidence rates of FGM. Virtually all Somali women are circumcised and it is estimated that nine out of ten are infibulated (see below).[11] As Edna Adan Ismail, who in recent years headed the Midwifery Training Department of the Ministry of Health in Somalia, asserts: "Infibulation [the most severe form of FGM] continues to be done today on almost all female children throughout Somalia and wherever ethnic Somalis live."[12] Second, in recent years Somalis have been arriving as refugee claimants in Canada in record numbers. In the last decade more than 30,000 Somalis have come to Canada "to escape a brutal civil war and ensuing anarchy that have engulfed the impoverished East African country," bringing to 70,000 the total number of Somalis living in Canada.[13] In addition, Toronto, with nearly 40,000 recently arrived Somali residents, "is now the largest Somali city outside of Somalia itself."[14] Finally, I had the privilege of interviewing two members of the Toronto Somali community, Safia Hassan Ahmed, a direct service worker with the Rexdale Women's Centre, and Kowser Omer-Hashi, a community health educator and counsellor with the Birth Control and Venereal Disease Information Centre, and benefited tremendously from their insights into this complex issue.[15] Both of these women oppose the practice and are involved in education initiatives related to FGM.

Before analyzing the specifics of the Canadian situation, however, we need to briefly examine the nature of this practice, its associated health complications, as well as some of the reasons it is practised.

FGM IN AFRICA

Scholars distinguish between three to five basic types of FGM in accordance with the severity of the procedure.[16] These types range from the mildest and rarest form, which involves the removal of only the tip of the clitoris, to the most radical operation, known as infibulation or Pharaonic circumcision, in which virtually the entire vaginal lips are removed and the raw walls of the vulva are stitched shut leaving only a tiny opening. As I have already indicated, this latter, most severe form of FGM is the most common type practised in Somalia. Kowser Omer-Hashi, one of the Somali professionals whom I interviewed, was infibulated as a young child of four years and described her painful experience in *Healthsharing* magazine:

> A group of women came to my home. I was told to sit on the floor. One woman sat behind me to support me. She opened my legs and two women held them down. My mother supervised the procedure and told the woman with the razor blade to remove everything.

She injected some fluid into me, which was supposed to be an anaesthetic. Then she cut off my clitoris, my labia majora, and part of my labia minora while I screamed in pain. Then she stitched my vulva closed, leaving an opening the size of a corn kernel for urine and menstrual blood.

My legs were tied together from my waist to my feet. I stayed bound like that for nearly three weeks so my vulva could heal shut. Urinating was excruciatingly painful. I had to be turned on my side so the urine could drip out of an opening.[17]

Girls are most often circumcised prior to menarche (the onset of menstruation) between the ages of three and twelve years.[18] Traditionally, the operation is performed with improvised instruments—kitchen knives, old razor blades, broken glass, or sharp stones—under unsanitary conditions and without anaesthetic. Because of the child's struggles and the crude nature of the procedure a more severe form of FGM than was intended may result. In addition, it is not uncommon for a girl to die as a result of the immediate complications of this operation, such as shock, prolonged hemorrhaging, or infection.

The survivors, however, can experience a lifetime of health problems including vaginal and urinary infections, menstrual problems, painful sexual intercourse, infertility, and serious birth complications, depending on the severity of the procedure.[19] If the mother has been infibulated, special obstetrical care is required and the risk of both fetal and maternal mortality during childbirth, and/or infant brain damage, is quite high.

Tragically and paradoxically, "the victims of the practice" are often "its strongest proponents."[20] While the ritual is valued as a symbol of cultural identity and purity, women bear the costs of maintaining this tradition disproportionally. They are the ones who bear the pain, increased health risk, and lack of sexual pleasure. In addition, in Somalia and many other countries, it is the responsibility of the women in the family to make all the arrangements for a young girl's circumcision. As in Omer-Hashi's experience, female relatives may even be given the task of holding the child down while a paid exciser performs the grisly operation. While the girl's father may pay for the initiation rite, men generally regard FGM as women's business and by tradition are not allowed to witness the procedure.[21] Thus, most often the people who benefit most from this "tradition of pain"[22]—men—are shielded from the gruesome details.

The reasons that women continue to subject their daughters to this brutal procedure are numerous and complex. A perceived need to control female sexuality is the most common reason given for this practice. Ultimately, however, it is the insistence by men that their wives be mutilated which ensures the continuation of this practice.[23] In the traditional societies which practice FGM, paramount importance is placed on female virginity prior to marriage. At stake is not only the family's honour and the girl's economic survival, but also in some cases the family's economic future since a bride price can only be secured if the girl is a virgin.[24] Infibulation is regarded as the most effective way to prevent female promiscuity and guarantee a bride's virginity.[25] Thus, as Kouba and Murasher note, despite the serious health consequences of this procedure, the social and economic "benefits gained from these operations by the recipient and her family far outweigh any potential danger."[26]

In addition, many people who practise FGM mistakenly believe that it is a requirement of Islam. Although female circumcision is not required by the Koran or by any formal religious doctrine, some religious leaders endorse it and, therefore, practitioners may regard it as an important part of their faith.[27] Since FGM is practised in some Muslim countries but not in others, and because forms of female circumcision have been practised by most major religious groups including Christians,[28] the ritual is more accurately seen as a cultural practice particular to specific countries rather than as a religious practice.

Furthermore, a number of unfounded beliefs concerning the alleged dangers of the clitoris together with an ignorance of basic human biology serve to perpetuate this practice.[29] Uncircumcised girls are seen as dirty and hypersexual and are frequently severely ostracized. In impoverished areas where "social acceptance and support may mean the difference between life and death,"[30] such girls may be disowned or forced into prostitution. Even in more affluent communities the social pressure to be genitally mutilated may be very strong. One study examining the prevalence of FGM among more affluent and educated Sudanese found that some high school students had actually demanded that their parents have them circumcised because they could not endure the relentless name-calling they experienced at school.[31]

CULTURE CLASH

Although many traditional customs are disappearing as a result of pressures to modernize, FGM continues to be a deeply ingrained custom in many societies and an important source of cultural identification for those ethnic groups which still practise it. Newcomers to Canada who desire to continue this harmful tradition, however, encounter a completely different cultural situation when they arrive. Initially, many Somali refugees are surprised to find that women in Canada are not circumcised, since most have probably never met a woman who has not been genitally mutilated before.[32] In addition, they soon discover that Canadians are appalled by a practice which their mothers, grandmothers, and great-grandmothers have done for centuries. The rite of passage which at home is marked by celebration and gift-giving is, in Canada, considered a form of child abuse. The resulting clash of cultures raises some difficult questions for Canadians who, on the one hand, want to ensure that young girls living in Canada are not subjected to what they perceive as a horrendous practice, but who, on the other hand, out of a genuine concern not to repeat the mistakes of the colonial past, approach this issue gingerly.

The problem is that while an overwhelming majority of Canadians from all backgrounds would oppose the practice of female genital mutilation, a small minority of new Canadians evidently believe that it is a legitimate cultural practice which they should be allowed to continue. We know from the anecdotal reports of physicians that some requests to have FGM performed in Canada have been made, but it is difficult to accurately assess the views of these individuals since the voices of practitioners of FGM have been virtually excluded from media coverage of this issue.[33] The closest the Canadian media has come to presenting a pro-FGM point of view was in 1992 when the *Ottawa Citizen* quoted the president of the Canadian African Women's Organization, a group which at that time had taken no official position for or against FGM. The president, Louise Dourado, implied, however, that there should be room for parental choice on the matter: "We are saying they should have a choice, parents have to decide."[34] Although little direct information on the views of potential practitioners is available, it is clear from other contexts that attempts to abolish FGM are certainly experienced by some groups as an attack on their cultural and/or religious values.[35] Defenders of this custom generally argue that it is an essential part of their culture and believe that it is wrong for those who disapprove of the practice to attempt to abolish it. Jomo Kenyatta, who became Kenya's first prime minister, is perhaps the most well-known advocate of FGM, arguing that for the Gikuyu people, female circumcision symbolized the essence of their tribal culture and "had enormous educational, social, moral and religious implications."[36]

With respect to the issue of FGM, then, Canadians find themselves in a pluralist dilemma. To allow the practice of FGM in Canada violates the deepest convictions of the vast majority of Canadians, while non-participation in this ritual violates traditional practitioners' deeply held convictions. In other words, the issue of FGM in Canada involves a fundamental conflict of worldviews. Given this situation, the key question for Canadians is, "When is it justifiable to interfere with the cultural practices of a particular segment of society?" Or put another way, "What are the limits of cultural expression?"

Discerning the point at which the need to oppose the destructive consequences of a practice outweigh the need to protect cultural freedoms is no easy task. Like Alison Slack, however, I would argue that an important consideration in making this judgment is "the extent to which the 'victim' of a certain harmful tradition" participates voluntarily.[37] An act is voluntary if the participant is conscious of the nature of the act and its probable consequences, and chooses or consents to the act. To describe an act as voluntary also implies that the participant has a significant degree of freedom of choice in the matter and is not compelled or constrained by an external force to act in a certain way.[38] To illustrate how the criteria of volition functions, I will show its applicability to another pluralist dilemma regarding the right of individuals to refuse Western medical treatment for religious reasons and then suggest how this criteria might apply to FGM. An adult who refuses emergency medical treatment for a life-threatening condition (e.g., a blood transfusion) for religious reasons and who has been informed by doctors that s/he will probably die is acting voluntarily. Therefore, although I may strongly believe that the person is making an unwise decision and regret the likely and (from my perspective) unnecessary consequences, I would argue that in the interest of preserving religious freedom society should allow the person the freedom to make this decision. In other words, despite the undesirable consequences, society should tolerate the refusal of medical treatment in this case since the person is acting voluntarily. On the other hand, in my view, state interference is warranted in the case of a parent who wishes to refuse essential medical treatment for a child. The parent's decision will in all likelihood result in the death of the child and the child is too young to consciously participate in such a weighty decision. In this situation since the child does not participate voluntarily, then, I would argue that state interference, rather than toleration is warranted.

VOLITION AND FGM

Young girls who are circumcised are in a similar position to the child in the above example. They are too young to refuse the procedure and therefore do not participate voluntarily. The volition criteria, however, can also be applied to the adult women who participate in this ritual. We need to consider the extent to which their actions may be constrained by their social position and powerful external social and cultural forces. Regrettably, as Fran Hosken asserts in her discussion of the Kenyan circumcision controversy,[39] this is an angle which has been overlooked in past debates about this issue. It is one thing for Jomo Kenyatta to claim that: "No proper Gikuyu [man] would dream of marrying a girl who has not been circumcised,"[40] but we need to consider the implications of such a stance for women living in a society in which their economic security depends on marriage. Do Gikuyu women have any genuine alternative to this practice? I think a strong case can be made that where FGM is an indigenous practice, the adult women who have their daughters circumcised or who perform the procedure themselves lack the education and social and economic freedom to make non-participation in this ritual a viable option. In effect, the mothers' social and economic situation prevents them from fully exercising their responsibility to care for and protect their children from harm. The degree to which these women's actions are circumscribed by external forces provides some basis for opposition to the practice on moral grounds.

HEALTH EFFECTS AND FGM

Another related criterion that should be considered in relation to cultural practices such as FGM and the limits of tolerable cultural expression is the seriousness of the associated health effects. The fewer and milder the associated effects, the more tolerable a given cultural practice becomes.[41] As I have already indicated, however, the health consequences related to FGM are serious. Thus, while there are some health risks associated with various forms of body piercing (arguably, another form of mutilation) this practice is much less objectionable from a health point of view than female genital mutilation. When applying this criterion, however, it is important to bear in mind that perceptions of health, illness, and pain can vary cross-culturally and are shaped to some extent by worldviews. Since a circumcised state is the norm for females in the communities which maintain this traditional practice, it is unlikely to be viewed as unhealthy. Thus, in making a case against FGM an appeal to the health problems associated with the ritual cannot be seen as an appeal to an objective and universally held standard. Nevertheless, it is significant that when circumcised women become aware that uncircumcised women do not experience the same pain which they do, they are increasingly likely to reject this practice. Many hope to spare their daughters from the negative health effects which they endured as the "normal" lot of females.

For supporters of FGM like Jomo Kenyatta, however, evidently the importance of FGM as a mark of cultural identity is such that it may be preferable to them for Gikuyu women to endure health problems, and increased risk of maternal and fetal mortality, rather than to abandon this custom. This scenario brings us back full circle to the question of volition and FGM.

In view of the serious health consequences associated with FGM and the vulnerable position of women in societies which practice it, I believe that this traditional practice should not be tolerated.[42] The girls who are subjected to FGM are too young to refuse it and their mothers lack the education and social and economic freedom to make not circumcising their daughters a viable option.

Advocates of FGM, however, could still challenge this verdict on two grounds. First, they could point out the hypocrisy of Westerners in disallowing this harmful practice while tolerating a number of unhealthy and dangerous practices ranging "from smoking cigarettes and drinking alcohol to participating in dangerous sports."[43] An argument such as this, however, is not very compelling since just because one tolerates one bad practice, does not make it right to tolerate another one. However, if we consider the Western acceptance of forms of cosmetic surgery which enable women to physically alter their healthy bodies so that they can better conform to prevailing beauty norms, this argument hits a little closer to home.[44] As Hazelle Palmer observes, while such practices are perhaps less extreme, they are not dissimilar to female circumcision: "FGM is at the far end of a continuum which has young girls and women having their bodies redefined in order to be more attractive and pleasing to men."[45]

While I would certainly favour increased regulation of the cosmetic surgery industry and recognize that the pressures on women to conform to beauty ideals are significant, in contrast to the situation with FGM, women in North America have a high degree of control over their participation in such cosmetic operations. As Alison Slack indicates, "there is no social requirement for women to undergo cosmetic surgery in the United States."[46] Moreover, while greater monitoring of the health risks related to these beauty procedures is necessary, the health complications associated with female genital mutilation are much greater.

Second, defenders of FGM could charge that Westerners are simply imposing their beliefs on other people without respecting the integrity and complexity of the others' own cultural systems. While there is a very real sense in which to oppose FGM through education programs or social policy is to take a deliberate stance against practitioners of FGM, I reject the implication that this kind of imposition of beliefs is always wrong. In contrast to Joan Gullen, then, who asserts that: "we must not remain silent about...[FGM] in the mistaken belief that we might be interfering in someone else's culture,"[47] I submit that we cannot evade the reality that to oppose FGM in this way is precisely to interfere in someone else's culture.[48] As I have already indicated, however, the real question is not whether or not opposing female genital mutilation constitutes interference in another's culture, but rather whether such cultural intervention is justified in this case. In this specific case, I believe it is.

However, even as I advocate the prevention and—to the extent that it might already exist—the elimination of FGM in Canada, I recognize, as legitimate, the concern that such actions might repeat the racism and paternalism that has too often characterized past Western relationships with the original inhabitants of the colonies. Canadians, for example, need only consider the situation of Native peoples in this country to see ample evidence of the injustices wrought when governments and churches arrogantly assumed that they knew what was best for Native groups.[49] Westerners, then, are certainly not immune to being blind to the ways in which we ourselves may culturally sanction cruelty.[50]

However, while it is important (especially for members of culturally dominant groups) to be mindful of the dangers of cultural arrogance and to be appropriately self-reflective, in the case of FGM, a number of factors mitigate the concern that Westerners who oppose FGM are simply being culturally arrogant. First, there is a growing international movement against this practice which has the support of many reputable international organizations such as the World Health Organization and UNICEF.[51] In other words, opposition to FGM is coming from a variety of cultures, not just Western culture. Second, in many cases, the laws of the country from which a family has emigrated already prohibit this practice. For example, in the Sudan female circumcision was officially outlawed in 1946. Or alternatively, the government may have launched education campaigns with the aim of eradicating it. Prior to current political unrest in Somalia, for example, the government officially sponsored anti-FGM education programs. Third, increasingly, courageous members of ethnic groups which practice FGM are themselves opposing it. Finally, although a practice like FGM may become important to immigrants for preserving cultural identity in a new context, the factors which motivate the practice at home frequently do not apply in mainstream Canadian society. For example, in Canada circumcision is not considered a necessary prerequisite for marriage and therefore there is no external reinforcement for this practice. Moreover, while Kenyatta maintained that the abolition of FGM would destroy very essence of his tribal culture, no parallel tribal system exists in the immigrant communities of North America. The structure of immigrant communities, of necessity, changes considerably in response to new circumstances and pressures.

TREATING NEIGHBOURS WITH RESPECT

One way to guard against any latent paternalistic or racist tendencies which might inform Canadian actions is to ensure that our interest in our Somali neighbours extends beyond our strong disapproval of this particular ritual to an understanding and appreciation of both their traditional culture and their current contribution to Canadian society as a whole. Canadians do injustice to this community if we give this one aspect of their culture, reprehensible though it maybe, our exclusive attention. Articles stressing the harmful nature of this traditional practice, important as they are, need to be balanced by positive stories about the lives being built in Canada by people from societies that traditionally practise FGM. In addition, discussion of the relationship of this practice to Islam need to be handled sensitively to minimize the risk that communities of potential practitioners will feel that their religious convictions are under attack. In the wake of a landmark Canadian decision to allow a Somali woman and her daughter to stay in Canada because of the mother's realistic fear that her daughter would be genitally mutilated, for example, the Somali community was concerned that negative publicity had "embarrassed the Muslim faith."[52]

Respect for our neighbours also implies that when policy-makers take specific actions against genital mutilation, they should at a minimum ensure that their decisions are clearly communicated to members of cultural groups that traditionally practise FGM. Unfortunately, this kind of basic courtesy has not always characterized Canadian efforts to combat this traditional practise. When the College of Physicians and Surgeons of Ontario (CPSO), the regulatory body which governs Ontario doctors, banned the performance of FGM by health professionals in 1992, Safia Hassan Ahmed of the Rexdale Women's Centre expressed frustration that the doctors had neglected to even translate their policy statement into Somali (and possibly other key languages). Warning that approaches to this sensitive issue which fail to meaningfully involve potential practitioners of FGM will be ineffective, the Somali social worker commented that: "The target audience [for the doctors' policy] was this group of people. Whatever decisions you make, you don't make them without informing the people who are going to be affected!"[53]

Furthermore, health professionals and community workers need to work cooperatively and collaboratively with members of affected communities to find ways of addressing the cultural concerns which motivate the practice that are acceptable to both the ethnic community itself and the wider society. Opposition to the practice of FGM need not translate into opposition to the cultural beliefs which undergird the ritual. Somalis, for example, need not alter their high view of virginity. The elimination of FGM does require, however, that they cease to identify virginity with infibulation. In conclusion, actions such as these would help ensure that the mistakes of the past are not repeated.

Fortunately, it appears that Canadian education and healthcare initiatives with respect to FGM have been characterized by greater cultural sensitivity and community involvement than the CPSO efforts to publicize their anti-FGM policy. In Ottawa, the Somali Women's Community Education Project, sponsored by the Family Service Centre of Ottawa-Carleton and funded by the Ontario Women's Directorate, seems to be off to a good start. The program is run by Somali women and addresses FGM in the context of a wide range of issues relevant to recent female immigrants (including housing, recreation, counselling, ESL classes, job searches and child care). In addition, "educating and sensitizing Canadian service providers and caregivers such as social workers, teachers, Children's Aid workers, nurses, obstetricians, gynecologists, and pediatricians, to give them a better understanding of the their Somali clients and the health issues associated with FGM" is another important component of this initiative.[54]

We turn now to a consideration of some of the actions which Canadians have already taken to combat FGM, beginning with the important decision made by Canadian doctors with respect to the practice alluded to above, and concluding with an examination of the debate over specific legislation for FGM.

PHYSICIANS

Since most Western doctors have never even heard of female genital mutilation, they are frequently unprepared to handle requests to perform this procedure. In the absence of professional guidance on this issue, such requests create an ethical dilemma for doctors. Should they refuse and report the request to an appropriate social agency, perhaps the Children's Aid Society? What if the parents opt instead to have the operation performed covertly without anaesthetic under unsanitary conditions or send the child back home for the procedure?

Whether motivated out of a desire to at least alleviate the pain and risk of infection the young girl would experience in a traditional circumcision, or unscrupulously by the lure of under-the-table profits, or by a belief that they should not interfere in an ancient tradition, the procedure has been performed by Western doctors in modern medical facilities on a number of occasions.

One of the most publicized cases occurred in England, where in 1982 a Harley Street doctor admitted to performing the procedure on two Nigerian clients in a private London clinic.[55] The resulting controversy led eventually to the passing of a specific law in Britain banning the practice. In contrast to the British situation, however, as far as I am aware there is no evidence that Canadian doctors have performed this procedure. In fact, whereas the Royal College of Obstetricians and Gynaecologists (RCOG) were initially unconvinced of the need for the British bill, in Canada physicians have taken the lead in addressing this issue and have called on the Canadian government to legislate against FGM.

The CPSO banned doctors from performing FGM in January 1992. They were the first provincial medical body to take this stance and since then the equivalent Alberta body has taken similar steps.[56] "We have a general rule in medicine: Do not harm," Roy Beckett, associate registrar of the college, said in explaining the need for a ban.[57] The college's official position statement on FGM defines the performance of any form of FGM by a physician who is licensed in Ontario as "professional misconduct." The policy states specifically that "A physician who is requested to perform this procedure must decline and also refuse to refer the matter to any other person."[58] This stance is consistent with that of the World Health Organization which has expressed "its unequivocal opposition to any medicalization of the operation, advising that under no circumstances should it ever be performed by health professionals or in health establishments."[59]

TO LEGISLATE OR NOT TO LEGISLATE

While Canadians are generally united in their opposition to FGM and in their support for the measures taken by Canadian physicians, opinions vary as to the merits of passing specific legislation banning this practice in Canada. Such legislation against female genital mutilation already exists in several countries including Sweden and Great Britain, where the performance of this procedure carries a penalty of imprisonment. At present, however, Canadian policy is closer to that of the Netherlands where no specific law has been passed. As a spokesperson from the Dutch Health ministry explains: "Netherlands [sic] policy in the matter is generally geared to information and prevention, while the penalties enshrined in criminal law serve as a final deterrent."[60]

Similarly, in Canada the federal Department of Justice has concluded that at present "no amendment to Canadian law is necessary" to address the practice of female genital mutilation, since if it occurred in Canada, it "would be found to violate several existing Criminal Code provisions."[61]   In view of this decision, I feel that the most compelling reason for specific legislation in Canada is that it would clarify exactly where Canada stands with respect to FGM. Special legislation would add official weight to the assertions of doctors, healthcare professionals, and community workers that FGM is an unacceptable practice in Canada. However, before Canadians opt for this change in policy, a number of complicating factors need to be considered.

First, we need to determine the scale of the problem and whether it warrants special legislation. Based on the anecdotal evidence we have from doctors who have been asked to perform this procedure, it is difficult to determine how many girls are genuinely at risk of being circumcised in Canada. On the one hand, we cannot afford to wait, as France did, until a child dies as a result of FGM before clamping down hard on this practice.[62]   On the other hand, if the problem can be effectively handled by documenting requests and having an appropriate social agency intervene on a child's behalf if necessary, there is no point in embarking on a complicated and time-consuming legislative process.

As far as I am aware, there are no documented cases of FGM occurring in Canada and the ban on the procedure imposed by Alberta and Ontario medical regulatory bodies should effectively guard against its practice by physicians. In addition, if effective preventative education programs are implemented which alert newcomers to Canada to the dangers of this traditional practice immediately upon their arrival, then likely few parents will want to continue this practice. As Safia Ahmed indicates: "Many people in the community don't like...[FGM] and don't want it and I believe many, many more would not want it if they knew the whole story."[63]   Furthermore, as Kowser Omer-Hashi suggests, it may be that the long immigration process during which claimants must maintain residency in Canada and the expense of a trip home will effectively deter the few who adamantly assert: "I can always take my child back to Somalia, I don't have to do it here!"

Second, if the legislative process in Britain is any indication, passing a law in Canada could be a very difficult, long, and expensive process. As Elise Sochart asserts, although the Prohibition of Female Circumcision Bill "appeared relatively mundane and uncontroversial in parliamentary terms" when it was initially introduced by Lord Kennet in March 1983, "as the bill passed through the legislative process, the issue was transformed into one of great personal, moral and political sensitivity."[64] It took almost two and a half years before the bill received royal assent on 16 July 1985, and numerous redrafts of the bill and amendments were required. Moreover, such a lengthy process in no way guarantees that the final product will be a good piece of legislation. As Sochart noted: "formal monitoring arrangements, although suggested many times during the closing debates, had not been embodied in the [British] act—suggesting that it was indeed more of a placebo policy than a piece of social reform."[65]   In contrast, effective Canadian legislation would have to have a strong emphasis on preventative measures and not simply punitive ones.

Assuming that the risk of this procedure being performed in Canada is fairly small and that the existing Criminal Code already provides authorities with appropriate legal sanctions, I remain unconvinced that specific legislation is warranted at this time. As Barbara Fulford indicates, "prohibitions and legal sanctions—necessary as they are—are a measure of last resort" in this sensitive matter. Undoubtedly, our major efforts should be directed toward culturally sensitive educational programs and toward supporting the efforts of pioneers like Safia Ahmed and Kowser Omer-Hashi who are working to ensure that another generation of girls is not subjected to this cruel practice.

Clearly, significant, lasting social change in relation to female genital mutilation cannot be achieved by the passing of a single piece of legislation. It requires the commitment of health professionals, governments and specialized community agencies and, most importantly, the involvement of members of ethnic groups which have traditionally practised FGM in both the planning and implementation of policies and educational programs. As Safia Ahmed repeatedly stressed, culturally sensitive ways of approaching this sensitive topic need to be found so that members of practising groups themselves will come to the realization that FGM is, in Charles Kyazze's words, "not contributing positively to" their culture.[66]

Notes

1. (New York: Pocket Star Books, 1992), pp. 8-9.
2. As cited in "Kenya Elders Defend Circumcision," *Women's International Network News* 16, 4 (Autumn 1990): 40. (Cited as *WIN News*.)
3. As cited by Sherri Davis-Barron, "Doctors drafting policy on female circumcision" *Ottawa Citizen* (4 January 1992): A11. (Cited as Davis-Barron.)
4. This is a rather conservative figure. The World Health Organization (WHO) estimates that between 85 million and 115 million women have had their genitals mutilated. The WHO figure is cited in Storer Rowley's "Worldwide ban on circumcision of women urged," *Calgary Herald* (11 September 1994): A1. Furthermore, Fran Hosken estimates that in Africa alone more than 110 million females have been genitally mutilated (*WIN News* 19, 1 [Winter 1993]). Leonard Kouba and Judith Murasher have suggested that previous estimates made by Hosken were somewhat inflated. See "Female circumcision in Africa," *African Studies Review* 28, 1 (March 1985): 95-110. (Cited as Kouba and Murasher.)
5. Alison Slack, "Female Circumcision: A Critical Appraisal," *Human Rights Quarterly* 10 (1988): 462. (Cited as Slack.)
6. As cited in Paul Taylor's, "MDs unite against surgical ritual: Circumcision of females banned," *Globe & Mail* (3 December 1991): A1, A6. (Cited as Taylor.)
7. Interestingly enough, even the very mild procedure of male circumcision has become the subject of recent public and medical debate. See John McGrath's "Controversy surrounds circumcision," *Toronto Star* (26 December 1992): J14.
8. The purposes of male circumcision and female circumcision also differ markedly. The

former practice is essentially a ceremonial one with religious significance, whereas in addition to its value as a rite of passage, female circumcision is specifically intended to curb both female sexual desire and activity.

9. Sue Armstrong, "Female Circumcision: Call to Outlaw Needless Mutilation," *New Scientist* 15 (December 1990): 11.

10. Lawrence P. Cutner as cited in Slack, p. 439 n. 4. Currently practised in over forty countries on every continent, FGM is most prevalent in Africa and the Middle East. There have also been documented cases in France, Britain, Sweden, and Germany (Slack, p. 439).

11. Slack, p. 443.

12. Edna Adan Ismail as cited in Fran Hosken, *The Hosken Report: Genital and Sexual Mutilation of Females* (Lexington, MA: WIN News, 1992), p. 121.

13. Shawn McCarthy, "Starting Over: Fleeing war and chaos, Somali refugees struggle to adjust to a new life in Canada," *Canadian Geographic* (January/February 1993): 68-75.

14. Janet Sommerville, "Coalition draws diverse Somalis into citizen diplomacy," *Catholic New Times* 17, 4 (11 July 1993): 14. Kowser Omer-Hashi places the number of Somalis living in Metropolitan Toronto at 50,000. See "Female Genital Mutilation," *Treating the Female Patient* 3, 2 (May 1993): 12-13. (Cited as Omer-Hashi.)

15. Personal Interview with Safia Hussan Ahmed (Toronto: Rexdale Women's Centre, 17 March 1993). Telephone Interview with Kowser Omer-Hashi (Toronto, 5 April 1993). (Cited as Ahmed Interview and Omer-Hashi Interview, respectively.)

16. See Kouba and Murasher, pp. 96-97, for a more detailed discussion of these types.

17. Kowser Omer-Hashi as cited by Virginia Mak in "Female Genital Mutilation: A Tradition of Pain," *Healthsharing* 13, 4 (Winter/Spring 1993): 10-13. (Cited as Mak.)

18. The age at which girls are circumcised varies both geographically and ethnically (Slack, pp. 442-43).

19. For a detailed description of the immediate and long-term health effects of FGM see Slack, pp. 450-55.

20. *WHO Chronicle* 33.

21. See Pia Gallo and Franco Viviani, "Female Circumcision in Somalia," *The Mankind Quarterly* 29 (1988): 165-80, especially p. 171. In some countries men take a more active role in the rite. In September 1994 CNN filmed the clitoridectomy (removal of the clitoris) of a ten-year-old Egyptian girl by two males, a florist and plumber, in the presence of her father and other relatives. See Jill Smolowe's "A Right of Passage—or Mutilation?" *Time* (26 September 1994): 39.

22. The phrase "tradition of pain" is borrowed from Mak, p. 10.

23. Indeed, a very important intermediary step toward eliminating FGM would be a cessation of an identification of moral and sexual purity with the circumcised state. Carolyn Fluehr-Lobban observes that, "In Egypt, the Cairo Institute for Human Rights has reported the first publicly acknowledged marriage of an uncircumcised woman." See Fluehr-Lobban, "Cultural Relativism and Universal Rights," *The Chronicle of Higher Education* (9 June 1995): Section 2.

24. In traditional societies marriage represents the only way in which women can obtain a measure of economic security. In some cultures, a marriage contract is sealed with the payment of a dowry by the bride's family to her future husband. In other cultures, the groom pays his bride's family a substantial bride price in order to marry her. The desirability of the daughter determines the bride price and therefore also the economic benefit to her family.

25. As Paul Taylor notes, this radical procedure "in effect produces a chastity belt of thick scar tissue," Taylor, A6.

26. Kouba and Murasher, p. 107.

27. Preventative education facilitated by religious leaders and scholars, which highlights the

fact that there is no religious basis for the practice, will likely be effective in challenging those who practise FGM for religious reasons to rethink their attitudes (Ahmed Interview).

28. In the nineteenth century British and North American doctors often treated female "hysteria" by surgically removing the clitoris. See Naomi Wolf, "Violence," *The Beauty Myth* (Toronto: Vintage Books, 1990, 1991) pp. 244-45. (Cited as Wolf.)

29. For a brief discussion of some of these myths and misunderstandings see Kouba and Murasher, pp. 103-104 or Slack, pp. 459-61.

30. *WHO Chronicle* 33.

31. Amna El Sadik Badri, "Female Circumcision in the Sudan," *Ahfad Journal* 1 (1984): 11-21, especially p. 16.

32. Ahmed Interview. See also "Experience with Somali Women Refugees at Vive in New York," *WIN News* 19, 1 (Winter 1993): 39.

33. This gap in media coverage likely reflects both the abhorrence with which the vast majority of Canadians view this practice and the secrecy which surrounds the practice in general. Such private matters are not considered appropriate topics of conversation within communities which practise FGM.

34. Davis-Barron, A11.

35. For example, following a 1990 presidential decision to outlaw female circumcision in Kenya, some tribes accused "others of engineering the ban to destroy their culture and customs," *WIN News* 16, 4 (Autumn 1990): 40.

36. Kouba and Murasher pp. 102-103.

37. Slack, p. 468.

38. Dick Keyes defines tolerance as "living side by side with others who have real and deep difference with us, but living with respect and civility in our personal attitude, and as much as is possible, in public policy." Both toleration and interference are ways of responding to the fact of pluralism. See Dick Keyes, "Pluralism, Relativism and Tolerance," *The Third Way* (December/January 1992-93): 30-33.

39. See Fran Hosken's case study on Kenya in *The Hosken Report*. She argues that Jomo Kenyatta, Kenya's first prime minister—who likely had never seen the procedure and yet insisted that it was not harmful—used the issue of FGM and its importance to tribal unity as an effective political ploy to secure Kenya's independence. The perspective of Gikuyu women was never considered.

40. Jomo Kenyatta as cited in Slack, p. 463.

41. Similarly, in the case of the refusal of medical treatment for religious reasons, few people would oppose a person's right to refuse treatment if the health consequences were relatively minor and posed little long-term risk.

42. At their deeper levels, my convictions that this practice should not be tolerated go beyond such real health concerns and the belief that women's sexuality should not be forcibly controlled nor women's bodies violated, to the Christian conviction that for all these reasons this practice fundamentally violates the sanctity of women and girls, created as they are in the image of God.

43. Slack, p. 473.

44. For a more detailed discussion of the cosmetic industry see Wolf, pp. 218-69.

45. Hazelle Palmer, "Unimaginable? Not really...," *Healthsharing* 13, 4 (Winter/Spring 1993): 3.

46. Slack, p. 464.

47. Joan Gullen, "Female Genital Mutilation," *Vis-a-Vis* 10, 3 (Winter 1993). (Cited as Gullen.)

48. Gullen's reluctance to admit that to actively oppose FGM does involve a form of cultural interference likely stems from conflicting loyalties. She desires both to adhere to the popular liberal dogma that we ought not to impose our personal beliefs on another person

nor interfere with another individual's cultural expression, and to oppose what she considers, for feminist or other reasons, an unconscionable practice. The faulty logic of Gullen's position takes the following form: Premise 1—It is wrong to interfere with someone else's cultural expression; Premise 2—It is right to oppose the practice of FGM; Conclusion—Opposing FGM is not interfering with someone else's cultural expression.

49. Charges of cultural arrogance and racism were raised in the British debate (March 1983-July 1985) over specific legislation to ban female circumcision. The Department of Health and Services wanted the cutting away of part of the clitoris or labia majora to be allowed for certain mental health reasons, but forbidden for reasons of custom or ritual (*WIN News* 10, 2 [Spring 1984]: 40) and as a result the legislation was deemed racist. Lord Kennet asserted: "Now this is clearly racial discrimination. White depression ('I don't believe the doctor when he says I am like other girls of my people') would secure an operation; black depression ('It is better for me to be like other girls of my people') would not secure one. To allow the mutilation of a deluded white girl and not of a deluded black girl is indefensible.... What the law bans, and must ban, is acts of cruelty and harm as such." Lord Kennet as cited in "The Prohibition of Female Genital Mutilation (Circumcision) Bill in UK," *WIN News* 10, 2 (Spring 1984): 40. See also Elise Sochart, "Agenda Setting, the Role of Groups and the Legislative Process: The Prohibition of Female Circumcision in Britain," *Parliamentary Affairs* 41, 4 (October 1988): 519-20. (Cited as Sochart.)

50. Western treatment of senior citizens, for example, is regarded as barbaric by cultures who revere the elderly for their wisdom.

51. In 1994, delegates at the International Conference on Population and Development in Cairo made the following declaration: "Governments are urged to prohibit female genital mutilation wherever it exists and to give vigorous support to efforts among non-government and community organizations and religious institutions to eliminate such practices." As cited in A. M. Rosenthal, "Sentence on mutilation speaks loudly," *Winnipeg Free Press* (7 September 1994): A7.

52. Tom Fennel, "Finding new grounds for refuge," *Maclean's* (9 August 1994): 18-19.

53. Ahmed Interview, p. 51

54. Citation from Gullen. The St. Joseph's Health Centre in the greater Toronto area has developed a special prenatal class for Somali women. See Gigi Suhanic, "Somali prenatal classes link culture and maternity wards," *The Villager* (May 1993): 15. In addition, Kowser Omer-Hashi gives regular workshops to healthcare professionals in Toronto, directs Somali women to sensitive service providers, and counsels couples in which the female partner has been circumcised on ways of enriching their sex life (Omer-Hashi Interview).

55. Sochart, p. 510.

56. Robert Walker, "Female Circumcision Forbidden in Alberta," *The Calgary Herald* (14 February 1992): B1.

57. Beckett as cited in Taylor, A6.

58. College of Physicians and Surgeons of Ontario (CPSO), "New Policy: Female Circumcision, Excision and Infibulation," *College Notices* 25 (March 1992).

59. *WHO Chronicle* 33, p. 35.

60. *WIN News* 19, 1 (Winter 1993): 34.

61. Citation taken from an April 1992 Federal Justice Department letter quoted by Barbara Fulford in her letter to the *Globe and Mail* (27 August 1993).

62. *WIN News* 10, 2 (Spring 1984): 39.

63. Ahmed Interview.

64. Sochart, p. 508.

65. Ibid., p. 523.

66. Charles Kyazze as cited in Taylor, A6.

8

Violent Asymmetry: The Shape of Power in the Current Debate over the Morality of Homosexuality

RONALD A. KUIPERS

Our society is currently in the throes of an emotionally exhausting dispute over what constitutes appropriate levels of tolerance, recognition, and acceptance of the homosexual sisters and brothers who live in, and contribute to, our communities. This dispute is so charged because, in the growing lesbian and gay political struggle for protection, recognition, and justice, many heterosexuals perceive a threat to their historically entrenched moral standards.[1] Because of the homosexual community's vigilance and willingness to assume personal risk in this struggle, its visibility has finally reached a point where its claims can no longer be ignored. But challenging the traditional morality of human sexuality is not the only effect this community's struggle has had. It has also helped many people at the centre notice and begin to address the many different sufferings this peripheral community has endured. Our new-found capacity to notice the suffering of lesbians and gays enables us to respond to their pleas for justice.

The honesty, candour, and courage that gays and lesbians have exhibited in this struggle, along with the personal risk they assume by engaging in it, convince me that silence and ignorance are no longer options for anyone in this cultural debate. In particular, two things occur to me that the previous silence and ignorance concerning homosexuality have made it sadly impossible to address: First, the pernicious ethical ramifications of a Western inability to cope with difference clearly surface in this dispute.[2] Second, and related to the first, one also sees here a distinct asymmetry of power at work.[3] Those with power in this debate, those at the centre who represent, constitute, and prescribe the cultural norm for human sexuality, place an incredible amount of pressure on those in this debate who lack power, who come from the margins, who are singled out, and who are expected to prove beyond a shadow of a doubt why their lives are different but not deviant, alternative but not harmful.

In this chapter, I hope to contribute to a mediation of this imbalance. It is understandable that those who now enjoy cultural power, precisely because of this enjoyment, do not recognize the ways in which that power is withheld from others. It is also understandable that this group should need to be persuaded why those now excluded deserve to be included. It is not my desire to demonize the centre qua centre and valorize the margins qua margins. I only hope to encourage those at the centre to show solidarity with those who, in my opinion, suffer unnecessarily at the margins of our society.

In particular, I would like to encourage the heterosexual majority to see that the difference between itself and the homosexual community is not a threatening one. After examining in thick detail the sufferings this minority community has endured, I hope to help persuade those heterosexuals who now understand homosexual difference as deviance that this difference, when compared with the many similarities between both groups, is not a difference that should make a difference when it comes to the issues of inclusion and sharing cultural power. To paraphrase philosopher Richard Rorty, the difference between the heterosexual majority and the homosexual minority is unimportant when compared with the similarity both groups have with respect to their ability to suffer pain and humiliation.[4] In the suffering of the homosexual minority, both groups may begin to recognize a shared humanity, one that transcends the difference of sexual orientation, enabling both groups to achieve a more expansive sense of solidarity than now exists.

Simply put, the playing field in this cultural dispute is at present far from level. These debates hide the fact that those who represent the heterosexist point of view should recognize how their historically constituted subjectivities affect or obscure the terms of the debate.[5] Only the morality of homosexuality is on the table here, not the various moral dangers that can be shown to flow from our culture's strict adherence to the heterosexist standard.

These two observations have suggested several questions, which I hope to raise in this chapter: What threat is perceived in the existence of homosexuality and the political assertiveness of homosexuals? Is this perception justified, or is it chimerical? How has heterosexuality been inscribed so decisively as the norm for human sexuality in contemporary society? What are the effects of this inscription? In what ways are we now able to begin to think otherwise about these norms? What would be the pragmatic consequences of thinking differently?

However one answers such questions, it is becoming extremely difficult for ethically sensitive people to tolerate the current treatment of homosexuals in our society. Given the gravity of the violence that a homophobic society inflicts upon the homosexual, it is also doubtful that an attitude of mere tolerance can even begin to address the rightful demands for justice now being voiced by this community. For this reason, I hope that we may find cultural space in which to think otherwise about homosexuality than we have previously. Perhaps the time has come, for ethical reasons, to be suspicious of the universality, immutability, and naturalness that our society claims for the cultural norms we use to proscribe homosexuality and banish the homosexual. Such suspicion should not be read as a version of moral relativism, but conversely, as a strengthening of our resolve to pursue justice and procure freedom for all.

One strong reason for recommending such a change in societal attitude is the suffering face of the gay brother or lesbian sister in our community. If the cries, the faces, and the stories of suffering and hope shared by many brave homosexual sisters and brothers do not supply sufficient motivation for us to change our thinking and acting, then surely our society has lost all hope of responding ethically to the widow, the orphan, and the stranger.

STORIES FROM THE WRONG SIDE OF POWER

North American communities have amassed an appalling ethical record concerning the treatment of gays and lesbians. The suffering that homosexuals have endured in our society runs a vast gamut from employment discrimination to violent murder. The blanket condemnation of homosexuality is so strong in our culture that many homosexuals themselves go through a destructive stage of internalized homophobia; a stage which, if they survive, often leaves lasting emotional scars.[6] Many homosexuals face banishment from family and friends for revealing this aspect of their identity. Homosexuals face constant threats of discrimination, exclusion, and violence. Simply put, the perceived threat that homosexuals pose to the stability of North American society pales in comparison to the real threats to life and livelihood that they themselves confront each day.

The extent of homosexual suffering in our society is overwhelming. Although the numerous, sad statistics compiled on this matter (the volumes of which fill library shelves) can never adequately capture the singularity of the suffering inflicted upon members of the homosexual community, a look at these statistics can help begin to paint an (incomplete) picture of a life lived on the wrong side of power. When one stops to consider the many different trials a homosexual faces while moving from adolescence through adulthood, every surviving homosexual life seems miraculous.[7]

First, we may be struck by the tragic suicide of a young homosexual who fails to find a livable path between society's condemnation and her or his strong, affective attraction toward a member of the same sex. Sadly, young homosexuals often resort to suicide, seeing it as their only option when all routes of continuing life appear foreclosed. A recent American study discovered that "queer teenagers are two to three times likelier to attempt suicide, and to accomplish it, than others;...up to 30 percent of teen suicides are likely to be gay or lesbian;...a third of lesbian and gay teenagers say they have attempted suicide;...minority queer adolescents are at more extreme risk."[8]

Sadly, an intense feeling of social isolation drives many young homosexuals to pursue such a desperate measure. Eric Rofes, a gay man who studies the phenomenon of suicide among gays and lesbians, says that such drastic action is a direct result of the "estrangement" that gays and lesbians experience in Western society:

> One of the major factors contributing to the suicides of lesbians and gay men is our estrangement from the traditional support systems within our culture that people turn to in times of crisis. For a young person, these institutions would ordinarily be their family, church, and school.... If young gay people are deprived of these traditional support systems, where can they receive the help and support they need?[9]

The fact that so many young homosexuals see suicide as the only option is not only a state of affairs to be mourned, but a call to recognize and address the many ways our culture has failed to provide a safe place for young homosexuals to understand and come to terms with their sexuality. The fact that such support mechanisms are available for heterosexual youth is yet another indication of the lopsided playing field upon which gays and lesbians must continually struggle uphill.

But let us suppose this young homosexual does not become another in a long line of such hard statistics. Suppose he or she manages to survive a period of internalizing society's condemnation and hatred. What does he or she have to look forward to? Unfortunately, the picture is rather gloomy. If, for instance, a gay man comes out to family and friends, he often risks losing them. "In one survey, 26 percent of young gay men had been forced to leave home because of conflicts with parents over their sexual identity."[10] Many of these youths are left to fend for their survival on cruel urban streets. "Young gays and lesbians, many of them throwaways, comprise as many as a quarter of all homeless youth in the US."[11]

Yet let us assume even further that the surviving homosexual also manages to avoid this fate. Even this particular homosexual stands a good chance of becoming a victim of violence in his or her lifetime:

> Direct violence against lesbians and gays is a nationwide phenomenon. The National Gay and Lesbian Task Force published a study involving over two thousand lesbians and gay males in eight major US cities (Atlanta, Boston, Dallas, Denver, Los Angeles, New York, St. Louis, and Seattle). The results showed that over 90 percent of the respondents experienced some form of victimization on account of their sexual orientation—greater than one out of three had been threatened directly with violence.[12]

If the person we are talking about is Charlie Howard from Bangor, Maine, or Harvey Milk from San Francisco, he would meet, as have many others, a violent end.[13]

Nevertheless, let us pretend still further that this homosexual survivor never becomes the victim of physical violence (save by living in constant fear of it). This person still faces many other forms of discrimination. "Sexual minorities are, in many instances, excluded from protections regulating fair employment practices, housing discrimination, rights of child custody, immigration, inheritance, security clearances, public accommodations, and police protection."[14]

Having painted this picture, I have admiration for—but am not envious of—homosexual survivors. Given the violence and condemnation they face each day, I am surprised by their graceful willingness to suffer those who condemn them, to patiently tell their stories, to eagerly offer their gifts, and desperately hope that those gifts may find a place to be received.

Such graciousness has led me to examine my own complicity, as a heterosexually identified man, in the high level of abuse and marginalization the homosexual experiences. For insofar as we in the heterosexual community do anything to affirm societal homophobia, we contribute to the considerable suffering that the homosexual endures each day. While we may not condone violent attacks or murder, these attacks nevertheless find their sanction in society's negative attitudes.[15]

The need to change society's attitudes toward homosexuals is even more urgent now that many homosexuals find themselves to be physically ill and in even greater need of compassion. For example, Eve Kosofsky Sedgwick, a prominent scholar of gay studies who has been stricken with breast cancer, has been pilloried by the intellectual right in America as but one more example of the left-wing decadence that is harming the moral fibre of American youth. Normally, she would not let such uninformed criticism affect her. Yet, when joined with her illness, she explains how such condemnation both saddens and wearies her:

> If the journalistic hologram bearing my name seemed a relatively easy thing to dis-identify from, though, I couldn't help registering with much greater intimacy a much more lethal damage. I don't know a gentler way to say it than that at a time when I've needed to make especially deep draughts on the reservoir of a desire to live and thrive, that resource has shown the cumulative effects of my culture's wasting depletion of it.[16]

This is indeed a scathing indictment of Western attitudes toward homosexuals, attitudes enforced and institutionalized by the clergy, the intelligentsia, and many other people in positions of cultural authority.[17]

Sedgwick's response to her marginalization also shows the painful, cumulative effect that societal homophobia, of which none of us are innocent, has on the homosexual: "Such things as these are facts, but at the same time they are piercing or murmuring voices in the heads of those struggling to marshal 'our' resources against illness, dread, and devaluation. They speak to us. They have an amazing clarity."[18]

From the point of view of people like Sedgwick, North American society is a scary place in which to dwell. These voices from the wrong side of power provide the most poignant reasons in favour of a call for cultural change. Perhaps, then, the role of the intellectual is to marshal his or her theoretical abilities in order to "change something in the minds of people"[19]; if for no other reason than to avoid being the society that "wants its children to know nothing; wants its queer children to conform or (and this is not a figure of speech) die; and wants not to know that it is getting what it wants."[20]

ROOM TO THINK OTHERWISE: A HISTORICAL EXCURSUS

The extreme violence that is the ultimate expression of societal homophobia portrays, among other things, the depth, pervasiveness, and strength of negative attitudes toward homosexuals in our society. The fact that those offenders who manifest such extreme homophobia are often punished less harshly than those who commit equally severe crimes against other sectors of society shows a deep societal sympathy with homophobic attitudes.[21] It is not surprising, then, that we ontologize homosexual behaviour, describing it as "unnatural" or "abnormal." It is also not surprising that we view the norm of heterosexuality as writ large into the eternal, immutable structure of the universe.

If heterosexism and homophobia have become culturally normative in our day, it is important to remember that this was not always the case. By now many people are aware of the widespread practice of homosexuality in ancient Greece and Rome. Yet many associate homosexual practice at this time with promiscuity and a patriarchal abuse of power. There is a growing body of historical evidence, however, which also suggests that in premodern European society reciprocal same-sex relationships were not only licit, but officially recognized. "Though certainly not a golden age of pluralism, the 7th to the middle of the 12th centuries was an era (except in Spain) of relative calm and acceptance of same sex acts."[22]

In a thorough study of the premodern ecclesiastical archive, the late John Boswell analyzes premodern liturgies for same-sex unions and argues compellingly that these liturgies evince the fact that homosexual unions were licit and publicly recognized during this time. Boswell admits, however, that, given the ascetic attitude toward human sexuality in general in premodern Europe, he is not able to show that these same-sex unions were erotic. He also makes the valid point, however, that neither is there any strong reason to presume they were not.[23] The major strength of Boswell's argument here, I think, is his emphasis that in all measurable ways these unions were like heterosexual couplings.[24] The burning desire to prove or disprove the existence of an erotic component, to find a smoking bed, is, Boswell argues, just the anachronistic imposition of a contemporary cultural obsession with the physical part of human sexuality. Boswell does argue, however, that sexuality between persons joined in some sort of ecclesiastical union would not have seemed even mildly sinful to people at this time.[25]

Boswell argues further that, in most important ways, ceremonies of same-sex union were very similar to their heterosexual counterparts. He is vigilant to point out all similarities where they occur, and they are numerous.[26] He is also honest about pointing out the differences between the same-sex and heterosexual ceremonies.[27] Boswell argues, however, that the similarities outweigh the differences. The elements of heterosexual ceremonies that are missing in the same-sex union, he says, usually had to do with symbolizing the virginity of the bride, or they were elements that were also not mandatory for heterosexual unions but often present in them.[28]

Boswell bolsters his interpretation of these documents by citing many subsequent legal texts (post-twelfth century) which prohibit the performance of same-sex unions on the basis that they were perceived to sanction homosexual behaviour. The existence of such legal prohibitions not only helps explain the demise of the same-sex union, but also bears witness to the fact that, indeed, these unions were understood to be very similar to heterosexual marriages.[29] But there is more than just negative evidence. For instance, Boswell points out that in eleventh century Byzantine society same-sex unions were licit and recognized.[30]

By exploring such diversity of historical opinion on homosexuality, Boswell shows that the historical spread of homophobic attitudes in the West was gradual. Such attitudes were not always culturally normative, nor did they appear suddenly. The strength of Boswell's close historical analysis is that it shows how something with a grip as strong and ubiquitous as modern homophobia is, despite such pervasiveness, not writ large into the nature of things, but a historically contingent cultural phenomenon that might have been otherwise.[31]

Given Boswell's historical evidence, the emergence of homophobia in the West presents somewhat of a mystery. One reason why homophobia became such a cultural force, I think, is because it has shown itself to be an extremely functional tool for those with an interest in acquiring and maintaining cultural power. Of course, a complex cultural phenomenon like homophobia defies such simplistic analysis. It is multifaceted, with sociological, psychological, and other components. It shows itself in many forms from mild, if tolerant, revulsion, to outright violence. So I am not putting forward this suggestion as an exhaustive explanation of cultural homophobia. Nonetheless, it appears plausible that homophobia is integrally related to the centres of power in our culture, and if we understand this, we may begin to put our cultural power in the service of something less damaging.[32]

REPRESSIVE POWER

In his book *The Formation of a Persecuting Society: Power and Deviance in Western Europe*,[33] historian R. I. Moore puts forward the thesis that a persecuting society in Europe grew out of a desire among ecclesiastical and secular authorities to consolidate their cultural power. In the twelfth century there was a power struggle between a centralizing, bureaucratizing authority and local, popular jurisdictions. Moore argues that the power to ascribe normalcy and name deviancy did much to shore up the fortunes of the centralizing power at this time.[34] Medieval historian Robert Sweetman summarizes Moore's point here, saying, "it is the princes, whether ecclesiastical or secular, who called for a re-affirmation of social unity and hence the naming of the few 'deviants'."[35] The power to name deviants not only ensures social unity, it also gives those who do the naming the power to decide what shape that social unity will assume.

Moore argues that, from the twelfth century onward, deviance becomes generalized to the point where all forms of deviance come to be caricatured by a single, overarching stereotype. Moore concludes his chapter on persecution saying that for "all imaginative purposes, heretics, Jews, and lepers were interchangeable. They had the same qualities, from the same source, and they presented the same threat: through them the Devil was at work to subvert the Christian order and bring the world to chaos."[36] It is not difficult to see how in the thirteenth century all difference becomes demonized in the interests of centralized power, and that the newly introduced "machinery for persecution" described in such documents as the canons of the Fourth Lateran Council would be used against homosexuals, prostitutes, and witches, in addition to the religious heretic.[37]

While Sweetman notes problems with the historical accuracy of some of Moore's conclusions, he does agree with Moore that "there does seem to be an important shift in Western European attitudes to its marginal groups in the course of the eleventh and twelfth centuries, a shift by which people came to see them as so many modalities of a single threat to right order in church and society."[38] During this time we also find that those in power assume a heightened vigilance over the moral and physical health of their subjects. This heightened vigilance serves them because it suppresses resistance to the exercise of power over the population at large.

So when we look back in history we find not only a time when homosexual relationships may have been affirmed and recognized, but we also find some of the roots of our society's current attitude toward homosexuals. Homophobia grew in part because it helped define the normality of a central power by serving as a foil to it. These historical roots help explain many of the manifestations of homophobia in our society today.

Simply put, prejudice and discrimination are often functional for those in power. Homophobia is one form of discrimination that helps solidify a central power's claim to normativity. A dominant group can define itself as normal only against the ascription of deviance to marginal groups. In fact the recent "family values" movement in America can be interpreted as in part an upsurge of old homophobic attitudes: "At a time when the family is undergoing change and many traditional values are being questioned, lesbians, gays, and bisexuals may serve as a convenient scapegoat for those who fear what those changes will mean."[39]

PRODUCTIVE POWER

To this point, I have attempted to examine the contours of the current moral debate on homosexuality from both sides of the structure of power that manifests itself in the debate. Such an analysis, however, tends to monsterize those at the centre. Indeed, from the point of view of the marginalized homosexual, those who have cultural power do not come out looking so good. Still, such an analysis would be overly simplistic and would not do justice to the insidious ways power takes shape in this dispute. I also doubt whether reversing the polarity of this debate and demonizing those at the centre is an effective strategy. Societal homophobia is a broken cultural situation in which we all need healing.

Continental philosopher and historian of ideas Michel Foucault spent much of his academic career researching the relationship between truth and power in human discourse. His analyses may further clarify the way in which power comes to manifest itself in the dispute over homosexuality, and how we might go about resisting this particular manifestation of cultural power.

Foucault questions what he calls the "repressive hypothesis" in which repression is taken to be the paradigmatic mode in which power operates:

> What makes power hold good, what makes it accepted, is simply the fact that it doesn't only weigh on us as a force that says no, but that it traverses and produces things, it induces pleasure, forms knowledge, produces discourse. It needs to be considered as a productive network which runs through the whole social body, much more than as a negative instance whose function is repression.[40]

Foucault was one of the first thinkers to realize that, around the seventeenth and eighteenth centuries, the shape of power fundamentally changed. At this time, power began to function more invisibly and anonymously. Today, we find ourselves no longer certain about exactly who or what the word "centre" describes. We should remember this when analyzing the shape that power assumes in the current dispute. Homophobia emerged at a time in history when deviance was dealt with overtly and repressively. In order to accurately describe the way homosexuality is handled today, however, we must pay heed to the productive, and not just the repressive, aspects of cultural power.[41]

Foucault argues that if we wish to understand the way in which power functions in our discourse today, we should begin our analyses not with the intention of those who possess power, but from the point of view of the material effects that power has on its targets. "We should try to grasp subjection in its material instance as a constitution of subjects."[42] In this paper, I have tried to take up power from this perspective. When we see how cultural power affects the homosexual, we see an arrangement of power that should be changed, but we also see that such change will be a difficult purchase. Liberation for the homosexual is no longer a matter of overthrowing an oppressive sovereign authority, but instead one of rooting out a deeply seated and highly functional prejudice.

Foucault says that, after the seventeenth and eighteenth centuries, "as power becomes more anonymous and more functional, those on whom it is exercised tend to be more strongly individualized; it is exercised by surveillance rather than ceremonies, by observation rather than commemorative accounts, by comparative measures that have the 'norm' as reference rather than genealogies giving ancestors as points of reference."[43] As power becomes more functional and less overtly repressive, the "norm" that gets used as a point of reference for power also becomes more anonymous. We forget its historical origins, and it becomes difficult to think that it is possible to criticize or change that standard.

So homosexual survivors are caught up in a system of power that excludes them from the authority of normativity, and in which those who are included within the boundaries of the norm fail to recognize its historical contingency. The norm becomes understood as universal, permanent, and necessary, and any deviation from the norm threatens to bring on chaos and disorder. "What haunts us," Foucault says, "is no longer offense, or attacks on common interest, but departure from norm, anomaly. Social enemies are deviants, bringers of disorder."[44]

Ironically, Foucault's disciplinary society sounds much like Moore's persecuting one.[45] The difference, I think, involves the constitution of the centre. Unlike repressive societies, we are no longer certain what power the centre serves. The status quo, if vacuous, still functions as the ensurer of cultural stability. Foucault paints a picture of a society in which normality becomes a pervasive, yet empty, shrine.

> The judges of normality are everywhere. We are in the society of the teacher-judge, the doctor-judge, the educator-judge, the "social worker"-judge; it is on them that the universal reign of the normative is based; and each individual, wherever he may find himself, subjects to it his body, his gestures, his behaviour, his attitudes, his achievements.[46]

We are all subject to the age of normality. Unfortunately, however, some people in our society are more scathed by this state of affairs than others.

The obviousness of the discrimination and violence perpetrated against the homosexual community would lead us to believe that here we have an unproblematic instance of repressive power at work. While this is perhaps the most salient way in which power shows up in this area, researchers like Herek and Foucault warn us that we will not be able to criticize and dismantle this pernicious manifestation of power unless we recognize its productive aspects. Says Foucault: "It is not a matter of denying sexual misery, nor is it however one of explaining it negatively by a repression. The entire problem is to grasp the positive mechanism which, producing sexuality in this or that fashion, results in misery."[47] Our Western socialization into the sex roles which help constitute our sexuality (as described by Herek[48]), with its deep historical and cultural roots (as described by Boswell), along with the way in which this socialization continues to serve the interests of those with cultural power (as described by Moore and Foucault), all result in misery for the homosexual.

The way power is used to the disadvantage of the homosexual minority in our culture is depressing. But thinkers like Herek, Boswell, Moore, and Foucault give us more than a negative description of one manifestation of cultural power. Their work also helps us see that there is nothing universal, necessary, or immutable about this particular manifestation of cultural power. Given the amount of damage that has been inflicted upon the homosexual community, these thinkers give us more than ample reason to change our minds about this contentious cultural issue.

CONCLUSION

Hopefully, our culture is now in a position to question our unquestioned acceptance of the good of "normativity." If we are no longer certain of what constitutes the cultural norms we serve, and if indeed these can be shown to be damaging and lethal, not to mention contingent and unnecessary, then perhaps it has become time to renovate our society's normative framework. Perhaps the homosexuals' cry for justice can encourage us to stir our collective moral imagination in order to reinvigorate our moral vocabulary. To be sure, we will not need to create a new vocabulary *ex nihilo*, for there are many resources remaining in our Western moral, intellectual, and religious heritage which may help redirect our ethical vision. The importance of the need for such a revamped ethical vision, however, cannot be questioned. The lives of homosexuals, as well as many other minorities in Western culture, hang in the balance. We can no longer assume the innocence of what we consider to be "normal," for, as Bruce Cockburn aptly says, "the trouble with normal is it always gets worse."[49]

Notes

1.   See Gregory M. Herek, "Psychological Heterosexism and Anti-Gay Violence: The Social Psychology of Bigotry and Bashing" in Gregory M. Herek, ed., *Hate Crimes: Confronting Violence Against Lesbians and Gay Men* (Newbury Park, CA: Sage Publications, 1992), pp.149-69. Herek points out that, not only do our society's anti-homosexual attitudes work on the negative level of cultural response to a perceived threat, but that

"psychological heterosexism and anti-gay violence are often functional for the person who manifests them; the principal function served by these attitudes and actions differs for each person, depending upon her or his psychological needs; and the translation of individual needs into anti-gay attitudes and behaviours involves a complex interaction of deep-seated personality characteristics, salient aspects of the immediate situation, and cultural definitions of sexuality and gender" (p. 151). See also Herek's "On Heterosexual Masculinity," *American Behavioral Scientist* 29, 5 (May/June 1986): 563-77. In this article, Herek describes homophobia as a large-scale societal prejudice that is back-grounded by socially constructed gender roles, roles that are themselves problematic (p. 568). Such attitudes help reinforce and stabilize the sexual identity of individuals in a society whose roles are determined by the traditional gender role model. In the particular case of heterosexual masculinity, Herek claims that homophobia serves three expressive functions in male heterosexual identity. These are defensive, social, and value-expressive functions. "For each of these expressive functions, homophobia helps to define what one is not and direct hostility toward that symbol.... Under normal circumstances, homo-phobic men will not give up their prejudice as long as it continues to be functional" (pp. 572, 573).

2.   I explore the specific contours of our culture's intolerance toward this different minority in more detail below. Many surveys have been conducted, as well as books written, on the discrimination that homosexuals face daily, in differing degrees of strength, because of their different sexual orientation. See, for example, Alan P. Bell and Martin S. Weinberg, *Homosexualities: A Study of Diversity Among Men and Women* (New York: Simon and Schuster, 1978), pp. 188-200. (Cited as Bell and Weinberg.) Bell and Weinberg's study was conducted in the San Francisco area, a community noted for its tolerant attitude toward its sizable homosexual population. Nevertheless, the authors notice that the homosexual respondents of their survey suffered a significant level of social abuse. While they are quick to point out that a homosexual lifestyle is not necessarily a dangerous one, they do claim that a sizable minority of their respondents reported incidents of assault and robbery directly related to their homosexuality. The authors also point out that a survey performed in a less permissive community might well show higher incidences of discrimination and abuse. See also William Paul, et al., eds., *Homosexuality: Social, Psychological, and Biological Issues* (Beverly Hills, CA: Sage Publications, 1982). (Cited as William Paul.)

3.   The fact that the homosexual minority suffers various forms of discrimination at the hands of a heterosexual majority shows that this cultural dispute does not operate on a level playing field. As I have already stated, there exists abundant documentation to show this asymmetry. The way in which homosexuals have been dealt with by the Western legal system provides a salient example of such asymmetry. For example, in the case of *Halm v. Canada*, an American man convicted of criminal offenses in the United States contests his ordered deportation from Canada by the minister of Employment and Immigration. In Halm's case, the adjudicator for the ministry of Employment and Immigration ruled that the offenses of which Halm was convicted in the US had equivalencies in Canadian law, and he should therefore not be granted immigration to Canada. The Canadian Criminal Code offense to which Halm's offenses were found to be equivalent is section 159. This section of the code, however, has been contested as unconstitutional, because it unfairly discriminates against homosexuals (see the "Factum of the Interveners Canadian AIDS Society and Coalition For Lesbian and Gay Rights in Ontario" Ontario Court of Appeal, Court file no. C.12929). While—at the time of writing—sexual orientation is still not explicitly listed in the Canadian Human Rights Act as an illegal ground for discrimination, there have been many cases, including the 1992 case of *Haig and Birch v. Canada*, in which such discrimination was ruled unconstitutional. Given that the federal government does not plan to challenge this ruling, it is ironic that it would use

section 159 of the Criminal Code to bar a gay man from entering Canada.

4. *CIS*, p. 192.

5. Herek's work, cited in note 2, is a rather lonely exception in that it probes the effects of Western cultural socialization on our society's attitudes toward sexuality, as well as our negative and often violent attitude toward homosexuality. See also Herek's article "Social Stigma, Prejudice, and Violence Against Lesbians and Gay Men" in John C. Gonsiorek and James D. Weinrich, eds., *Homosexuality: Research Implications for Public Policy* (London: Sage, 1991). Another factor that contributes to the unreflective acceptance of this attitude (which acceptance is gradually changing) is its deep historical roots, which I will explore below.

6. See Eli Coleman, "Developmental Stages of the Coming-Out Process" in William Paul, pp. 149-51. One should keep in mind, as Coleman points out, that "[m]any people who have identified themselves as gay or lesbian, despite the pressure by society to view themselves in [a] negative manner, develop into mentally healthy individuals with positive self-concepts." The point is not that homosexuals are necessarily doomed, but that society places unfair and unreasonable obstacles before their efforts to achieve and maintain happy lives and healthy relationships.

7. In drawing the following portrait, my intention is to indict an oppressive attitude held by many people in Western society. I do not intend to imply that homosexuals are masochistic, to deny that many homosexuals do lead happy, productive, and ethical lives, or to say that all homosexuals are affected to the same degree by society's attitude toward them. Yet while the following may read as a "worst-case scenario," it is nonetheless supported by empirical evidence.

8. Paul Gibson, "Gay Male and Lesbian Youth Suicide" in the US Department of Health and Human Services Report of the Secretary's Task Force on Youth Suicide, pp. 110-42, cited in Eve Kosofsky Sedgwick, "Queer and Now" in Mark Edmundson, ed., *Wild Orchids and Trotsky: Messages from American Universities* (New York: Penguin, 1993), p. 239. (Cited as Sedgwick.) Several other studies have confirmed this finding. In a study of a Canadian and American population, authors Karla Jay and Allen Young discovered the following: "In response to the statistical questions, 40% of the men and 39% of the women say they attempted or seriously contemplated suicide. Fifty-three percent of the men and 33% of the women who had considered or attempted suicide said their homosexuality was a factor." See *The Gay Report: Lesbians and Gay Men Speak Out About Sexual Experiences and Lifestyles* (New York: Summit, 1979), pp. 729-31. See also Bell and Weinberg, p. 454; and Marcel T. Saghir and Eli Robin, *Male and Female Homosexuality: A Comprehensive Investigation* (Baltimore: Williams and Wilkins, 1973), p. 276. In *"I Thought People Like That Killed Themselves": Lesbians, Gay Men, and Suicide* (San Francisco: Grey Fox Press, 1983), author Eric E. Rofes summarizes these studies on pp. 36-37: "Existing statistics indicate that lesbian and gay youth may experience tremendous feelings of self-destructiveness. In Bell and Weinberg's study, over half of the Lesbians and Gay men who attempted suicide had made the attempt at the age of 20 or below. A startling 36% of black lesbians' attempted suicides had occurred when they where 17 years old or younger, as had 21% of the white lesbians', 32% of the black gay men's, and 27% of the white gay men's." In Saghir and Robin's study, five out of six homosexual men who had attempted suicide did so prior to the age of twenty, or, as the authors state, "during the latter part of adolescent years, when conflict at home and with one's self concerning homosexuality was intense."

9. *"I Thought People Like That Killed Themselves,"* p. 47.

10. G. Remafedi, "Male Homosexuality: The Adolescent's Perspective," *Adolescent Health Program*, University of Minnesota (Unpublished), 1985. Cited in Sedgwick, p. 240.

11. Gibson, pp. 113-15. Cited in Sedgwick, p. 240.

12. Warren J. Blumenfeld and Dianne Redmond, *Looking at Gay and Lesbian Life* (Boston:

Beacon Press, 1993), p. 250. (Cited as Blumenfeld and Redmond.) See also William Paul, p. 360: "An informal pilot survey reported that among 50 fairly visible Gay men (mean age 34, living openly in San Francisco), 20 percent had encountered some form of anti-Gay violence. These data are consistent with victimization reports compiled there by Community United Against Violence.... The attackers are predominantly young males (aged 15-24) who usually operate in groups that outnumber victims. These groups deliberately enter areas with large Gay populations, searching for victims. Data from emergency room admissions during the same period showed Gay people accounting for 27 percent of the street attack victims in an area with a heterosexual majority."

13. For a detailed account of the political events surrounding Harvey Milk's assassination, see David J. Thomas, "San Francisco's 1979 White Night Riot: Injustice, Vengeance and Beyond" in William Paul, pp. 337-50.

14. Blumenfeld and Redmond, p. 252.

15. Ibid., p. 247: "The assailants [of homosexuals] tend to be white males in their teens or early twenties who are acting out society's prejudices.... Intimidation and humiliation are the instruments by which [the assailants] make their beliefs known—beliefs which very often receive community sanction." See also William Paul, pp. 359-61. At one time, violent attacks on homosexuals were ascribed to an individual psychosis called "homosexual panic." More recently, however, psychologists have come to doubt that these attacks can be divorced from larger societal prejudices. See Henry T. Chuang and Donald Addington, "Homosexual Panic: A Review of its Concept," *Canadian Journal of Psychiatry* 33 (October 1988): 613-17, especially p. 615: "In dealing with acts of violence attributed to "homosexual panic", one cannot dissociate from how society, with contributions from psychiatric, legal, and religious sources, views homosexual behaviour." The *Toronto Star* confirmed such findings when it reported that incidents of violence against homosexuals increased dramatically during the public debate of Bill 167, a debate which galvanized anti-gay groups. ("How the Death of Ontario's Bill 167 Brought Misery to Three Families," *Toronto Star* 13 September 1994, A17.) See also William Paul, "Minority Status for Gay People: Majority Reaction and Social Context" in William Paul, p. 363: "there have been numerous examples of violent attacks against Gay individuals and Gay groups that seem undeniably correlated with anti-Gay rhetorical campaigns. During the campaign by Bryant's followers...there were apparently systematic violent attacks against both Gay and heterosexual civil rights workers—including beatings and fire-bombings" (*Miami News*, 22 March 1977). Data gathered by Stingel...indicated a sharp rise in anti-gay violence in San Francisco after the CBS special "Gay Power, Gay Politics."

16. Sedgwick, p. 259.

17. See Blumenfeld and Redmond, pp. 252-62.

18. Sedgwick, p. 260.

19. In Luther H. Martin, et al., eds., *Technologies of the Self: A Seminar with Michel Foucault* (Amherst: University of Massachusetts Press, 1988), p. 10, Foucault describes this as "the role of an intellectual."

20. Sedgwick, p. 241.

21. See Blumenfeld and Redmond, pp. 247-52. The teenage murderers of Charlie Howard did not go to trial, instead they accepted guilty pleas to the lesser charge of manslaughter and were sent to a youth centre for a short time after which they rejoined their families. The killer of Harvey Milk, Dan White, was also convicted of the reduced charge of manslaughter and sentenced to a relatively light prison term of six years (given that he premeditatedly shot and killed two city officials in cold blood). See also William Paul, p. 359, for a record of an Arizona case in which teenage murderers were released without sentence.

22. Blumenfeld and Redmond, p. 237.

23. John Boswell, *Same-Sex Unions in Pre-modern Europe*, p. 182 n. 101.
24. Ibid., pp. 185, 190-91. Some of these similarities include the facts that the joined couple lived together and that the ceremony only ever applied to two people.
25. Ibid., p. 188.
26. Ibid., pp. 204, 206, 207, 210, 211-12, 217. Some of the similarities between same-sex and heterosexual unions listed here include the fact that similar litanies were used in both ceremonies, they were both usually followed by some sort of communal feast, in both ceremonies the parties joined right hands. All the different liturgies for same-sex unions shared at least four out of ten elements of medieval marriage symbolism.
27. Ibid., pp. 207, 209, 215, 216. These differences include the absence of rings in ceremonies of same-sex union, the fact that such ceremonies rarely mentioned crowning, the fact that different Biblical texts were used for each ceremony, and the fact that a formal expression of consent is missing in the liturgy for same-sex unions.
28. Ibid., pp. 209, 215.
29. Ibid., pp. 225-26, cf. 249.
30. Ibid., pp. 229, 246-48, cf. 281: "In almost every age and place the [same-sex union] ceremony fulfilled what most people today regard as the essence of marriage: a permanent romantic commitment between two people, witnessed and recognized by the community."
31. Ibid., p. 243: "in fact sustained and effective oppression of those who engaged in homosexual behavior was not known in Europe until the thirteenth century, and was never common in the Byzantine East."
32. In *Christianity, Social Tolerance, and Homosexuality: Gay People in Western Europe from the Beginning of the Christian Era to the Fourteenth Century* (Chicago: University of Chicago Press, 1980), Boswell offers the following (p. 37): "The transition from tolerance to hostility [towards homosexuals] ... was almost wholly the consequence of the rise of corporate states and institutions with the power and desire to regulate increasingly personal aspects of human life." See also p. 302: "Change in public attitudes had a profound and lasting impact on European institutions and culture as a result of the permanent and official expression it achieved in thirteenth century laws, literature, theology, all of which continued to influence Western thought and social patterns long after the disappearance of the particular circumstances which produced them."
33. Cited as *Persecuting Society*.
34. See *Persecuting Society*, pp. 133, 135, 144 and 146. On p. 140 Moore claims that persecution "served to stimulate and assist the development of the claims and techniques of government in church and state, as well as the cohesiveness and confidence of those who operated it."
35. Unpublished manuscript, Toronto: Institute for Christian Studies, 1995. (Cited as Sweetman.)
36. *Persecuting Society*, p. 65.
37. Ibid., p. 10.
38. Sweetman, p. 6.
39. Blumenfeld and Redmond, p. 233.
40. Michel Foucault, "Truth and Power" in *Power/Knowledge: Selected Interviews and Other Writings* (New York: Pantheon, 1980), p. 119.
41. As mentioned earlier, the work by Herek, cited above in note 2, begins to examine the productive aspects of the power exerted by a homophobic cultural majority.
42. Foucault, "Two Lectures" in *Power/Knowledge*, p. 97.
43. Michel Foucault, *Discipline and Punish: The Birth of the Prison* (New York: Vintage, 1979), p. 193.
44. Ibid., pp. 299-300.
45. In the interview "Sexual Choice, Sexual Act: Foucault and Homosexuality" in *Politics, Philosophy, Culture: Interviews and Other Writings, 1977-1984* (London: Routledge,

1988), Foucault notes that our society overtly represses homosexuality, "and severely so" (p. 293). Foucault recognizes that when it comes to homosexuality, cultural power is not very subtle. Boswell also observes that only when public antipathy abates, do the fortunes of marginal groups improve, and that for homosexuals, unlike usurers, this has yet to occur. See *Christianity, Social Tolerance, and Homosexuality*, p. 332.

46. *Discipline and Punish*, p. 304.
47. Foucault, "Power and Sex" in *Politics, Philosophy, Culture*, p. 113.
48. See note 2.
49. From the album "The Trouble with Normal" © 1983 True North Records.

9

Native Self-government: Between the Spiritual Fire and the Political Fire

GEORGE VANDERVELDE

My people, the Iroquois, were very powerful people. They had a coalition of forces that was governed by two fires: the spiritual fire and the political fire. The central fire, of course, was the spiritual fire. The primary law of Indian Government is the spiritual law. Spirituality is the highest form of politics, and our spirituality is directly involved in government.
OREN LYONS, *"Spirituality, Equality, and Natural Law"[1]*

News stories made much of the religious ceremonies surrounding the official signing of the historic Aboriginal self-government agreement in Manitoba on 17 December 1994: the opening prayer, the "sacred" peace pipe, the closing song.[2] By contrast, most writing about Aboriginal self-government is devoid of any mention of religion or spirituality. This silence is curious. After all, descriptions of Native spirituality emphasize its all-encompassing, holistic, integral character, its interwovenness with every aspect of existence.[3] It seems exceedingly strange then to observe that spirituality vanishes almost entirely from view when the spotlight illumines not merely an aspect of existence but its societal warp and woof, the governance structures of a self-governing community. A torrent of literature has appeared of late on Native spirituality, as well as on the issues surrounding Native self-government. But they exist as two separate worlds, it seems, without a link. That isolation is anomalous, since both are encompassing "worlds." As Oren Lyons rightly indicates, politics and spirituality are two fires that have "governing" force, are directly linked, and of which one has primacy, namely the spiritual fire.

In this chapter, I will explore the thesis that banishing reflection on the connection between the two fires may well prove to be a costly escape from its troublesome return in reality.

SPIRITUALITY

First, a few preliminary remarks about "spirituality." Although its abstractness makes it somewhat problematic, spirituality is a useful term to "express the subject of communion with God and the way of life which emanates from that."[4] To be useful for our purposes, however, it needs to be made at once more general and more specific. More generally, spirituality is a common human phenomenon, regardless of whether it is related to "God." More specifically, spirituality does not refer simply to the relation with "God" but to the particular ways in which this relation is maintained, nurtured, and directed. Accordingly, as used here, spirituality refers to the specific ways in which human beings attune life to what they consider to be ultimate, i.e., the source or matrix of life. Thus, spirituality suffuses all of life but comes to concentrated expression in rituals, rites, worship, and teachings.

Native Spirituality

To speak of Native spirituality is misleading in that its form varies among the diverse Native peoples. Christopher Vecsey mentions the following reasons for this difficulty:

1. the cultural-linguistic gap,
2. The considerable diversity among tribes, and even within a single community (monotheists, henotheists, and polytheists, as well as a variety of cultic traditions, may coexist in the same village),
3. the fluidity resulting from the absence of a written canon,
4. the comprehensiveness of such spirituality, making it difficult to circumscribe,
5. its syncretistic and mutable nature (Christian elements may be incorporated along with others),
6. the secrecy surrounding sacrality.[5]

Despite these difficulties, it is possible to identify some salient features of Native spirituality. In fact, merely describing aspects of Native spirituality reveals its intimate connection with the practicalities of governance. This is evident in several of the items in Deward Walker's enumeration of characteristics of Aboriginal spirituality:

1. "a special sense of the sacred that is centred in natural time and natural geography,"
2. "a set of rituals that express religious belief and provide social cohesion,"
3. "shamans ... who teach and lead group(s) in the conduct of their ritual life,"
4. "a set of prescriptive and proscriptive (ethical) guidelines establishing appropriate behaviour associated with the sacred,"

5. "a belief that harmony must be maintained with the sacred through the satisfactory conduct of rituals and adherence to sacred prescriptions and proscriptions."[6]

Given the obvious linkage between spirituality, ritual, authority, and governance, it is hard to envisage how Aboriginal spirituality can play anything other than a hegemonic role.

Native Self-government

The "natural" hegemony of Native spirituality is confirmed when one approaches the question at hand from the opposite direction, namely, self-government. Reflecting on the exigencies of Hawaiian Aboriginal peoples, Mililani Trask identifies several constitutive elements of "sovereignty":

1. a "strong and abiding faith in Creator: sovereignty cannot be achieved without a strong spiritual basis,"
2. "people with a common culture and history,"
3. "a land base—this consists not only of earth but also natural resources, and oceans,"
4. a "governance structure [in the Hawaiian situation, a monarchy].... Any groups seeking sovereignty must have a decision-making process,"
5. an "economic base—achieving economic self-sufficiency."[7]

In the Canadian context, David Hawkes lists rights as accruing to Aboriginal peoples in the following areas:

*   land, resources, and environment
*   collective self-determination or self-government
*   citizenship/membership in Aboriginal nations/communities
*   economic development, employment, and training
*   hunting, trapping, fishing, harvesting, gathering
*   customary law and enforcement
*   language, culture, religion
*   fiscal relations/arrangements
*   education
*   health and social services[8]

The Privileged Role of Native Spirituality

Only in Trask's description of "sovereignty" and "self-determination" does religion or spirituality play the dominant role that one would expect, given its central place in Native culture and way of life. Not only does he place religion first; he makes it the sine qua non of sovereignty: "sovereignty cannot be attained without a strong spiritual basis." Consequently, spirituality appears again in his description of self-rule, when he insists that room is to be created for the free exercise specifically of "traditional religion" and "traditional sacred ways." He does not indicate whether the same room is to be accorded to other "religions." But the earlier statement seems to indicate that Native spirituality has a privileged place.

Giving pride of place to Native spirituality is, on the one hand, to be expected. After all, Aboriginal cultic rites and practices, and sacred myths are the prime carriers of Native culture, traditions, and wisdom. Furthermore, Native spirituality is linked to the land, the key component to Native self-government. Since Native spirituality is so intrinsically linked to a Native way of life it seems destined to have a hegemonic role in a Native self-governing community.

The Problematic Role of Native Spirituality

Yet, this natural link of Native spirituality to Native self-government is fraught with problems. The potential problems are not recognized of course when the two "fires" are systematically separated from one another. This compartmentalization is precisely what happens within the academic tradition. Spirituality or religion is a private matter. Self-government is a socio-political matter; it lies in the public realm. This separation, however, works only in theory. The genius of Native spirituality is precisely that it resists compartmentalization.

Both the Western bias that eliminates spirituality when considering socio-political issues and the natural resistance of Native experience to this myopic approach is illustrated by a study commissioned by a church. Bishop Denis Croteau, of the MacKenzie-Fort Smith diocese initiated a study designed "to identify the major political, economic, social and cultural concerns of the people."[9] Given this clear focus on the structural and cultural concerns, the outcome is all the more striking: The two key concerns of the Dene and Inuit people were "spirituality and the land." Of these, spirituality, which was not even within the study's purview, was the most fundamental and encompassing. The element of surprise about this conclusion is evident in the report by Marie Zarowny, who undertook the study:

> Although some people expressed surprise that the Church was interested in hearing about their political and economic concerns, it quickly became evident that the Dene integrate the religious or spiritual with the secular. As they spoke they didn't separate their lives into compartments.... This was especially clear as they returned again and again to their yearnings for a deeper spirituality. Although this study was not intended to include spirituality, concerns in this area were so persistently expressed that I could not ignore them.[10]

The study mandate, at least in the mind of the investigator, placed spirituality beyond the study's parameters. Yet, spirituality could not be banished. It emerges, not as a personal dimension that is simply juxtaposed with socio-political concerns, but as a reality that lies at the very core of such concerns. Zarowny reports, "What became clear to me is that spirituality is at the heart of the struggle of the Native people to be strong and to be proud as individuals and as a people."[11] In the words of a Native person interviewed for the study, "We need an integrated approach to spirituality: it needs to be holistic, including politics, business, education and social" (sic.).[12] If a church-commissioned study was thus blinkered, the academic study of Native political issues is even more likely to ignore their connection with spirituality.

Perhaps the surprising silence regarding spirituality in discussions of Native self-government cannot be ascribed only to the scholarly habit of compartmentalization and the secular penchant for banishing religion and spirituality from political deliberations. Perhaps the silence regarding spirituality reflects premonitions about the dangers of a direct, intrinsic link between Native spirituality and Native self-government. The political fire alone is daunting enough. Add the spiritual fire and one fears a conflagration, especially if a particular spirituality were to be privileged.

The problematic character of ascribing a "natural" primacy to Native spirituality can be demonstrated by Chief Gordon Peters' description of its proper role. His assessment is all the more significant for our purposes in view of his affirmation of the privileged status of Native spirituality within a self-governing community.

> There is only one source of authority that we have, and that is the Creator, who put us here with a very distinct purpose in mind.... The original instructions that we were given as a people and the role we play was to take care of the earth. For us to understand the original instructions that we were given, it must be part and parcel of our understanding that we are not the Creator as man, but we are simply part of creation. We must live in harmony and share the power with all other beings—the animals, the birds —to keep in tune.[13]

Stated in such general terms, the primacy assigned to Native spirituality need not present a problem. But assumed are all the specifics of Native "religion" that must to be observed in order "to keep in tune" with creation.

> We must understand the legends and stories that we have about the creation of this land and why we call this land Turtle Island—our songs, our dances, our ceremonies—all of those oral things that tell us how we were put here and why we were put here and what we must continue to do in order to remain here. Those songs and those oral ways and those traditions are so strong and so powerful in being able to relate to us our existence that they were some of the first things that the European people tried to diminish, and

then to eliminate, so that we would no longer have the connection with the original instructions, so that our authority would then come from the same kind of documents that were being provided for their people.[14]

He concludes with a striking appeal:

There is a natural law that we must observe. There is a natural power that is greater than ours as man. Until we recognize that, legislation, constitutions, and all other forms of supposed authority and jurisdiction will be meaningless.[15]

A similar point is made by another author when he maintains that "Through (Native) spirituality the natural order of things was revealed and man's proper relationship to nature was established—a relationship of respect and preservation, not exploitation."[16] This presents no particular problem to pluralism when, strained through a Western utilitarian sieve, all that remains of this "spirituality" is its ecological distillate, namely, respect and care for creation. Left behind in the sifting process, however, is the particular web of spirituality within which this care is sustained. Harmony with creation is maintained not simply by "working at it" but by observing very specific rituals, by heeding the wisdom of "spiritual" elders. Speaking of the Iroquois, Oren Lyons maintains that "The primary law of Indian government is the spiritual law"; conversely, "Spirituality is the highest form of politics, and our spirituality is directly involved in government." It is difficult to understand spirituality here as simply referring to general values regarding care for the earth. These statements, after all, are immediately linked to the role of chiefs with regard to cultic rituals: "As chiefs we are told that our first and most important duty is to see that the spiritual ceremonies are carried out. Without the ceremonies, one does not have a basis on which to conduct government for the welfare of the people."[17] The chiefs are both cultic and political leaders. This intimate link comes to the fore also in Tom Porter's essay. Leadership in the community depends on one's involvement and leadership in the cultic practices of a particular community: the chief "has to know those ceremonies because the knowledge of the spiritual values of his nation is the chief's first mandate from the Creator."[18]

This conflation is embedded in the mythological stories of the origins of the Aboriginal peoples. The Creator and his "Messiah" have delineated a form of government, a "constitution" and handed down the "original instructions" that must be heeded.[19] From this is derived, according to Porter, the relationship of male and female chiefs, as well as the practice of banishing the "bad apple," the chief who does not act in the interest of the nation.[20] The spiritual and the political community are assumed to be one. Soteriology and politicology merge. Noel Lyon insists that the separation of church and state is "a concept almost sacrilegious to Aboriginal culture."[21] If this is meant literally, it presents a major problem, for it makes the problem of pluralism acute: which "church" is to be joined to the state? But even if Lyon here equates (as is more likely) separation of church and state with separation of religion and politics, the concomitant intertwinement of religion and politics presents a problem, when one religion is designated as the "official" religion.

PLURALIST CONUNDRUM?

Assigning a privileged place to Native spirituality presents a strange paradox. On the one hand, the existence of self-governing communities next to others and within a single state represents a supreme expression of structural or associational pluralism. On the other hand giving hegemony to Native spirituality within the self-governing community contradicts religious or directional pluralism.[22] This presents us with the following anomaly: pluralism makes room for Native self-government; Native self-government eliminates pluralism. Limiting directional pluralism need not present a problem as long as the non-pluralist entity is constituted by voluntary membership. Examples of this type of entity are a religious organization or a club. A self-governing community, however, is not a voluntary society. As a land-based entity, membership in the community is determined either by territory or by ethnicity. In both cases, membership is involuntary. Leaving this community—let alone being forced to do so—cannot be a solution, especially when Native identity is so closely related to geographic space. As Leslie Green points out, "when membership is partly ascriptive," i.e., membership by birth rather than choice, "exit is difficult and hardly a good substitute for rights."[23]

According Native spirituality a privileged place presents a problem because it appears to limit the public role of other religions. If more than half of the Native population considers itself Christian, as census figures indicate,[24] a large segment of Aboriginal people is marginalized by assigning a privileged public role to Native spirituality.

When presented with this problem, James Dumont of the Department of Native Studies at the University of Sudbury, made some intriguing observations. When asked, how he conceived of the place of spirituality in a self-governing Aboriginal community, he unhesitatingly replied that Native spirituality would constitute the common ethos. As to the situation in which a large percentage—perhaps the majority—of the Native peoples of a particular community would be Christian, Dumont did not consider this to be a problem. He cautioned that in considering these kinds of issues, one should not allow particular problems to determine (and hamper) one's approach to self-government. He suggested, as an analogy, the difficulties encountered in determining Native status. There are many cases in which it is not easy to determine who may legitimately claim this status. However, to start with the problematic claims, Dumont insisted, would probably lead to the conclusion that the problem is insoluble. It is better to take as one's point of departure the more general situation in which Indian status is clear.

This approach provided an opening to address the problem of spirituality more pointedly: assuming that one has determined which persons are legitimate members of a particular Native grouping, it is quite likely that a large proportion of this group is Christian; how can one insist that the spirituality of some of the members of a self-governing community will have privileged status in policy-setting, decision-making, and governance?

Reflecting on this situation, Dumont suggested that perhaps all Aboriginal peoples would have to go through a decolonization process in order to rediscover their identity. In this context, he appealed to "liberation theology" and the bondage (exodus/exile) return motif. Christianity, as brought by the colonizers, brought with it an alien culture, which was imposed on the indigenous peoples. Decolonization would involve a purification process in which the alien elements would be removed. As sound as this role of Native spirituality may be, the challenge of pluralism remains: what is the status of those who appeal to a different spirituality?

PLURALISM—IMPOSSIBLE NECESSITY?

One obvious way to deal with the potentially oppressive features of granting hegemonic status to Native spirituality is the recourse to rights, more specifically, individual rights. This approach is obvious, however, only from the vantage point of Western political liberalism. From the vantage point of Native aspirations, this recourse to individual rights is highly problematic. The very quest for Native self-government presents a critique of an individualist approach to the aspirations of a group. Because political liberalism denies that social groups have rights as a collective entity, the appeal to individual rights subverts the viability of existing distinctive groups.[25]

Avigail Eisenberg explores the problems inherent in casting Native rights issues as a conflict between individual and collective rights.[26] This approach, she argues, polarizes the issue as a contest between incommensurate, absolute values, and renders the decision in favour of one or the other to be either arbitrary or biased.[27] A more constructive approach opens up from what she calls "the difference perspective." This approach does not cast the problem abstractly in terms of competing rights, but takes into account the "differences between people that play a constitutive role in shaping their identities," such as culture, religion, language, and gender.[28] Some of these differences, such as a distinctive language, require a communal context in order to be maintained. Rather than having to decide between competing values represented by opposing sides as being absolute and incommensurable, the difference perspective weighs the various values that are at stake in terms of their importance for maintaining individual or group difference.

She discusses a case heard in the British Columbia Supreme Court, *Thomas v. Norris*. David Thomas was forcibly subjected to the Spirit Dance, an initiation rite of the Coast Salish people. Thomas sued representatives of the band for assault, battery, and false imprisonment.[29] This case is especially interesting because spirituality or religion plays a significant role. The defence claimed that the Spirit Dance "is part of the religious tradition" of the Coast Salish people and that they had a collective right to continue this tradition by forcibly initiating members. The plaintiff, by contrast, claimed that, though he was a member of this group, he had lived off the reserve most of his life, had not been raised in the religious tradition and knew little about it.[30]

The court decided in favour of Thomas. Unfortunately, the verdict does not fully clarify the nature of competing rights claims. The importance of group difference is obscured for two reasons. First, Thomas was not a full participant in Salish culture. Second, the court determined that "the Spirit Dance, and more specifically the involuntary aspect of it, was not a central feature of the Salish way of life."[31] Regarding the first, Eisenberg rightly raises the question whether the outcome would have been different if Thomas had been more fully part of Salish culture.[32] In determining the role of spirituality in a self-governing community, full participation in the community is crucial. What if members of a self-governing group who, rather than simply claiming ignorance of the religious tradition of the group, wish to dissociate themselves from its spirituality? As Frances Svenson remarks regarding Native communities, "Members of the community are expected to participate in communally-oriented functions, and to respect the authority of the community and its traditions and values; withdrawal from participation is equated with withdrawal from the community, since membership can mean nothing other than participation."[33] For that reason opting out of the Spirit Dance, or an equivalent Aboriginal rite, means removal from the community. Or, if they remain, these dissenters would lose the right to participate fully in the juridical and political decision-making processes within the self-governing community.

The difference perspective is helpful in unravelling various values underlying conflicting group and individual rights claims. Nevertheless, Eisenberg's analysis does not help to determine the appropriate role of Native spirituality in a self-governing community, because she marginalizes religion. In sifting through "identity conferring characteristics," she relegates religion to the realm of "individual difference," because it "depends on a personal relation to a deity." Thus it is assumed to have no "political significance within a community."[34] But this privatization of religion is a Western liberal intrusion that violates the holistic nature of Native spirituality.[35] Melissa Williams aptly criticizes this kind of dissection, when she states: "it strikes me as a tricky bit of surgery so neatly to separate religion from culture."[36]

Conversely, it could be argued that the insistence on the holistic character of Native spirituality is an unwelcome intrusion of an antiquated view of religion in the political realm. A compelling argument can be made, however, that politics itself cannot be shorn of convictions rooted in religious allegiances. Michael Perry makes that case when he contends that neutral politics is impossible.[37] He argues that all political choices involve convictions about human good, which, for some, include religious convictions. To exclude religious convictions from the political forum because they are not generally shared is arbitrary. It privileges the convictions of some at the expense of those who hold religious convictions pertaining to the human good.[38] Moreover, Perry is convinced that "only a politics in which beliefs about human good, including disputed [also religious] beliefs about human good, has a central place is capable of addressing" the most basic "political-moral questions, like questions about human rights."[39]

BEYOND PRIVATIZING AND PRIVILEGING SPIRITUALITY

If religion and spirituality cannot be banished from the political enterprise, the question remains regarding the appropriate role of spirituality in a community composed of groups with divergent basic religious convictions. This brings the discussion of spirituality and Native self-government in relation to pluralism full circle. We began by exploring the problem posed by granting privileged status to Native spirituality within a self-governing community. We acknowledged that such status can be defended on the grounds that it is intrinsically bound up with Native traditions and Native identity, that it is holistic, and fundamentally related to land as a habitat which evokes respect and care. Yet, granting this status to one particular spirituality obviously privileges some members of that community over others. Thus by redressing the injustices resulting from the marginalization of Native people within Canadian society, new injustices would be built into Native self-governing communities. But this anomaly exposes not merely a potential problem for self-governing communities. It poses a problem with respect to the viability of pluralism itself.

The problem which I have in mind is the same as that which Mouw and Griffioen address in terms of the metaphor "open horizon."[40] We can focus on this problem by posing pluralism as paradox. To have a unitary state one must devise a neutral state. It creates room for a diversity of competing and incompatible religions only by privatizing them. Yet, it is the genius of religion to be holistic and totalizing. Religions are therefore inherently "imperialistic" in that they vie for hegemony. Even a pluralist approach to society cannot escape proceeding from a fundamental commitment that guides a specific societal configuration of pluralism. There can be no pluralism of pluralisms. Within a single state there is a structure that limits diversity. There can be only one set of rules. And such rules cannot be neutral. They reflect a dominant ideology. Such ideology is rooted—whether implicitly or explicitly—in religion, in convictions about ultimate realities.

Perhaps a description of a the integrality of Native spirituality, worldview, order, ethic, and, by implication, governance raises the problem of pluralism itself. Discussing legal systems, James Youngblood Henderson describes the Native sense of an ordered, comprehensive, "normative universe" or "natural order." This unity is connected to the earth and to the spirit world that inhabits and animates it. The cohesion of this world lies, he says, in a "shared world-view," and comes to expression in language, which lies at the core of the normative order. In other words this cosmic order is a "sacred order," which is maintained by rituals and by a life led in accordance with the guidance of spiritual elders. "Violating the harmony of the natural order unleashes danger-ous forces," which need to be mollified and reintegrated to restore harmony.[41]

In this description the problem of directional pluralism again presents itself. If religion is by nature totalizing and holistic, is religious pluralism really viable? Is it possible to have a geographically determinate jurisdiction in which competing, holistic worldviews coexist? Or, to pose the same question from another angle, if religion is the deepest cohesive force in society, what in its absence holds a society together? A. James Reichley puts the question this way, "Can a nation that maintains no established church, and that regards religious pluralism as both socially inescapable and ethically desirable, confidently look to religion to generate and nurture its fundamental moral values?"[42]

If one refuses to solve this problem either by privileging a particular spirituality, which is to marginalise all who follow a different spiritual path, or by relegating religion to a private realm, which is to denature religion, the only way forward may be a pragmatic one. Any holistic spirituality fosters a basic wisdom tradition, seasoned discernment into the practicalities of daily life. What if the interaction among religions (or spiritualities) were to take place at the point of Native spirituality's strongest suit, namely, its creation-oriented holism? Through such interaction the earth-oriented bent of biblical revelation (to limit ourselves to the Judeo-Christian tradition) can also be recovered. This common quest would likely unearth the practical, experiential wisdom deposited in biblical and Aboriginal traditions. Or, approached from the viewpoint of practical issues confronted in a local setting, adherents of diverse faiths would all draw on their traditioned wisdom for guidance regarding concrete problems that face a community as a whole. A conviction regarding political issues within a community would not be given greater credence by virtue of the spirituality in which it is rooted. Rather, arguments for a particular political proposal would be weighed in terms of their practical sagacity.[43] Thus diverse spiritualities or religions are acknowledged as legitimate, even intrinsic, sources for political deliberations and decisions but no particular spirituality is privileged.

While Native decision-making processes work towards consensus, validating the public role of spirituality in no way ensures this result. In fact, the realization that public conflict has often been rooted in divergent religious convictions is precisely what has made the banishment of religion from the public sphere appear to be an attractive solution. If, however, the marginalization of spirituality militates against the nature of both the religious and the political fires, the public role of religion and the potential for the public clash of deeply held convictions cannot be averted. The solution is not to banish spirituality from the public square but to build into the public square ways of reconciling or living with opposing convictions.

Either to privatize or to privilege spiritualities is to diminish the socio-political well-being of a self-governing community. By declaring all religion or spirituality politically irrelevant, the privatization of spirituality robs political deliberation of the rich resources regarding the human good that are to be found in spirituality. Privatizing marginalizes all spirituality. Privileging a particular spirituality marginalizes all spiritualities but one. Honouring the two fires brings about not the conflagration but the vitalization of a self-governing community.

Notes

1.   Oren Lyons, "Spirituality, Equality, and Natural Law" in Leroy Little Bear, et al., eds., *Pathways to Self-Determination: Canadian Indians and the Canadian State* (Toronto: University of Toronto Press, 1984) p. 5. (Cited as *Pathways*.)
2.   *Toronto Star*, 18 December 1994.
3.   See, e.g., Christopher Vecsey, *Imagine Ourselves Richly: Mythic Narratives of North American Indians* (San Francisco: HarperCollins, 1991), p. 26.
4.   Frank C. Senn, *Protestant Spiritual Traditions* (New York: Paulist Press, 1986), p. 2.
5.   Christopher Vecsey, ed., *Handbook of American Indian Religious Freedom* (New York: Crossroads, 1991), pp. 12ff. (Cited as *Handbook*.)
6.   See Deward E. Walker "Protection of American Indian Sacred Geography" in *Handbook*, p. 102.
7.   "Global Consultation on Self-Determination," sponsored by the World Council of Churches, unpublished report, 1994, pp. 10, 11.
8.   David C. Hawkes, "Aboriginal Self-Government: What Does It Mean?" (Kingston: Institute of Intergovernmental Relations, 1985), pp. 11, 12.
9.   See "You Can Help Us to Become Strong Inside," *Insight* (1990): 77-85.
10. Ibid., p. 79.
11. Ibid.
12. Ibid., p. 80.
13. Chief Gordon Peters in Frank Cassidy, ed., *Aboriginal Self-Determination* (Lantzville, BC: Oolichan Books, 1991), pp. 33-34. For the intrinsic relationship between Native culture (including the prominence of spirituality and the sacred ways) and juridical issues, see James Dumont, "Justice and Aboriginal People" in *Royal Commission on Aboriginal People: Aboriginal Peoples and the Justice System* (Ottawa: Ministry of Supply and Services, 1993), pp. 42-85.
14. Peters in Cassidy.
15. Ibid.
16. *Pathways*, p. 4 (introduction to article by Oren Lyons).
17. Oren Lyons, "Spirituality, Equality, and Natural Law," *Pathways*, p. 5.

18. Tom Porter, "Traditions of the Constitution of the Six Nations," *Pathways*, p. 20.
19. Ibid., p. 15.
20. Ibid., pp. 17-18.
21. Noel Lyon, "Comments on Constitutional Interpretation" in David C. Hawkes and Evelyn Peters, eds., *Issues in Entrenching Aboriginal Self-Government* (Kingston: Queen's University Press, 1987), p. 58.
22. For the terms "associational" and "directional" pluralism, see Mouw and Griffioen, p. 16. "Associational" pluralism refers to membership in a diverse groups. "Directional" pluralism refers to the diversity of religions, worldviews, or value systems to which people are committed.
23. Leslie Green, "Internal Minorities and Their Rights" in Judith Baker, ed., *Group Rights* (Toronto: University of Toronto Press, 1994), p. 109.
24. Statistics Canada, *Aboriginal Peoples Survey 1991* (Ottawa: Statistics Canada, 1995): APS91A.C427.
25. For this reason, Aboriginal leaders have sought limitations on the applicability of the Charter of Rights and Freedoms to Native peoples. See Will Kymlicka, "Individual and Community Rights" in *Group Rights*, pp. 17-33. The issue of the relation of individual rights vis-à-vis those of the community becomes especially acute in the appeal to the charter of rights to assert the rights of Native women; see Teressa Nahanee, "Taking the Measure of Self-Government: For Native Women, It's a Bad Deal," *Compass* 10 (1992): 17-18. The dilemma regarding the role of Native women is well expressed in a statement quoted by Kathleen Jamieson, "Discrimination against women is a scandal but imposing the cultural standards of white society would be another scandal"; Kathleen Jamieson, *Indian Women and the Law in Canada: Citizens Minus* (Ottawa: Ministry of Supply and Services, 1978), p. 2. See also Teresa Nahanee, "Dancing with a Gorilla: Aboriginal Women, Justice, and the Charter" in *Royal Commission on Aboriginal People*, pp. 359-82.
26. Avigail Eisenberg, "The Politics of Individual and Group Difference in Canadian Jurisprudence," *Canadian Journal of Political Science* 27 (1994): 3-21.
27. Ibid., p. 8. Richard Simeon recognizes a strong bias in favour of individual rights. "The overwhelming thrust of the Charter of Rights is to give primacy to the rights of individuals and to see citizenship as an abstract, universal concept in which each individual is the same as every other, taken out of an historical or social context. The Charter is hostile to any subordination of the individual to the collective interest; it is hostile to any differentiation of rights; it is hostile to the maintenance of distinctive cultural values." Richard Simeon, "Aboriginal Self-Government and Canadian Political Values" in Hawkes and Peters, *Issues*, p. 52.
28. Ibid., p. 9.
29. Ibid., p. 3.
30. Ibid., pp. 17-18. See also Leslie Green's analysis of the same case, *Group Rights*, p. 109.
31. Ibid., p. 18.
32. Ibid.
33. Frances Svensson, "Liberal Democracy and Group Rights: The Legacy of Individualism and Its Impact on American Indian Tribes," *Liberal Democracy and Group Rights* 27 (1979): 431.
34. Ibid., p. 11.
35. Her own reference to "cultural or religious communities" (p. 12) indicates that it is difficult to banish religion to the private sphere.
36. Melissa Williams, "Group Inequality and the Public Culture of Justice" in *Group Rights*, p. 39 (here in critique of Kymlicka).
37. "The Impossibility of Neutral Politics" in Gordon L. Anderson and Morton A. Kaplan, eds., *Morality and Religion in Liberal Democratic Societies* (New York: Paragon House,

1992), pp. 41-72.

38. Ibid., pp. 42-48.
39. Ibid., p. 61.
40. Mouw and Griffioen, pp. 158-77.
41. James Youngblood Henderson, *First Nations' Legal Inheritance* (University of Winnipeg, Canadian Legal History Project, 1991), pp. 1-46.
42. James Reichley, "Religion and American Democracy" in *Morality and Religion in Liberal Democratic Societies*, p. 217.
43. Martha Johnson provides an example of the compatibility of approaches to environmental questions from two distinct worldviews, namely, that of Native spirituality and that of Western science. Unfortunately, the Native contribution is cast largely in negative terms: "Northern scientists are often reluctant to accept Dene TEK [Traditional Environmental Knowledge] as valid because of the spiritual explanation for environmental phenomena. What they often fail to recognize, however, is that the spiritual explanation often conceals conservation strategies and does not necessarily detract from the reality of a situation and the making of appropriate decisions about the wise use of resources." (Martha Johnson, "Documenting Dene Traditional Environmental Knowledge," *Akwe:kon Journal* 9 (1992): 72-79; citation from p. 76.)

10

On Identity and Aesthetic Voice
of the Culturally Displaced[1]

CALVIN SEERVELD

I will speak as a person who is handicapped by being culturally at home in a rich tradition of Reformation Christianity filtered through a Dutch ethnic background. Since my native cultural neighbourhood is on the other side of the secularist tracks, I feel kinship with the disadvantaged minorities overridden by both a former dominant rationalism and the current fashion of calling any eschatonic narrative into question as mastermindingly oppressive.

This simple declaration of my handicap for entering the academic chess game on an embroiled topic is not meant to be a polemical assertion of my Christianitude,[2] but rather it is meant to attest how difficult it is for the insiders of institutional power—which most of us present are[3]—to hear the voice of the other solitudes.[4] And to preclude your stereotyping the speaker, which Bhabha correctly says entails both phobia and fetish,[5] let me add that I am not politically far right, I do not believe in proselyting audiences, and though I am the son of a fishmonger, I have brown eyes, am left-handed, and have never, by sticking my finger in an earthen mass of dirt and stones, saved a Dutch town from flooding.

Let me focus on a fierce debate current among philosophically trained cultural leaders from various African countries, and just suggest how their struggle might relate to certain fundamental historical realities faced by the praxis of First Nation artistry of Canada in our generation. The complex problem I probe is this: is it possible for a fourth-world culture[6] to avoid both idols of the tribe and ethnocidal assimilation by the entrenched, dominant, civilizational power? Are there good ways for an other, diverse community to establish its own vibrant cultural and artistic identity in the world, or is such a prospect utopian?[7]

PROFESSIONAL PHILOSOPHY VS ETHNIC NATIVE CULTURES

In the African philosophical discussion of cultural identity, on the one hand Paul Hountondji (Benin-Nigeria), Peter Bodunrin (Nigeria), and Kwasi Wiredu

(Ghana) press for secularity, a neutral rationality (somewhat as Habermas does),[8] so that philosophy can be professional, scientifically critical philosophy the way mathematics is theoretical mathematics,[9] unencumbered by folkloric African residues.

Hountondji, Bodunrin, and Wiredu are current voices which reject leaders of the recent past. In order to combat a century of European colonializing exploitation, statesman Leopold Senghor (Senegal) had championed Negritude, to rally black self-respect throughout Africa, in the firm belief that cultural independence is a prerequisite for political independence.[10] Similarly, Sartre's ringing co-affirmation of the black Orpheus poet's going as *vates* to claim Eurydice from the European Pluto exile, using the French language![11] was a well-meant endorsement in 1949 of revolutionary activity, but was veritably an obfuscative romanticizing of the "pre-contact" African past.[12] There is, says Bodunrin, no pure original "Africa" on which to build an autochthonous African philosophy.[13]

The earlier Pan-Africanist movement forged by Afro-American Alexander Crumwell (1819-98), Edward W. Blyden (1832-1921), and W.H.B. DuBois (1868-1963), who were intent on fixing a non-European black identity, reached its culmination in Kwame Nkrumah's (Ghana) post-World War II speech in Liberia on "Africa for the Africans!" But we need to demythify Africa, says Hountondji. "Africa is no more than the geographical place name it is"[14] because the plurality of ancient *poleis* and multifariousness of indigenous tribal cultures on the continent called Africa belie any unanimous homogeneity.[15] Pan-Africanism, like Zionism, assumes an antiracial racism, and remains entrapped in the detractive, bogus problematics of the oppressors.[16] There is no essential African philosophy: there is only a set of written discourses, a collection of heterogeneous, open philosophical texts in Africa whose cultural values are like venereal diseases, owned by no one ethnic people.[17] "I speak as an anxious African," says Wiredu: we need to grow up and grow out of traditional "folk thinking," and separate worthwhile aspects of our tradition from what is superstitious, like "pouring of libations to the spirits of our ancestors on ceremonial occasions."[18]

On the other hand, figures like K. C. Anyanwu (Nigeria) and Ngugi wa Thiong'o (Kenya) find this (modernist) rejection of ethno-philosophy and native culture too antiseptically quick, committing the very error it faults—ethnocentrism. What in the world validates converting the particular Western mould of *philosophia perennis* secularized to neutral theoretical analysis, to be the universal criterion for all philosophy everywhere? Why should the paradigm of Plato's categorical framework, whose anthropology assumed slavery and whose theory on the nature of art was wrong, and Aristotle's logic, which pretends to go timelessly beyond dated, human experience,[19] be the norm for rigorous African (or Eastern) critical reflection and wisdom?[20]

If we grant that the era of Negritude counter-racism became itself counterproductive, because the *prises de parole* handicapped European-educated African thinkers and artists as "primitives" and disallowed their setting their own agenda;[21] and while it is indeed a mistake—to vaunt independent national identity nationalistically or fetishize one's tribal roots—there is no way to escape the ruinous imperialism overrunning African countries unless there be an African literature in African languages. The forced imposition of foreign languages—English, French, Portuguese—upon people speaking Hausa, Yoruba, Ibo, Zulu, Venda, Swahili, Kiswahili, says Ngugi wa Thiong'o, dislocated those unprotected people's actual lives, because language is the memory bank of a people, and literature in people's language defines its outlook, its own ethos. To have one's mother tongue repressed by bureaucratic governing overlords, and to find one's oral heritage of stories truncated, stunted from continuing in literature because one's tribal literati publish in world-market languages, is simply devastating to a people's dignity.[22]

So acclaimed Kenyan novelist Ngugi wa Thiong'o acted consequently from his jail cell in 1977 and decided henceforth to write novels only in the Gikuyu language. In 1986 he also wrote his last English essay, "Decolonising the Mind." "From now on it is Gikuyu and Kiswahili all the way,"[23] to service his people's deep-structural need for a self-respecting cultural identity and, along with world literature in translation, try to decentre from the Kenyan literary educational program stalwart pillars like Matthew Arnold, T. S. Eliot, and F. R. Leavis.[24]

COMPLICATIONS AND OPTIONS FOR AFRICANS

Despite the sharp leadership difference between what look like no-name philosophers to the adherents of native culture and what seems to be a hole-in-the-corner parochiality flirting with racism to the professional secular theorists, fairly common to all the disparate peoples and cultures of sub-Saharan Africa is the sorry past of colonialized defeat. Foreign explorers and enterprising merchants took charge of the land, domesticated the natives' ways to European customs, and introduced superior technology which along with medical and transportational benefits and sundry conveniences upset the local economies. Pertinent for our North American understanding of the aggrieved response of formerly colonized peoples in Africa (and the First Nations peoples of Canada) is to realize that their traditional mode of life with its spiritual framework was desecrated, decimated, and that the cultural body of their communal consciousness was violated, literally raped—penetrated and discarded.[25]

The philosophical conundrum is that violence, paved with the best intentions, happens whenever a secular culture, whether idealist or pragmatist, which is technologically more specialized and powerful, confronts a less differentiated society whose culture is less technically developed and still wrapped uncontroversially in the practice of worshipping invisible beings. For example, when written language and literacy invades an oral culture, the former full-orbed, preliterate world where the lore and rich consensus of age-old knowledge was passed on by word of mouth of the elders suddenly becomes an illiterate world, disadvantaged by not being able to keep records with abstract precision for unfriendly scrutiny.[26] Or, when a tribal culture which is open to the wild, wonderful, and fearful in terms of agency by familiar but uncanny spirits is breached by an industrialized, urban, urbane mentality that casts unsure societal relations into the functional matrix of inanimate billiard balls' causality, suddenly the *One Hundred Years of Solitude* kind of miraculous and magical earthy mix of strange realities is taken to be the superstition of mana and tabu, something "primitive," not really worthy of an enlightened humanity. So the Western secular mind trivializes a deeply committed acceptance of numinous presence and the power of curses in the world.[27]

Why does advanced *techne* paired with the concentrated reductive force of secularization apparently, as a matter of fact, always overpower the traditional, non-experimental, minding-its-own-regular-business kind of culture? Must the meeting of diverse cultures truly be confrontational, discriminatory, disruptive, cast in terms of the stronger and the weaker with winners and losers?

Cultural identity, like ethnic inheritance, I think, is seldom thoroughbred, never simple, but normally intricately compounded with a people's political identity, wealth-to-poverty identity, mother tongue and acquired languages identity, faith-in-where-the-buck-stops (Yahweh, Allah, Jesus Christ, the Almighty Dollar) trust identity.

Any kind of cohering community, civilization, any dated and located (also in diaspora) grouping of society with a proper nameable identity—Asante kingdom, Dutch, Muslim, Latin people, South African—has a polymorphous complexity to its particularity. Trouble comes when one relative feature of the community's identity is fixed upon absolutely, rigidly conceived, yoked with other characteristics as requirement, or given final binding authority also for persons who do not choose to belong, to identify with that given community. Whenever nationality, economic class, language or creed, ethnicity, the construct of race or gender, style or education, is given overriding exclusivist weight in defining an individual's adherence to a human community, the normal enrichment each factor brings to the particular identity goes askew. (Perhaps what one fundamentally trusts is non-negotiable; but while one has the right to be a martyr, it is not legitimate to make martyrs of others.) Naturally, says Al-Amin Mazrui (Nigeria), a novelist employs the language of one's people, in sheer thankfulness for the ethnic watershed which nurtured his or her writing artistry; but when Ngugi wa Thiong'o berates Chinua Achebe and Wole Soyinka as Afro-European turncoats to the political aspirations of their people, Ngugi wa Thiong'o has made language ideological, since linguistic heterogeneity is not determinative against political unity.[28]

Kwame Anthony Appiah (Ghana) supports the point that cultural identity is a crucial ingredient of peoplehood, but still relative, with the startling assertion, "The truth is that there are no races."[29] Todorov shows that racism and witch hunts do not entail the existence of races and witches, says Appiah, and adds, "Nations are real enough, however invented their traditions."[30] That is, Harvard professor Appiah does not suffer the embarassment Kwasi Wiredu has in pouring a libation of respect for one's ancestors. "I am an Asante man," says Appiah, "a Ghanaian, an ecumenical Methodist Christian, Cambridge educated, polyglot, and would not even mind throwing a sacrificial lamb to a river crocodile in the funeral ritual of determining who will inherit the authority as head of the *abusua*, my matriclan."[31] My melee of a cultural identity is not a shameful, uneasy syncretism, says Appiah, but still enjoys the oral accommodative, enchanted world Africans recognize as their traditional inheritance. My conglomerate cultural identity has not been shattered by the scientistic, positivistic, individualistic climate of aggression, mobility, and pointed oppositions with which modernity prickles. The crux for us people caught in the uncomfortable earthquake zones of deep underground cultural realignments today is to maintain a challenging cultural integrity rather than let cultural identity fall into an eclectic, confused, disparate muddle.[32]

V. Y. Mudimbe (Zaire), however, takes a more morose position than Appiah's brokering for a cultural identity, because Mudimbe believes the acculturation process of peoples, which is historically normal everywhere, world without end, has been warped on the African continent by colonialist discourses, which are still in force today, in spite of the occasional rousing Marxist, socialist, and nondescript angry spokespersons over the years. The Western invention of Africa rests on a triple subtext of the exotic savage, higher and lower cultures, and the ethnographic anthropological search for, and reification of, primitiveness. The *episteme* of conversion and conquest hidden in these patterning discourses, says Mudimbe, has robbed our peoples of their own stories; hence, the cultural identity crises. We intellectuals need to reinvent the African past, because the present legends conveniently mitigate the violence of the Same in dispensing with us Others.[33] "Western reception of artistry fashioned in Africa today, taking its otherness as both monstrosity and *corpus mirabiliorium*, has not qualitatively changed since the first reports of the sixteenth and seventeenth centuries,"[34] when the handiwork of craftsmen and women in Africa was collected as curios. Since Mudimbe considers history writing to be always a special pleading by the arrogant, self-centred Same, Mudimbe with Foucault would deny privilege to any centre, and find strategies for regional Others to permanently recapitulate history-keeping until they are free to think of themselves "as the starting point of an absolute discourse."[35] So Mudimbe puts artistic action more or less on hold.

Since artistry is critical for cultural identity, however, "What is to be done?" (as Lenin said). What is being done? Do not produce African art complicit with the national bourgeois and international elite market for exotica—do not become an Otherness machine, writes Sara Suleri with stilettoes of irony, because the exotic Other is, as Yambo Ouologuem (Mali) asserts, a cheap self-identity, still concocted within the master-slave dialectic.[36] African tourist airport-art is the epitome of "post-colonial" neocolonialism: there is no gunboat diplomacy and no political disenfranchisement in producing and distributing such "neo-traditional" craft for export, and money sends everybody home happy; but the African birthright of tigritude is sold for a mess of potage, consumed as bookends.[37]

If one looks philosophically upstream, as Mudimbe suggests,[38] to uncover the silent source of this denaturing exotic Africa locked in mortal embrace with monolithic Western commerce, one would begin to question, I think, the underlying same/other binary problematics, despite its fashionableness for rhetorical purposes today. If identity/difference, the same/other, centre/margin is all there is—*tertia non datur*—then one's artistic activity and hermeneutic is forced into a standoff of power plays.[39] The ontical possibility of mutual cultural reciprocity is denied. The oversimplified lineup also evacuates multiple, rich, circumstantial specificities which can frequently mediate longstanding difficulties.[40] Categorical binarisms usually falsify realities, and the resident conceptual stalemate only prolongs the culture wars which have been ontologically certified.

Once the underside of this basic ontological polemic is self-consciously adopted as point of entrance, and the Other has refused to be assimilated by the dominating centre, us/them induces "protest art." Art protesting "them" can be blatantly propagandistic like Msangi's "Bastion of Apartheid: The Dutch Reformed Church" (Tanzania, 1980s), or modified to political satire in a velvet corkwood painted caricature of Prime Minister P. W. Botha with white blinders on (Phutuma Seoka, 1985). The permutations for "protest art" in South Africa have been endless, often sadly mocking black compliance before the cement brick wall of Western "world" concerns.

But Albie Sachs (African National Congress minister of Culture in exile, who lost a whole arm to a car bomb planted by the political far right when he returned, and who is currently Supreme Court Justice of the united coalition government of South Africa) broke out of the self-perpetuating reactive aesthetics with an eloquent 1989 position paper on "Preparing ourselves for freedom." To make art a weapon of political struggle, a tool against apartheid, he contends, denatures the power of art to be nuanced and imaginatively ambiguous, restricts the full orb of themes which human art normally treats, harps on attacking the enemy, and tends to minimize art quality so long as the message is politically correct.[41] Whoever would be a free people and lead in a non-hegemonic manner toward the multilingual, multicultural, multifaith society of the new South Africa needs to celebrate artistically what one lives for: "culture is us"—in all our pied multifariousness, with the pulsing confident beat of our folk music and dance.[42] "[W]e do not plan to build a non-racial yuppie-dom which people may enter only by shedding and suppressing the cultural heritage of their specific community."[43]

ARTISTIC EVIDENCE OF HOPE IN SOUTH AFRICA

I have seen the kind of uncommercialized, non-protesting, ethnically flavoured open-to-the-neighbour art Albie Sachs' vision would engender. Even in the South African shantytowns presided over by police gun-control towers, not only is the wonderful aesthetic touch of a grass carpet tended to grow in the rubble before the communal toilet outhouse, but also at the edge where the squatters' camp meets a government road there will be a piece of what came to be called in the 1980s "township art" [illustration A]. A gaily painted, sculpted tree looks like an acrobatic dancer doing a headstand while juggling a doughnut of a tire between the legs, as a tread peels off; or is it an animated stand with ropes and lifesaver to rescue people in trouble?

Wood carvings by local black artists can snapshot an expert headblock in the secular religion of soccer, or portray a mother (Dian Cormick, 1990) straining to hold back her sons, with the theme Käthe Kollwitz often treated, "Don't let the men go to war." Or the celebrated Jackson Hlungwane (born c.1923) whose four-metre high *Adam and the Birth of Eve* (1985-88) presents a solemn, ungainly giant figure with Eve ethereally evolving out of the head and shoulder portions while the dangling legs, hand, and arms are from their children Cain and Abel [illustration B]; in the palm of the upper hand is an egg, not a stone, says Hlungwane, a hint on how men and women should treat one another. His *Altar of God* with figures of God, angel Gabriel, metal cross, and wooden solar arc over heaped stones blends Tsonga beliefs and articles of biblical faith idiosyncratically. The altar was more at home in the Mbhopkota village in Gazakulu, northern Transvaal, on the site Hlungwane calls "the New Jerusalem," where he lives, carves, and preaches to his following. In the Johannesburg Art Gallery it is gentrified, like taking the welter of cascading sound of black spirituals sung in a church on the south side of Chicago and having it concertized by the Robert Shaw Chorale, Schubertianized, you could say. But the fact that *Altar of God* was originally not made for sale or show still comes through.

If one wants to be pulled back to raw South African artistry, one can contemplate this small painted clay piece [illustration C done by a nine-year-old child in Durban whose craft-class school assignment was "Make something you've seen recently"], a tire-necklaced human figure burned beyond recognition.

Major Afrikaner artist Andries Botha learned indigenous crafts to acculturate his sophisticated artistic conceptions into pieces which reconcile quite divergent milieux, like this artwork [illustration D] entitled *For those taken darkly* (1991). It acts like an epitaph for those who have mysteriously died and been found—washed up face down by the waves, like the prone black figure. The eddy of water waves is woven from thatching grass by master Zulu builder Maviwa and women weavers Myra and Agnes Ntshalintshli from Drakensberg. It is difficult to see, but the upper half of a living woman-figure of wire mesh is emerging from a silver fish's mouth, whose scales are composed of soda-can tops. The waves of grass are warm and friendly, caressing the living and the dead. Some die in the flood of water; some like Jonah are saved by a fish—*ichthus*—and disengorged up on the shore.

A final example is a celebrative artwork in Pieter Maritsburg, Natal, where violence and murder have been almost the worst in South Africa [illustration E]. A Christian sculptor, white man Gert Zwart, together with various local black community artists and grassroots organizations, built *Peace Tree* with gaily painted tires around Christmas time in 1991. They put it in the very centre of the city near its old Boer War memorials, converting necklaces of death into suspended trinkets filled with laughter and a poignant hope, in public space, for "Cry, the beloved country."

CONCLUDING THESES TO ORIENT POLICIES

There are three theses I could distill from what I have analyzed so far:

1. While hatred for the former colonialist guardians and current neocolonialist manipulative policies may make some kind of sense, says Mudimbe, anger is no longer important or helpful for disadvantaged people to become culturally (artistically) mature.[44] To live from handouts and/or festering bitterness stymies a human community from ever taking root in what it stands for. Root art in what is an identifying goodness of one's diversity for the neighbour.

2. While the "once bitten, twice shy" postmodern mentality toward Archimedean point commitment for one's core identity is understandable, to avoid the fragmentation of legitimating any local cultural leftovers whatsoever, says Appiah, we would do well to follow the lead of those novelists and artists who identify with *la négraille*, the nigger-trash of whatever date and place,[45] the poor which you always universally have with you, especially if you are middle class. To enable the culturally weak and diverse to sound their voice in the human choir, the culturally dominant need to convert their strength into at least enough restraint to listen to the offbeat song, strange shapes, and speech only partially intelligible to them.[46] Let stifled, peaceable contributions to the commonweal be made public.

3. Mainstream connoisseurs, theorists, and educators need to relax enough to recognize that "cultural work" like agitprop theatre, didactic posters, protest songs, imaginative events like the *Peace Tree*, which are not refined art ready for gallery, museum, and concert hall do, however, belong in the

larger aesthetic world as critical training ground for grassroots culture to develop historically an artistic voice that has communal identity.[47] Without exacting conformity to mainstream quality art fashion, nurture what shows promise.

OUR CANADIAN SCENE

The struggle to be ethnically at home with a cultural identity even as one's community is in the process of change for good and/or ill in the world at large, which I have sketched, resonates with Canadian concern to make earnest with the multicultural perplexities of our inherited environs. I have not yet seen enough or talked with enough First Nation artists to try to formulate a taxonomy of our complex problematics. At the risk of being simply an academic WASP kibitzer from the sidelines let me end by noting very briefly three troubles, and make a wish.

1. George Swinton reports how amazed Inuit John Tiktak was when he was flown in from Rankin Inlet to Winnipeg in 1970 for his first ever "one-man show" which Swinton had arranged. Tiktak was flabbergasted to see dozens of his carvings to be held in the hand all exposed separately together. After the 1970 show Tiktak went home, writes Swinton, and started to mass produce pieces, which became hollow echoes of the original work.[48] And I have read testimonies by Inuit carvers in their own script which so painfully protest just a little too much that "Inuit carve, not just for the money."[49]

    Was Swinton's generous act the kiss of Midas? Are we *kabluna* prudent enough to let the Innu have their graphic art speak their own language, or has our touch made it pidgin Inuit artspeak, an astounding cold and remote voice—in exile?[50]

2. Bill Reid was trained in the European goldsmith speciality and describes himself in refashioning old West Coast Indian themes in today's world as an "artifaker."[51] When Reid fashioned his incredible *Phyllidula: The Shape of Frogs to Come* [illustration F] he invented something artistically new in cedar wood that is not faking migrant Haida mythical frogs, but astounds your imagination with its poised, froggy animal mystery. The impressive showpiece [illustration G] *The Spirit of Haida Gwaii* (1986-91) at the Canadian embassy in Washington, DC, however, seems to me to strain under the making of a Haida artist. The official video, *The Spirit of Haida Gwaii* (48 minutes, 1991)[52] presents the Haida creation myth in Walt Disney animated cartoon form(!), calling into question, it seems to me, the very authenticity of taking Haida ethnicity seriously, especially when Reid's piece has a tongue-in-cheek resemblance to Emanuel Leutze's staged icon of *Washington Crossing the Delaware* (1851).

Or is Bill Reid's black canoe with shaman and undomesticated animals afloat, without a flag to plant somewhere, precisely the kind of ironic fillip Neil Bissoondath recommends—speaking from the privilege of success—to keep ethnicity from narrow-minding our humanity?[53]

3. After designing St. Mary's Church in Red Deer (1968) with its campanile-type towers and an almost Romanesque softness, with walls undulating curves, Plains Metis Douglas Cardinal has gone on to put his trademark on the Canadian architectural landscape [illustration H]. A Plains Indian experiences the aggressive, motorized, urban, North American environment, says Cardinal, like a momentary lapse of reason, which has become permanent. You are no longer an earthling walking upright on the sacred earth among fellow creatures, grasses and animals, to whom you are connected; in the secular city all the people seem bent on adversarial destruction. But "every act is spiritual," says Cardinal,[54] and to stay sane you have to carry "your own native reality" around with you into the killing fields of a government-sponsored major architectural project made of stone. Cardinal believes in soft power, he says, female power, because it is resilient.[55]

Cardinal's Metis wisdom sometimes sounds like Tao philosophy crossed with Norman Vincent Peale's "positive thinking," but Cardinal is resolutely hi-tech: there is not a single drafting board in his entire architectural firm headquarters in Ottawa; all architectural planning and designing is done on computers. But Cardinal returns, as an Orthodox believer would to Mount Athos, to a Native camp for the sweat-house healing and centring of Metis rituals. "The Canadian Museum of Civilization," he writes, "is a true monument to our people. I went to the ceremonial lodge and I was given the vision. It is a vision of taking technology and creating something positive with it and maintaining my way of being in doing it."[56] How could Cardinal's brilliant idiolect in Metis dialect giving colour to the Canadian idiom be complemented by other rooted ethnic diversities, rather than remain a brilliant solo?

My wish is that mainline intellectuals who are serious about furthering the identity and aesthetic voice of the culturally diverse, who have become displaced in our secularized Western culture, think long range and slowly, even to the extent of learning, let's say, the Ojibwa language.[57] My wish is that without losing a systematic philosophical rigour the theoretical aesthetics we practise could pull the horizon of wisdom into focus so we could proactively, at arm's length recognize the neighbourhooded nature of humans (cf. Heidegger's *Mitsein* of *Dasein*), the normality of different faith-deep communities,[58] where vision permeates one's varied relative ethnic, political, economic, lingual, philosophical identities, and then foreground the surprising complementary joy there can be in sharing diversity by way of artistry, or even philosophical discourse, in the press of life and death affairs.

Notes

1. Written with special thanks to Gideon Strauss, University of the Free Orange State in Bloemfontein, who introduced me to Mudimbe and Appiah's writings, and to Phyllis Rozendal, York University in Toronto, for discussion on the "other solitudes." Thanks also go to Ruth Kerkham, Hamish Robertson, and Scott Macklin, who diligently assisted me with library research.

2. This is an allusion to Wole Soyinka's critique of Leopold Senghor's concept of "Negritude" when Soyinka remarked that a genuine tiger does not need to proclaim its own tigritude.

3. This is the text of a lecture presented at the Learned Societies of Canada meeting in Montreal on 1 July 1995, before the Canadian Society of Aesthetics.

4. Linda Hutcheon and Marion Richmond, eds., *Other Solitudes: Canadian Multicultural Fictions* (Toronto: Oxford University Press, 1990), pp. 1-5, 7-12.

5. Homi K. Bhabha, "The Other Question: Homi K. Bhabha Reconsiders the Stereotype and Colonial Discourse." *Screen* 24, 6 (November-December 1983): 18-36.

6. "The Fourth World is the collective name for all aboriginal or native peoples whose lands fall within the national boundaries and techno-bureaucratic administrations of the countries of the First, Second, and Third Worlds. As such, they are peoples without countries of their own, peoples who are usually in the minority and without the power to direct the course of their collective lives" Nelson H. H. Graburn, ed. *Ethnic and Tourist Arts: Cultural Expressions from the Fourth World* (Los Angeles: University of California Press, 1976), p. 1.

7. Rasheed Araeen, *The Other Story: Afro-Asian Artists in Postwar Britain* (London: Haywood Gallery, 1989), p. 83.

8. Sander Griffioen, "De betekenis van Dooyeweerds ontwikkelingsidee," *Philosophia Reformata* 51 (1986): 83-109, especially 101-102.

9. Alwin Diemer, ed., *Symposium on Philosophy in the Present Situation of Africa* 30 August 1978 (Wiesbaden: Franz Steiner Verlag, 1981), p. 9. (Cited as Diemer.) With contributions by Odera Oruka, Peter Bodunrin, Paulin J. Hountondji, and others.

10. Olusegun Gbadegesin, "Negritude and Its Contribution to the Civilization of the Universal: Leopold Senghor and the Question of Ultimate Reality and Meaning" in *Ultimate Reality and Meaning* 14, 1 (March 1991): 30-45, especially 31, 37. (Cited as Gbadegesin.)

11. Jean-Paul Sartre, "Orphé Noir," trans., John MacCombie in *"What Is Literature?" and Other Essays* (Cambridge: Harvard University Press, 1988), pp. 296-98, 300.

12. Godwin Sogolo, *Foundations of African Philosophy: A Definitive Analysis of Conceptual Issues in African Thought* (Ibadan, Nigeria: Ibadan University Press, 1993), p. 203.

13. Bodunrin in Diemer, p. 13.

14. Hountondji in Diemer, p. 41.

15. Gbadegesin, p. 43.

16. Kwame Anthony Appiah, *In My Father's House: Africa in the Philosophy of Culture* (New York: Oxford University Press, 1992), pp. 43f. (Cited as Appiah.)

17. Paulin J. Hountondji, *African Philosophy: Myth and Reality [1976]*, trans. Henri Evan with Jonathan Ree (Johannesburg: Hutchinson University Library for Africa, 1983), pp. 175-79.

18. K. Wiredu, "How Not to Compare African Thought with Western Thought" from *Ch'indaba*, republished in Richard A. Wright, ed., *African Philosophy* (Lanham, MD: University Press of America, 1984), pp. 149-62, especially pp. 150, 152, 159.

19. D. H. Th. Vollenhoven, *De Noodzakelijkeheid eener Christelijke Logica* (Amsterdam: H. J. Paris, 1932), pp. 48-50.

20. K. C. Anyanwu, "The Idea of Art in African Thought" in *Contemporary Philosophy, A New Survey, African Philosophy*, vol. 5 (Dordrecht: Martinus Nijhoff, 1987), pp. 235-60, especially 237-40.

21. V. Y. Mudimbe, *The Invention of Africa: Gnosis, Philosophy, and the Order of Knowledge* (Bloomington, IN: Indiana University Press, 1988), p. 39. (Cited as Mudimbe.)

22. Ngugi wa Thiong'o, *Decolonizing the Mind: The Politics of Language in African Literature* (Nairobi: Heinemann Kenya, 1986), pp. 310-17, 327-30.

23. Ibid., xiv.

24. Ibid., pp. 90, 98-101.

25. Mudimbe, pp. 2-4.

26. Appiah, pp. 130-33.

27. Ibid., pp. 120-24.

28. Al-Amin M. Mazrui, "Ideology or Pedagogy: the Linguistic Indigenisation of African Literature." *Race and Class* 1 (Summer 1986): 63-72, especially 64-65, 69-70.

29. Appiah, p. 45.

30. Ibid., p. 175.

31. Ibid., epilogue, pp. 181-92.

32. Ibid., pp. 54, 119-30, 134-36

33. Mudimbe, pp. 67-69, 192-96.

34. Ibid., p. 191.

35. Ibid., pp. 27, 33-34, 198-200.

36. Cited in Appiah, pp. 156-57.

37. Appiah, pp. 148-49; Mudimbe, pp. 11-12.

38. Mudimbe, pp. x-xi.

39. Wlad Godzich, "The further possibility of knowledge" in Michel de Certeau, *Heterologies: Discourse on the Other*, trans. Brian Massumi (Minneapolis, MN: University of Minnesota Press, 1989), pp. ix-xi.

40. "I, at least, worry about our entrancement with the polarities of identity and difference; partly because the rhetoric of alterity has too often meant the evacuation of specificity; partly because too many African intellectuals, captivated by this Western thematic, seek to fashion themselves as the (image of the) Other" Appiah, p.72.

41. Ingrid de Kok and Karen Press, eds., *Spring Is Rebellious: Arguments about Cultural Freedom by Albie Sachs and Respondents* (Cape Town: Buchu Books, 1990), pp. 19-22. (Cited as de Kok and Press.)

42. Ibid., p. 21-23, 27-28.

43. Ibid., p. 25.

44. Mudimbe, p. 36.

45. Appiah, p. 152.

46. "To keep multiculturalism from becoming just a complacent cliché, we must work to grant everyone access to the material and cultural conditions that will enable the many voices of contemporary Canada, to speak—and be heard—for themselves" (Hutcheon:15-16).

47. Junaid Ahmed in de Kok and Press, pp. 123-25.

48. George Swinton, "About My Collecting Inuit Art" in *The Swinton Collection of Inuit Art* (Winnipeg Art Gallery, 13 September to 8 November 1987) p. 8.

49. ᐃᓄᐃᑦ ᐸᐅᕐᖅᑦᑎᒪᔭᖓᔪᑦ ᐱᔭᖓᕐᕆᑦ (Repulse Bay: 25).

50. "Currently there exists a growing degree of Eskimo [*sic*] ethno-centricity, and the political pressures are such that the governmental agencies—more so the federal than the territorial—are vitally interested in supporting the Inuit's cultural aspirations. On the other hand, economic pressures and so-called 'purely commercial' pragmatism are posing an almost irresistible threat. In spite of good intentions, our white culture together with our educational system (which is at best inadequate and at worst corrosive) plus the

increasing influx of transient and inherently parasitical whites further menace the Eskimo's [*sic*] chances of continued existence and identity." George Swinton, *Sculpture of the Inuit [1972]*, rev. ed. (Toronto: McClelland & Stewart, 1992), p. 143.

51.   The term "artifaker" comes from Bill Holm in Karen Duffek and Bill Reid, *Beyond the Essential Form* (Vancouver, BC: University of British Columbia Press with UBC Museum of Anthropology, 1986), p. 40.

52.   *The Spirit of Haida Gwaii* was directed by Alan C. Clapp, scripted by Robert Bringhurst, produced by Deluxe Production Canada Ltd. in Vancouver, and funded from the Montreal Office of the Royal Bank of Canada.

53.   Neil Bissoondath, "I am Canadian," *Saturday Night* (October 1994): 11-22, especially 18.

54.   Douglas Cardinal, *The Native Creative Process: A collaborative discourse between Douglas Cardinal and Jeanette Armstrong* (Penticton: Theytus Books, 1991), p. 92.

55.   Ibid., p. 96.

56.   Ibid., p. 112.

57.   Basil H. Johnson in Daniel David Moses and Terry Goldie, eds. *An Anthology of Canadian Native Literature in English* (Toronto: Oxford University Press, 1992), pp. 99-104.

58.   "If modernization is conceived of, in part, as the acceptance of science, we have to decide whether we think the evidence obliges us to give up the invisible ontology. We can easily be misled here by the accommodation between science and religion that has occurred among educated people in the industrialized world, in general, and in the United States, in particular. For this has involved a considerable limitation of the domains in which it is permissible for intellectuals to invoke spiritual agency. The question how much of the world of the spirits we intellectuals must give up (or transform into something ceremonial without the old literal ontology) is one we must face: and I do not think the answer is obvious" (Appiah 1992:135).

(A) Anonymous piece near shantytown outside Cape Town, South Africa.

(B) Jackson Hlungwane, *Adam and the Birth of Eve* (1985-88). Collection: Johannesburg Art Gallery. By permission.

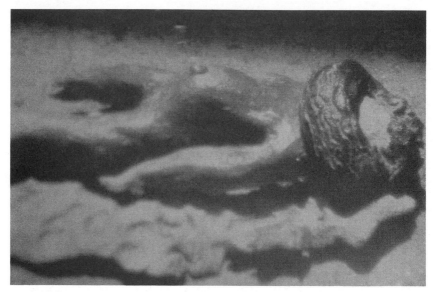

(C) Anonymous piece from school class in Durban, South Africa.

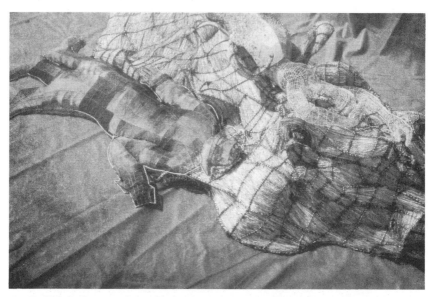

(D) Andries Botha, *For those taken darkly* (1990-93). Collection: Johannesburg Art Gallery. By permission.

214

(E) Gert Zwart and friends, *Peace Tree* (1991-92), Pieter Maritsburg, Natal, South Africa. Photo by Zak Benjamin. By permission.

(F) Bill Reid, *Phyllidula—the Shape of Frogs to Come* (1984-85), VAG 86.16. Collection: Vancouver Art Gallery. Permission granted by Vancouver Art Gallery and Dr. Martine Reid.

(G) Bill Reid and assistants, *The Spirit of Haida Gwaii* (1991) at the Canadian Embassy, Washington, DC. Permission granted by the Government of Canada and Dr. Martine Reid.

(H) Douglas Cardinal Associates, Canadian Museum of Civilization (1980s), Hull, Quebec. Photo by Malak.

Notes on Contributors

KEN BADLEY served as the senior member in educational foundations at the Institute for Christian Studies from 1992-96. He now teaches social studies and ethics at a Christian secondary school and carries on research as a visiting research scholar at King's University College in Edmonton, Alberta.

LISA CHISHOLM-SMITH completed her master's thesis at the Institute for Christian Studies on the subject of menstruation in Western society and has a keen interest in women's studies. She lives in the village of Bath and directs a regionally based program of adult Christian education for the Anglican Church of Canada in eastern Ontario.

HENDRIK HART is professor of philosophy at the Institute for Christian Studies, where he has taught since 1966. He has published *Communal Certainty and Authorized Truth; Understanding Our World; Setting Our Sights by the Morning Star;* and (with Kai Nielsen) *Search for Truth in a Withering Tradition.*

RONALD A. KUIPERS is a Ph.D. candidate in philosophy in the joint doctoral program of the Vrije Universiteit (Free University) in Amsterdam and the Institute for Christian Studies in Toronto. He is the author of *Solidarity and the Stranger: Themes in the Social Philosophy of Richard Rorty* (1997) and co-editor of *Walking the Tightrope of Faith: Philosophical Conversations about Reason and Religion* (1999). He is concentrating on contemporary under-standings of truth, rationality, and language, especially as these bear upon the themes of cultural pluralism and interreligious dialogue in the philosophy of religion.

JAMES H. OLTHUIS is professor of philosophical theology at the Institute for Christian Studies, where he has taught since 1968. He is the author of *Facts, Values and Ethics; I Pledge You My Troth; Keeping Our Troth: Staying in Love During the Five Stages of Marriage; A Hermeneutics of Ultimacy: Peril or Promise;* and recently edited *Knowing* Other-*wise: Philosophy at the Threshold of Spirituality.* He is also a psychotherapist in private practice in Toronto.

CALVIN SEERVELD is emeritated professor of philosophical aesthetics at the Institute for Christian Studies in Toronto. He was co-chair, 1984-1987, of the Canadian Society for Aesthetics when it was founded. His special interest is the methodology of art historiography, and his hobby is wisdom literature of the Older Testament.

ROBERT SWEETMAN is professor in the history of philosophy at the Institute for Christian Studies specializing in medieval philosophy, in particular, scholastic moral philosophy of the thirteenth century. His publications focus on the intersection of moral philosophical ideas and pastoral care, medieval hermeneutics, spirituality, and preaching.

GEORGE VANDERVELDE is professor of systematic theology at the Institute for Christian Studies. He has published in the areas of contemporary Roman Catholic theology, ecclesiology, and ecumenical hermeneutics. He co-chairs a consultation between the Roman Catholic Church and the World Evangelical Fellowship, and is a member of the Faith and Order Commissions of the Canadian Council of Churches, and the National Council of Churches of Christ, USA.

JANET CATHERINA WESSELIUS is a Ph.D. candidate in philosophy in the joint doctoral program of the Vrije Universiteit (Free University) in Amsterdam and the Institute for Christian Studies in Toronto. She is completing a dissertation on notions of objectivity in feminist epistemology. She teaches courses in feminist philosophy, women's studies, and religious studies, and has published several articles on feminist philosophy.

Subject Index

Aboriginal, 53, 58-61, 186-96, 200
Aboriginal self-government, 186, 191
Aboriginal spirituality, 58-60, 187-88
abortion, 55, 108, 137
abuse, 8, 44, 46, 127-46, 157, 170-75
Act of Toleration, 54
affirmation and negation, 27-30
Africa, African, 9, 154-58, 200-206
alterity, 134, 205
ambiguity, 8, 65, 100-17
androgyny, 77
antisemitism, 17
antithesis, 27
argument, 23, 37-46, 77, 82, 96-117, 160,
    175, 195
Aristotelian corpus, 26
Aristotle's Categories, 27
assimilation, 7, 9, 51-69, 200
authoritarian, 100, 127-31
authority, 8, 14-20, 42, 65-66, 91-122,
    131, 138-41, 174-79, 188-94,
    203-204
beliefs, 37-44, 52-64, 95-100, 117, 137,
    157-63, 174, 195, 206
belonging, 8, 102, 127-47
Bible, 94-119
boundaries, 3, 18, 62, 91-98, 113,
    120-122, 130-46, 179, 200
bureaucratic government, 21
Cartesian egos, 134
centralization, 19
Christian, 6-7, 13-31, 52-69, 91-122, 160,
    175-76, 186-95, 203-206
church, 17, 31, 56, 64, 92-93, 102-116,
    139, 146, 172-76, 188-95, 205-
    208
class, 2, 21-23, 30, 58-59, 66, 77-85, 118,
    128, 163, 202-206, 213
clergy, 16, 21-25, 31, 173
clerical class, 21
coherence, 16, 82
collective right, 194
colonialized, 202
common basis, 37-46, 74-86, 95
Common schools, 51-63

community, communities, 2-9, 18-26, 39-
    47, 53-62, 91-102, 110-22, 134-
    47, 155-66, 170-80, 186-97,
    200-209
compassion, 6-7, 110, 135, 144, 174
competing rights, 193-94
conflict, 6, 24-26, 42, 46, 56, 61, 92-97,
    119-22, 129-30, 146, 158, 172,
    193-96
connection, 5-6, 20-25, 41, 93, 107, 129-
    47, 186-91
consensus, 116-20, 196, 203
consequences, 37-46, 75, 97, 104-105,
    114, 121, 157-60, 171
constructivism, 74
contraries, 27-28
control, 6, 19-23, 46, 55, 97, 120, 128-39,
    155-61, 206
conversation, 37-46, 158
correlatives, 27-30
cosmetic surgery, 160-61
cosmic order, 196
cultural authority, 174
cultural change, 175
cultural expression, 158-61
cultural identity, 3, 156-62, 200-208
cultural plurality, 7, 13
deviance, 5, 9, 13, 19, 56, 171-78
deviants, 20, 177-79
dialectic, 25-27, 131, 205
difference, 1-9, 14-30, 39-46, 53-65,
    74-86, 91-109, 114-22, 131-46,
    157-58, 170-79, 193-96, 202-
    209
dilemma, dilemmas, 1-8, 85, 129, 154-63,
    193
directional pluralism, 192-96
discrimination, 93-94, 161, 170-80
divinities, 37
dominance, 1-7, 37-47, 53-60, 75, 107,
    131, 138, 161, 177, 188, 195,
    200, 207
education, 7-8, 24-27, 43, 51-69, 77-79,
    118-21, 144-47, 155-65, 188-
    90, 203

Enlightenment, 5, 37-45, 75, 84, 100, 117
epistemological, 56-63, 75
equality, 37-38, 67, 76, 96, 119-21
essence, 74, 84-86, 158-62, 176
essentialism, 74-78, 84-85
excluded, exclusion, 2-5, 44-46, 77-86,
        121, 158, 171-74
exegetical, 25, 102-17
family, 8, 118, 127-147, 156-63, 172-78
family values, 146
female circumcision, 153-65
Female Genital Mutilation, 8, 98, 153-66
feminine, feminist, 6-8, 45-46, 60-61,
        74-86, 112, 117, 127-35, 161
fideles, 29
Fire in the Rose, 146
First Crusade, 20
formation, 13-31, 56, 131, 146, 177
freedom, 8, 42-52, 75, 81, 92-99, 114-21,
        130-34, 158-60, 172, 187, 205
gay, 14, 22, 91-121, 170-76
gender, 1-8, 66, 74-86, 119, 127, 133-35,
        170, 193, 203
Genesis, 109-12
government, 9, 21-24, 43, 92-97, 146,
        161-77, 186-95, 205-209
Greek, 26, 109-12
Gregorian Reform, 16
Hawaiian Aboriginal peoples, 188
heart, 39, 40-47, 139, 190
hegemony, hegemonic, 7-9, 43, 55-57,
        188-93, 195
hermeneutical, 102-17
heterosexism, -sexist, -sexual 83, 112,
        170-75
Hincks Centre for Children's Mental
        Health, 140
homeless youth, 173
homophobia, 100, 170-78
homosexual, 8-9, 91-94, 101-17, 170-80
hope, 9, 39-47, 53, 94-95, 115, 122, 160,
        170-74, 206-207
human sexuality, 112, 170-75
humiliation, 9, 140, 171-74
identity, 3-9, 21, 41-45, 81-85, 95, 107,
        130-46, 156-62, 170-73, 192-
        95, 200-209
ideology, 37-43, 65, 195
imagination, 41, 97, 180, 208
imitatio, 25-26
immutable, 38, 78, 171, 175, 180
inclusion, 3-5, 14, 46, 86, 171

inclusive, 7, 25, 55, 113-19
individual rights, 193-94
indoctrination, 7, 51-67
infideles, 29
institutional, institutions, 3-4, 14-15, 22-
        25, 43-46, 54, 93-94, 146, 161,
        173-76, 200
intersubjectivity, 5, 134
intimacy, 8, 92, 119, 128-45, 174
intolerance, 13, 39, 46, 54, 101-17, 170
Iroquois, 186, 191
Islam, 56-64, 157-62
Jew, 15-23, 109-13
justice, 2-8, 23, 43-44, 51, 65-67, 76, 85-
        122, 146, 153, 164, 170-80,
        190-93, 205
law, 41-42, 61-69, 83, 92-98, 109-13, 121,
        136, 154, 161-65, 170, 186-93
legislation, 8, 91-99, 115-22, 161-66, 191
Leibnizian monads, 134
lepers, 14-20, 177
lesbian, 80, 114, 170-73
liberalism, 2, 7, 37-46, 61, 118, 193
liberation, 37, 47, 75, 86, 179
limits, 8, 41-42, 63-69, 93-100, 119-21,
        132, 140, 154-59, 195
liturgies, 175-76
local communities, 20
logical opposition, 27-31
marginalized, 1-2, 56-60, 85, 146, 178,
        192
marriage, 66, 106, 113, 119, 133, 156-62,
        176
masculine, masculinity, 77-84, 138, 170
metaphilosophical, 37
misery, 174, 180
modernity, modernization, 1-5, 31, 37, 75-
        78, 104, 134, 204, 209
moral, morality, 3-8, 19-20, 41-44, 52, 61-
        66, 80-86, 91-122, 130-36, 156-
        65, 170-80, 195-96
moral relativism, 172
moralitas, 25-26
mosques, 146
multiplicity, 134-37
muslim, 56-61, 157-62, 203
Native, 7-9, 24, 58-59, 161, 186-96,
        200-202, 209
Native self-government, 186-95
Native spirituality, 9, 186-96
naturalization, 38
naturalness, 171

necessary, 14-30, 58-68, 81, 99, 107-116,
    131, 142-44, 154, 161-65, 179-
    80
negotiations, 8
negritude, 201
neutral, 2-7, 37-41, 51-68, 77, 154, 195,
    200-201
norm, normativity, 51-56, 77-83, 105, 119,
    160, 170-79, 201
normality, 133, 177-79
objective, objectivism, 37, 46, 57-61, 96,
    160
oppression, 7-8, 75-86, 176
ordeal, 20-23
order, 16-19, 30, 40-41, 77-85, 95,
    104-14, 130-42, 157-60, 175-
    80, 190-96, 201-202
other, 3-6, 14-30, 38-47, 51-68, 75-86,
    91-120, 128-47, 154-65,
    172-80, 188-96, 200-209
pedagogy, 25-27, 138, 203
permanent, 14, 110, 154, 176-79, 209
persecuting society, 13-31, 56, 177-79
physicians, 20, 95, 154-65
plural society, 8, 38, 91, 118-22
pluralism, pluralist, 2-9, 37-46, 51-69, 74,
    92-101, 116-20, 154-58, 175,
    191-96
policy, 1-8, 15-18, 39-47, 51-67, 91, 101-
    103, 144-45, 153-65, 171, 193
political liberalism, 193
postmodern, 1-6, 13, 74-86, 102, 109,
    127-34, 207
power, 4-8, 13, 19-28, 41, 56-61, 79, 98,
    108-109, 120, 131-46, 170-80,
    190-91, 200-209
practices, 2-4, 23, 46, 85-96, 104-22, 138,
    158-61, 174, 189-91
pragmatic attitudes, 25, 171, 196
prejudice, 111, 118, 146, 170-79
premodern European society, 175
principles, 4, 76, 92-95, 118-19
privation and possession, 27-29
privileging spirituality, 195
professionalization, 21
public, 1-8, 14-15, 37-47, 51-69, 91-101,
    109, 116-22, 129, 144, 154-58,
    171-79, 189-97, 207
public justice, 8, 43, 91-100, 109, 116-22
public school, 55, 64
public/private, 7, 37-45, 97
radical feminism, 78

rationalism, 40-45, 60-61, 78, 200
realism, 37
reason, 3-5, 13-29, 37-46, 57-58, 67,
    76-97, 115-21, 137, 156, 164,
    171-80, 193-94, 209
Reformed, 61, 97, 108-109, 205
relation,-al, -s, 8, 15-16, 27, 37, 44, 56,
    64, 75-78, 85, 93-119, 129-45,
    153, 159, 166, 187-95, 203
relationship, 23-27, 57, 65, 92-120, 135-
    45, 162, 178, 190-91
relativisation, relativizing, 66, 109
religion, 1-9, 13-31, 37-46, 51-69, 91-110,
    116-22, 146, 154-62, 174-80,
    186-97, 206-209
religious pluralism, 196
religious violence, 55
repression, 6, 20, 77, 131, 178-80
reproductive, 79, 154
respect, 6-9, 13, 43-46, 54-60, 85, 92-100,
    114-22, 128-41, 147, 154-64,
    171, 191-95, 201-204
revelation, 39, 96, 115, 196
rhetoric, 18-31, 64, 205
rights, 2, 28, 52, 66, 76-77, 91-98, 117-21,
    130, 154-56, 170-74, 188-95
role, 3, 8, 18-20, 30, 39-46, 53-54, 65-66,
    80-81, 96-99, 107-109, 118-22,
    129-45, 156-61, 170-80, 188-97
Roman, 22-26, 62, 105-107, 112
Romans, 102-15
romantic, 1, 79-81, 176
sacrality, 187
sacred, 23, 56-57, 94, 110, 187-90, 209
sacred text, 110
Salish, 194
same-sex, 92-119, 127, 145, 175
schools, 8, 25-27, 43, 51-69, 145-46
scripture, 108-16
secular, 15-25, 31, 51-69, 96-101, 177,
    189-90, 202-209
secularizing logicization, 13
self, 4-9, 40-45, 66, 78-82, 95, 102, 111-
    14, 131-46, 161, 172-75,
    186-97, 201-205
self-government, 186-195
separation of church and state, 64, 191-92
sexism, sexist, 75-85, 130, 146
sexual orientation, 8, 66, 79-83, 91-94,
    105-107, 114, 170-71
sexuality, 112, 130, 146, 156, 160, 170-80
social change, 18-22, 56, 166

social plurality, 7, 13, 31
sociology, 127-33
solidarity, 21-23, 30, 37, 83, 118, 171
sovereignty, 188
Spirit Dance, 194
spiritual, spirituality, 5-9, 25-26, 41-43,
        57-60, 95, 115, 186-197, 202-
        209
strangers, 1-4, 115
structure, 8, 60-67, 76-80, 96-102, 130,
        136-38, 162, 175-78, 188, 195
subjective, subjectivities, 61, 96, 171
suffering, 6, 44-47, 137-41, 170-74
suicide, 137, 144, 172-73
surveillance, 179
synagogues, 146
theological, 8, 26-29, 101-11
tolerance, 8, 14-24, 37-42, 54, 62, 69, 81,
        101, 111-17, 154-58, 170-79
troth, 128-45
unavoidable, 42-46, 93-99, 110, 119-22,
        140
universal, -ity, -ization, 4, 18-19, 38, 79-
        85, 91-122, 133-36, 156, 171,
        179-80, 193, 201
universities, 25-27, 172
Vanier Institute of the Family, 133
violence, 4-8, 14-18, 38, 44, 55, 127-47,
        170-80, 202-207
voluntary, 130, 145, 158
voluntary society, 192
Weberian models, 19
wisdom, 161, 189-96, 201, 209
wisdom tradition, 196
Woodbine Heights Baptist Church, 146
World Health Organization, 153-64
worldviews, 38, 52-64, 95, 158-60, 192-96
Yonge Street Mission, 128

Name Index

Abelard, Peter, 26
Addington, Donald, 174
Ahmed, S. H., 155-57, 162, 165-66, 207
Anselm of Loan, 26
Anyanwu, K. C., 201
Appiah, K. A., 201-209
Araeen, R., 200
Aristotle, 27-30, 96
Armstrong, Sue, 154, 209
Ashraf, S. A., 57
Audi, Robert, 40, 99
Augustine, 23
Babbit, S. E., 46
Badri, A., 157
Bailey, D. Sherwin, 106
Baldwin, J. W., 24
Barth, Karl, 108
Bartlett, R., 23
Bauman, Zygmaunt, 1
Beaudin, M., 41
Beckett, Thomas, 26, 164
Bell, Alan P., 170, 172
Benson, R. L., 21
Berkhof, Hendrikus, 108
Berkouwer, Gerrit, 108
Bernstein, Richard, 37, 39, 44, 45
Bhabha, H. K., 200
Bissoondath, Neil, 208
Blumenfeld, Warren J., 20, 1734-75, 178
Bodunrin, P., 200, 201
Booth, Wayne C., 54
Bordo, Susan, 80, 85, 86
Boswell, John, 14, 101-17, 121, 175-80
Boyle, L. E., 27
Bradshaw, John, 138
Bredero, A., 23
Breyer, Q. J., 64
Broderick, C., 130
Brody, S. N., 14
Brown, Peter, 23, 64, 200
Buchanan, G. Sidney, 64
Bussert, Joy M. K., 139
Butler, Judith, 81-83
Bynum, C. W., 26
Byock, J., 23

Calvin, John, 9, 13, 108-109, 200
Cardinal, D., 209, 216-17
Chaplin, Jonathan, 99
Cheal, David, 129-30, 134
Chodorow, Nancy, 78-80
Chrysostom, John, 23, 107, 111-12
Chuang, Henry T., 174
Clanchey, M. T., 24
Clark, S., 29
Cockburn, Bruce, 180
Code, Lorraine, 45, 60-61
Cohn, N., 20
Coleman, Eli., 172
Collier, J., 127
Constable, G., 21
Copeland, R., 26
Croteau, Denis, 189
Cutner, Lawrence P., 155
d'Alverny, M., 26
Daly, Mary, 78
de Kok, I., 205, 207
Denzin, Norman, 133
Derrida, Jacques, 5
Dewey, John, 39, 42, 46, 63, 97
Di Stefano, Christine, 75, 77-79, 83
Diemer, A., 201
Douglas, Mary, 18, 23, 209, 216-17
Dover, G. K., 29
Dumont, James, 190-93
Durkheim, 19
Dworkin, Gerald, 65
Eichler, Margrit, 133
Eisenberg, Avigail, 193-94
Erasmus, 24
Erler, A., 23
Fennel, Tom, 162
Fish, Stanley, 39-40
Flax, Jane, 75
Flew, Anthony, 61
Foucault, Michel, 175, 178-80, 204
Fox, Bonnie, 127, 136, 172
Fraser, Nancy, 45, 81-83
Furnish, Victor, P., 106-107
Fuss, Diana, 83
Gadamer, Hans-Georg, 96

Gallo, Pia, 156
Gatchel, Richard, 53
Gbadegesin, O., 201
Gibson, Paul, 25, 172-73
Gittins, Dianna, 136
Godzich, W., 205
Goering, J., 25
Goldner, Virginia, 133
Gonsiorek, John C., 171
Goode, William, 129
Goodin, Robert E., 65
Grabmann, M., 26
Graburn, N. H. H., 200
Graham, J. R., 64
Green, Thomas F., 52, 192
Greer, G., 79
Griffioen, Sander, 99, 192, 195, 201
Grundmann, H., 23
Gullen, J., 161, 163
Hannon, Gerald, 98, 120
Harding, Sandra, 45, 75, 84-86
Hare, R. M., 52
Hare-Mustin, R., 133
Hart, Hendrik, 7, 8, 37, 91, 109-10
Hawkes, David, 188, 191, 193
Hays, Richard, 8, 94, 101-17
Heidegger, Martin, 38
Henderson, James Y., 196
Hengel, Martin, 109
Henry of Lausanne, 16
Herek, G. H., 170, 178, 180
Hill, R., 55, 68, 130
Hobbes, Thomas, 130
Hollins, T. H. B., 52
Hollister, C. W., 24
Holm, B., 208
Horn, Carl, 62, 64
Hosken, Fran, 154-55, 159
Hountondji, P. J., 200-201
Howard, Charlie, 173, 175
Hudson, W. D., 63
Hunt, R. W., 25
Hutcheon, L., 200, 207
Ismail, Edna Aden 155
Jaeger, C. Stephen, 25-26
Jaffee, Peter, 146
Jaggar, Alison M., 75-78
Jamieson, K., 193
Jaspers, Karl, 95
Jay, Karla, 172
Jeauneau, E., 26
Johnson, Mark, 97

Johnson, Martha, 196
Jordan, J. V., 129
Kant, Immanuel, 130
Kaplan, A. G., 129, 195
Keyes, D., 158
Kieckhefer, R., 20, 23
Kenyatta, J., 158-62
Kliever, Lonnie D., 53
Kouba, Leonard, 154-58
Kramer, H., 29
Kristeva, Julia, 4, 6
Kyazze, Charles, 166
Kymlicka, Will, 193-94
Lanham, C. D., 21, 99, 110, 201
Larner, Christine, 14, 20
Laura, R. S., 61
Le Bras, G., 22-24
Le Goff, K., 23-25
Little, Lester K., 22
Levinas, Emmanuel, 5
Lieder, M. D., 62, 64
Lloyd, Genevieve, 59, 77, 80
Locke, John, 38, 85, 96, 130
Longenecker, R., 110
Luepnitz, Deborah Anna, 130, 133, 135
Lyon, Noel, 191-92
Lyons, Oren, 186, 191
Lyotard, Jean-Francois, 5
Machiavelli, N., 24
Maddock, J., 130
Mak, Virginia, 156
Marshall, Paul, 53, 99
Martin, Luther H., 175
Mazrui, A. M., 203
McCarthy, Shawn, 155
McMillan, Carol, 80
Middleton, Richard J., 109
Miethke, J., 25
Milk, Harvey, 173, 175
Mill, John Stuart, 63
Miller, Alice, 129, 138, 141
Millet, Kate, 76
Minuchin, Salvador, 130
Mollat, M., 14, 19, 22
Mooney, C. F, 62
Moore, R. I., 14-24, 27-30, 177, 180
Mouw, Richard, 99, 192, 195
Mudimbe, V. Y., 200-207
Murasher, Judith, 154-58
Murray, A., 19, 22
Musschenga, Bert., 96
Nahanee, T., 193

Nasr, S. H., 56-57
Ngugi wa, Thiong'o, 201-203
Niblett, W. R., 69
Nicholson, Linda, 75, 81-83
Nielsen, Kai, 41, 85
Njeri, Mama Philomena, 153
Noddings, Nell, 61
Norman, Richard, 20, 64, 209
Novick, Marvyn, 130
Nye, F. I., 130
Oakley, Ann, 76
Olthuis, James H., 1, 5, 127, 129, 139
Otis, L. L., 14
O'Neill, John, 130, 147
Palmer, H., 159
Parsons, Talcott, 129
Paul, William, 170, 172-75
Perry, Michael, 195
Peters, Gordon, 53, 190, 191-93
Peuchmard, M., 23
Pfaff, William, 55
Plato, 96
Polanyi, Michael, 61, 95
Pontal, O., 22
Popper, Karl, 38
Powell, J. P., 69
Press, Karen, 205
Qadir, C. A., 57
Rahim, Bartholomew, 55
Redmond, Dianne, 173-175, 178
Reeve, Andrew, 65
Reichley, A. James, 196
Remafedi, G., 173
Reynolds, R. E., 23
Rich, Adrienne, 79
Richards, Janet R., 76-77
Richmond, M., 200
Robert of Arbrissel, 16
Roberts, G. O., 54
Robin, Eli, 104, 172
Rofes, Eric, 172
Rorty, 37-45, 61, 95, 171
Rosalto, M., 127
Saghir, Marcel T., 172
Saint Paul, 95-99, 104-115, 122
Sawatsky, Kevin G., 93
Schneider, R., 27
Scroggs, Robin, 104, 106-107
Sedgwick, Eve Kosofsky, 172-75
Segal, Alan F., 109
Senn, Frank C., 187
Slack, Alison, 154-61

Smith, J., 130
Smith, Mark D., 105
Smith, Steven D., 64
Smart, Ninian, 52, 64
Smart, Patricia, 52
Snook, I. A., 52-53
Sochart, E., 161, 164-65
Sogolo, G., 201
Solterer, H., 27
Sommerville, Janet, 155
Sprenger, J., 29
Stingel, 174
Stiver, I. P., 129, 141
Stock, Brian, 23
Stolzenberg, Nomi Maya, 61
Suhanic, G., 163
Surrey, J. L., 129
Sutherland, John R., 93
Svensson, Frances, 194
Sweetman, Robert, 7, 13, 67, 74, 177
Swinton, G., 208
Tash, Robert, 62
Taylor, Charles, 41, 95
Taylor, Paul, 157
Thiessen, Elmer, 52
Thomas of Monmouth, 20
Thompson, Catherine Crawford, 128, 133, 146
Thorne-Finch, Ron, 138
Tillich, Paul, 41, 95
Porter, Tom, 191
Tooker, Elizabeth, 58, 60
Trask, Mililani, 188
Turner, R., 24-25
Valauri, John, 64-65
Vauchez, A., 20
Vecsey, Chriostopher, 186-87
Viviani, Franco, 156
Vollenhoven, D. H. Th., 201
Walker, Deward E., 26, 153, 164, 188
Walsh, Brian J., 109-10
Walsh, Froma, 134
Weber, Max, 19
Weigel, G., 69
Weinberg, Martin S., 170, 172
Weinrich, James D., 171
Wesselius, Janet Catherine, 8, 51, 74
White, Dan, 175
William of Champeaux, 26
Williams, Melissa, 172, 194
Wilson, John, 52
Wiredu, K., 200-201, 204

Wittgenstein, Ludwig, 95
Wolf, N., 157, 160
Wollstonecraft, Mary, 76
Wolterstorff, Nicholas, 99
Woolf, Virginia, 79
Wright, N. T., 114, 201
Wylie, Alison, 85
Yanagisake, S., 127
Yeats, W. B., 2
Yerby, Winton E., 64
Young, Allen, 172
Zarowny, Marie, 189-90

Series Published by Wilfrid Laurier University Press for the Canadian Corporation for Studies in Religion / Corporation Canadienne des Sciences Religieuses

Editions SR

1. *La langue de Ya'udi : description et classement de l'ancien parler de Zencircli dans le cadre des langues sémitiques du nord-ouest*
   Paul-Eugène Dion, O.P. / 1974 / viii + 511 p. / OUT OF PRINT
2. *The Conception of Punishment in Early Indian Literature*
   Terence P. Day / 1982 / iv + 328 pp.
3. *Traditions in Contact and Change: Selected Proceedings of the XIVth Congress of the International Association for the History of Religions*
   Edited by Peter Slater and Donald Wiebe with Maurice Boutin and Harold Coward
   1983 / x + 758 pp. / OUT OF PRINT
4. *Le messianisme de Louis Riel*
   Gilles Martel / 1984 / xviii + 483 p.
5. *Mythologies and Philosophies of Salvation in the Theistic Traditions of India*
   Klaus K. Klostermaier / 1984 / xvi + 549 pp. / OUT OF PRINT
6. *Averroes' Doctrine of Immortality: A Matter of Controversy*
   Ovey N. Mohammed / 1984 / vi + 202 pp. / OUT OF PRINT
7. *L'étude des religions dans les écoles : l'expérience américaine, anglaise et canadienne*
   Fernand Ouellet / 1985 / xvi + 666 p.
8. *Of God and Maxim Guns: Presbyterianism in Nigeria, 1846-1966*
   Geoffrey Johnston / 1988 / iv + 322 pp.
9. *A Victorian Missionary and Canadian Indian Policy: Cultural Synthesis vs Cultural Replacement*
   David A. Nock / 1988 / x + 194 pp. / OUT OF PRINT
10. *Prometheus Rebound: The Irony of Atheism*
    Joseph C. McLelland / 1988 / xvi + 366 pp.
11. *Competition in Religious Life*
    Jay Newman / 1989 / viii + 237 pp.
12. *The Huguenots and French Opinion, 1685-1787: The Enlightenment Debate on Toleration*
    Geoffrey Adams / 1991 / xiv + 335 pp.
13. *Religion in History: The Word, the Idea, the Reality/ La religion dans l'histoire : le mot, l'idée, la réalité*
    Edited by/Sous la direction de Michel Despland and/et Gérard Vallée
    1992 / x + 252 pp.
14. *Sharing Without Reckoning: Imperfect Right and the Norms of Reciprocity*
    Millard Schumaker / 1992 / xiv + 112 pp.
15. *Love and the Soul: Psychological Interpretations of the Eros and Psyche Myth*
    James Gollnick / 1992 / viii + 174 pp.
16. *The Promise of Critical Theology: Essays in Honour of Charles Davis*
    Edited by Marc P. Lalonde / 1995 / xii + 146 pp.
17. *The Five Aggregates: Understanding Theravāda Psychology and Soteriology*
    Mathieu Boisvert / 1995 / xii + 166 pp.
18. *Mysticism and Vocation*
    James R. Horne / 1996 / vi + 110 pp.

19. *Memory and Hope: Strands of Canadian Baptist History*
Edited by David T. Priestley / 1996 / viii + 211 pp.

20. *The Concept of Equity in Calvin's Ethics**
Guenther H. Haas / 1997 / xii + 205 pp.
* Available in the United Kingdom and Europe from Paternoster Press.

21. *The Call of Conscience: French Protestant Responses to the Algerian War, 1954-1962*
Geoffrey Adams / 1998 / xxii + 270 pp.

22. *Clinical Pastoral Supervision and the Theology of Charles Gerkin*
Thomas St. James O'Connor / 1998 / x + 152 pp.

23. *Faith and Fiction: A Theological Critique of the Narrative Strategies of Hugh MacLennan and Morley Callaghan*
Barbara Pell / 1998 / v + 141 pp.

24. *God and the Chip: Religion and the Culture of Technology*
William A. Stahl / 1999 / vi + 186 pp.

25. *The Religious Dreamworld of Appuleius'* Metamorphoses: *Recovering a Forgotten Hermeneutic*
James Gollnick / 1999 /xiv + 178 pp.

Comparative Ethics Series/ Collection d'Éthique Comparée

1. *Muslim Ethics and Modernity: A Comparative Study of the Ethical Thought of Sayyid Ahmad Khan and Mawlana Mawdudi*
Sheila McDonough / 1984 / x + 130 pp. / OUT OF PRINT

2. *Methodist Education in Peru: Social Gospel, Politics, and American Ideological and Economic Penetration, 1888-1930*
Rosa del Carmen Bruno-Jofré / 1988 / xiv + 223 pp.

3. *Prophets, Pastors and Public Choices: Canadian Churches and the Mackenzie Valley Pipeline Debate*
Roger Hutchinson / 1992 / xiv + 142 pp. / OUT OF PRINT

4. *In Good Faith: Canadian Churches Against Apartheid*
Renate Pratt / 1997 / xii + 366 pp.

5. *Towards an Ethics of Community: Negotiations of Difference in a Pluralist Society*
James H. Olthuis, editor / 2000 / x + 230 pp.

Dissertations SR

1. *The Social Setting of the Ministry as Reflected in the Writings of Hermas, Clement and Ignatius*
Harry O. Maier / 1991 / viii + 230 pp. / OUT OF PRINT

2. *Literature as Pulpit: The Christian Social Activism of Nellie L. McClung*
Randi R. Warne / 1993 / viii + 236 pp.

Studies in Christianity and Judaism/ Études sur le christianisme et le judaïsme

1. *A Study in Anti-Gnostic Polemics: Irenaeus, Hippolytus, and Epiphanius*
Gérard Vallée / 1981 / xii + 114 pp. / OUT OF PRINT

2. *Anti-Judaism in Early Christianity*
Vol. 1, *Paul and the Gospels*
Edited by Peter Richardson with David Granskou / 1986 / x + 232 pp.
Vol. 2, *Separation and Polemic*
Edited by Stephen G. Wilson / 1986 / xii + 185 pp.

3. *Society, the Sacred, and Scripture in Ancient Judaism: A Sociology of Knowledge*
   Jack N. Lightstone / 1988 / xiv + 126 pp.
4. *Law in Religious Communities in the Roman Period: The Debate Over* Torah *and* Nomos *in Post-Biblical Judaism and Early Christianity*
   Peter Richardson and Stephen Westerholm with A. I. Baumgarten, Michael Pettem and Cecilia Wassén / 1991 / x + 164 pp.
5. *Dangerous Food: 1 Corinthians 8-10 in Its Context*
   Peter D. Gooch / 1993 / xviii + 178 pp.
6. *The Rhetoric of the Babylonian Talmud, Its Social Meaning and Context*
   Jack N. Lightstone / 1994 / xiv + 317 pp.
7. *Whose Historical Jesus?*
   Edited by William E. Arnal and Michel Desjardins / 1997 / vi + 337 pp.

The Study of Religion in Canada /
Sciences Religieuses au Canada

1. *Religious Studies in Alberta: A State-of-the-Art Review*
   Ronald W. Neufeldt / 1983 / xiv + 145 pp.
2. *Les sciences religieuses au Québec depuis 1972*
   Louis Rousseau et Michel Despland / 1988 / 158 p.
3. *Religious Studies in Ontario: A State-of-the-Art Review*
   Harold Remus, William Closson James and Daniel Fraikin / 1992 / xviii + 422 pp.
4. *Religious Studies in Manitoba and Saskatchewan: A State-of-the-Art Review*
   John M. Badertscher, Gordon Harland and Roland E. Miller / 1993 / vi + 166 pp.
5. *The Study of Religion in British Columbia: A State-of-the-Art Review*
   Brian J. Fraser / 1995 / x + 127 pp.

Studies in Women and Religion /
Études sur les femmes et la religion

1. *Femmes et religions**
   Sous la direction de Denise Veillette / 1995 / xviii + 466 p.
   Only available from Les Presses de l'Université Laval
2. *The Work of Their Hands: Mennonite Women's Societies in Canada*
   Gloria Neufeld Redekop / 1996 / xvi + 172 pp.
3. *Profiles of Anabaptist Women: Sixteenth-Century Reforming Pioneers*
   Edited by C. Arnold Snyder and Linda A. Huebert Hecht / 1996 / xxii + 438 pp.
4. *Voices and Echoes: Canadian Women's Spirituality*
   Edited by Jo-Anne Elder and Colin O'Connell / 1997 / xxviii + 237 pp.
5. *Obedience, Suspicion and the Gospel of Mark: A Mennonite-Feminist Exploration of Biblical Authority*
   Lydia Neufeld Harder / 1998 / xiv + 168 pp.

SR Supplements

1. *Footnotes to a Theology: The Karl Barth Colloquium of 1972*
   Edited and Introduced by Martin Rumscheidt / 1974 / viii + 151 pp. / OUT OF PRINT
2. *Martin Heidegger's Philosophy of Religion*
   John R. Williams / 1977 / x + 190 pp. / OUT OF PRINT
3. *Mystics and Scholars: The Calgary Conference on Mysticism 1976*
   Edited by Harold Coward and Terence Penelhum / 1977 / viii + 121 pp. / OUT OF PRINT
4. *God's Intention for Man: Essays in Christian Anthropology*
   William O. Fennell / 1977 / xii + 56 pp. / OUT OF PRINT

5. *"Language" in Indian Philosophy and Religion*
   Edited and Introduced by Harold G. Coward / 1978 / x + 98 pp. / OUT OF PRINT
6. *Beyond Mysticism*
   James R. Horne / 1978 / vi + 158 pp. / OUT OF PRINT
7. *The Religious Dimension of Socrates' Thought*
   James Beckman / 1979 / xii + 276 pp. / OUT OF PRINT
8. *Native Religious Traditions*
   Edited by Earle H. Waugh and K. Dad Prithipaul / 1979 / xii + 244 pp. / OUT OF PRINT
9. *Developments in Buddhist Thought: Canadian Contributions to Buddhist Studies*
   Edited by Roy C. Amore / 1979 / iv + 196 pp.
10. *The Bodhisattva Doctrine in Buddhism*
    Edited and Introduced by Leslie S. Kawamura / 1981 / xxii + 274 pp. / OUT OF PRINT
11. *Political Theology in the Canadian Context*
    Edited by Benjamin G. Smillie / 1982 / xii + 260 pp.
12. *Truth and Compassion: Essays on Judaism and Religion in Memory of Rabbi Dr. Solomon Frank*
    Edited by Howard Joseph, Jack N. Lightstone and Michael D. Oppenheim
    1983 / vi + 217 pp.
13. *Craving and Salvation: A Study in Buddhist Soteriology*
    Bruce Matthews / 1983 / xiv + 138 pp. / OUT OF PRINT
14. *The Moral Mystic*
    James R. Horne / 1983 / x + 134 pp.
15. *Ignatian Spirituality in a Secular Age*
    Edited by George P. Schner / 1984 / viii + 128 pp. / OUT OF PRINT
16. *Studies in the Book of Job*
    Edited by Walter E. Aufrecht / 1985 / xii + 76 pp.
17. *Christ and Modernity: Christian Self-Understanding in a Technological Age*
    David J. Hawkin / 1985 / x + 181 pp.
18. *Young Man Shinran: A Reappraisal of Shinran's Life*
    Takamichi Takahatake / 1987 / xvi + 228 pp. / OUT OF PRINT
19. *Modernity and Religion*
    Edited by William Nicholls / 1987 / vi + 191 pp.
20. *The Social Uplifters: Presbyterian Progressives and the Social Gospel in Canada, 1875-1915*
    Brian J. Fraser / 1988 / xvi + 212 pp. / OUT OF PRINT

Available from:

Wilfrid Laurier University Press

Waterloo, Ontario, Canada   N2L 3C5
Telephone: (519) 884-0710, ext. 6124
Fax: (519) 725-1399
E-mail: press@wlu.ca
World Wide Web: http://www.wlu.ca/~wwwpress/